OVERCONFIDENCE
AND WAR

OVERCONFIDENCE AND WAR

The Havoc and Glory of Positive Illusions

DOMINIC D. P. JOHNSON

Harvard University Press

Cambridge, Massachusetts, and London, England

2004

Copyright © 2004 by the President and Fellows of Harvard College
All rights reserved
Printed in the United States of America

Library of Congress Cataloging-in-Publication Data
Johnson, Dominic D. P., 1974–
Overconfidence and war : the havoc and glory of positive illusions /
Dominic D. P. Johnson
p.   cm.
Includes bibliographical references and index.
ISBN 0-674-01576-2 (alk. paper)
1. War—Psychological aspects.   2. War, Causes of.   3. Military history,
Modern—20th century.   4. Military history, Modern—21st century.
I. Title.
U22.3.J64   2004
355.02/7 22
2004047524

For my parents,
Roger and Jenny,
to whom I owe everything

Contents

1. War and Illusions   I

2. Looking for Illusions   35

3. World War I   58

4. The Munich Crisis   85

5. The Cuban Missile Crisis   108

6. Vietnam   125

7. Vanity Dies Hard   173

8. Iraq, 2003   191

Appendix   221

Notes   239

Acknowledgments   271

Index   273

In what field of human activity is boldness more at home than in war?

—Carl von Clausewitz

Chapter 1

War and Illusions

Always remember, however sure you are that you can easily win, that there would not be a war if the other man did not think he also had a chance.

—Winston Churchill

O God of battles! Steel my soldiers' hearts;
Possess them not with fear: take from them now
The sense of reckoning, if th'opposed numbers
Pluck their hearts from them!

—Shakespeare's Henry V

On 16 November 1532 the Spanish explorer Francisco Pizarro and his modest force of 168 men attacked and defeated an Inca army of 80,000 soldiers at Cajamarca in Peru. Despite the incredible asymmetry in manpower, the Spaniards apparently won by means of superior weaponry and the effects of their opponents' surprise at the novelty of cannon, horses, and trumpets. The greater mystery is what led the conquistadors to believe they could win. There are accounts of the whole valley being full of Inca soldiers, filing out of their huge encampment for most of the morning. What gave the Spaniards the audacity to stay and fight? A Spanish eyewitness wrote that having arrived, they could not turn back or show fear, as it would have made them seem uncertain of victory. Pizarro had attempted to boost his soldiers' morale by telling them there were "only" 40,000 Inca soldiers. It seems as though the Spaniards were determined to maintain the illusion that they expected to win.[1]

Pizarro was evidently well served by his confidence: the victory was his. Often, however, such optimistic evaluations bring disaster. Consider General Custer's cry at the battle of the Little Big Horn in 1876, "Hurrah, boys, we've got them!"—after which his entire battalion of around two hundred men was annihilated to a man by what he had been reliably informed would be 3,000 Sioux and Cheyenne. Like Pizarro, Custer apparently attempted to raise morale by misleading his men about the enemy: he reported this figure to his officers as only 1,500.[2]

The history of warfare includes many other instances of apparently exaggerated confidence, sometimes leading to victory against daunting odds, sometimes to utter defeat. Were Pizarro's and Custer's optimistic estimates of their chances similar to that of Israeli chief of staff David Elazar, who said of the Syrian forces before the 1973 Yom Kippur war, "We'll have one hundred tanks against their eight hundred . . . That ought to be enough"? Or that of a Union general in the American Civil War, John Sedgwick, who declared "They couldn't hit an elephant at this distance" immediately before he was killed by enemy fire at the battle of Spotsylvania Court House in May 1864? Or that of the Frankish knight who charged into a sea of Saracens at the battle of Acre in 1291, even though his compatriots had already turned and fled? The Duke of Wellington famously noted the ambiguous difference between bravery and folly, and their attendant havoc and glory, when he suggested that "there is nothing on earth so stupid as a gallant officer."[3]

Are such anecdotes isolated cases of arrogance? Or is overconfidence an important factor in explaining what Lawrence LeShan calls "the enthusiasm with which we greet the onset of war"?[4] Not all of us are enthusiastic about war, of course, but it takes only a few influential enthusiasts to start one. Does a human tendency toward overconfidence lead us into wars when a more realistic assessment might keep the peace?

Many scholars suggest that indeed it does. For example, Geoffrey Blainey: "The outbreak of war during the last three centuries reveals recurrent clues which illuminate the causes of war and so of peace. One concealed clue—crucial to an understanding of war—is the optimism with which most wars were commenced by nations' leaders." "Recurring optimism is a vital prelude to war. Anything which increases that optimism is a cause of war. Anything which dampens that optimism is a cause of peace." Robert Jervis: "Excessive military optimism is frequently associated with the outbreak of war." Alfred Vagts: "With only a few exceptions, the wars of the century from 1815 to 1914 were undertaken with each side believing that it would win." Stephen Van Evera: "At least some false optimism about relative power preceded every major war since 1740, as well as many lesser and ancient wars." Norman Dixon found an "unrealistic overconfidence in rapid victory" to be a "notable feature of the Boer War, of World War I, of World War II, and even, through what was by now a quite extraordinary incapacity to profit from experience, of the Suez crisis and Bay of Pigs fiasco." Sumit Ganguly deduced overoptimism to be a root cause of the India-Pakistan wars.[5]

There is also evidence of unrealistic expectations in Vietnam, Russia's campaign in Afghanistan, Iraq's attack on Iran, the Falklands, Somalia, Kosovo, and, according to a number of authors, the U.S. invasion of Iraq in 2003.[6] A RAND study found that even limited wars "often cost more and last longer than anticipated." Richard Ned Lebow found that in brinkmanship crises that led to war, leaders "grossly misjudged the military balance between themselves and their adversaries. In every instance they were confident of victory." John Stoessinger discovered "a remarkable consistency in the self-images of most national leaders on the brink of war. Each confidently expects victory after a brief and triumphant campaign. This recurring optimism . . . assumes a powerful momentum of its own and thus becomes one of the causes of war." And despite the widely held idea that humans generally make rational decisions, the reality is that often, in Herbert Abrams's words, "the fog of hope and wishful thinking obscures the facts. Nations miscalculate and go to war believing that national goals will surely be attained."[7]

International conflict, then, is often characterized by two opponents both of whom believe they will gain from it. Usually, of course, one of them is wrong. Richard Betts cautions that, if a war has a winner and a loser, "false optimism" and "valid optimism" are both true by definition: "The victor's optimism proves correct and the loser's mistaken." However, even victors can find it harder, longer, or more costly to win than expected, just as losers can find it was easier, quicker, or more costly to lose than expected. Either side in any situation, whatever the outcome, can be overconfident. As Betts recognizes, unrealistic optimism is implicated in excessively costly "Pyrrhic" victories, and in stalemates, and when attackers that expect to win end up losing. Data indicate that, since around 1500, attackers have lost one-quarter to one-half of the wars they started (depending on the method of calculation), and many of their successes have come at unexpected cost. The rationalist view, that one side fights and wins "at acceptable cost," appears to be rare.[8]

This is the core of the so-called War Puzzle: states led by rational decisionmakers should not fight because both sides could avoid the costs and risks of war by negotiating a prewar bargain reflecting their relative power (that is, both sides could obtain a similar result without the costs and risks of war). Since wars do happen, it appears that states overestimate their relative power.[9] At the brink of war, history tells us, rivals' estimates of their chances of winning commonly sum to more than 100 percent—for example, both think they have more than a 50 percent chance of winning (or one thinks it has an 80 percent chance and the other thinks its chance is 40 percent), an attitude that betrays unwarranted confidence on one or both sides. "If neither side is optimistic about its chances," Betts points out, ". . . war is less probable, because neither side sees much to gain from starting it."[10] Even if overconfidence were random, therefore, when it occurred it would tend to cause war. But I argue that it is far from random: rather, that it is a baseline tendency in human psychology, and that it varies systematically with specific conditions.

As Barbara Tuchman has made clear, overassessment of one's relative capabilities is not limited to war. There are abundant examples of overconfidence in diverse professional contexts, from business to trade unions to government. Examples also abound throughout the world's cultures, over all of recorded human history, and from the battlefield decisions of military commanders to political group decisionmaking.[11] From where does this illusive bias toward optimism come? I propose that such a bias conferred significant advantages in our ancestral environment and therefore was selected for in our evolution.

In this book, I do three things. First, I argue that overconfidence in conflict was an adaptive trait in our evolutionary past, and as a result has become an integral aspect of the human psyche. Second, I argue that, *whether or not it has an evolutionary origin,* overconfidence is a widespread phenomenon that we cannot ignore in attempting to understand conflict. Third, I argue that overconfidence contributes to causing war. Each of these three claims is independently valid, but my task is to show that they are linked: I argue that the strategic advantage of a confident spirit was favored by natural selection in human evolution, hence is prevalent in our psychology today, and hence promotes war (see Figure 1). (I do not argue that overconfidence is the *only* cause of war.)

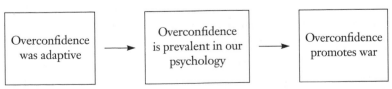

Figure 1. The three components of the positive illusions theory of war.

Adaptive Overconfidence

Systematic overconfidence is a widespread human trait that, I believe, was adaptive in our evolutionary past. (I use the term "adaptive" in the evolutionary biological sense, referring to a trait that provided a survival or reproductive advantage and therefore spread by natural selection.) Counterintuitive though it may seem, exaggerated confidence can bring numerous advantages. First, it can pay off in the long run because the costs of failure arising from overconfidence often matter less than the missed opportunities arising from accuracy or overcautiousness (see section 2 of the Appendix and the works cited there for details of this phenomenon). Second, it has been shown in numerous contexts to facilitate more effective mental, social, and physical functioning. Third, it can increase performance in conflict—even against a much stronger opponent—because it boosts resolve and/or bluffs the enemy into submission.[12] These findings suggest that overconfidence can provide significant advantages in challenging, competitive, or combative situations. Since opponents can exploit the same tactic, however, there will be a competitive escalation, an arms race, among adversaries to outdo one another. All other things being equal, in such an arms race high-confidence players will beat low-confidence players.

However, too much overconfidence can lead to disaster: overly confident actors may have their bluff called, in which case they may not only lose a conflict but also suffer high costs from having committed extra resources to stage the bluff. Clearly, then, there is some balance, in which a degree of staged confidence is "strategic," but too much is bad. For the Western Allies in the twentieth century, "the lesson of World War I is said to be: avoid provoking an aggressor with excessive strength; that of World War II: avoid encouraging an aggressor with excessive weakness."[13] While a fine balance must be struck, a certain amount of bluffing is critical to success in a world where everyone else is bluffing too (for more on this point, see section 4 of the Appendix).

The anthropologist Lionel Tiger argued that optimism is one

of humankind's most defining and adaptive features. The impact of "positive psychology," originally stemming from the work of Martin Seligman, on the behavioral sciences in recent years cannot be overstated. Reams of journal articles now document the evidence and utility of optimistic biases in pretty much any context one can imagine. Since the 1960s, carefully controlled psychological experiments have demonstrated that language, memory, and thought are systematically biased in a positive direction. For example, people use more positive than negative words, recall positive memories more readily than negative ones, evaluate themselves more positively than they do other people, attribute success to themselves but failure to others, and are overoptimistic about the future. In a review of the preponderance of optimism in human psychology, Christopher Peterson noted: "Apparently, in our minds, we are all children of [Garrison Keillor's imaginary] Lake Wobegon, all of whom are above average."[14]

According to Shelley Taylor and Jonathon Brown, two leading researchers on optimistic biases, accumulating evidence demonstrates that most people exhibit overconfidence in three key domains: "(a) They view themselves in unrealistically positive terms; (b) they believe they have greater control over environmental events than is actually the case; and (c) they hold views of the future that are more rosy than base-rate data can justify." Studies typically report that 67–96 percent of people rate their own qualities as better than those of their peers, and since it is "logically impossible for most people to be better than others," this tendency has been labeled "positive illusions." Note that even though some people may be correctly assessing themselves as superior to most others, a majority doing so cannot represent reality. Taylor and Brown also point out that "optimism as an illusion" is distinct from "optimism as a delusion": "illusions are responsive, albeit reluctantly, to reality, whereas delusions are not." Positive illusions do not blind us, they blinker us.[15]

There are various possible sources of overconfidence, such as excessive boldness after a string of successes, beliefs that supernatural forces offer superior powers and protection, certain personality types and disorders, and neurochemical stimuli such as hormones (see section 1 of the Appendix). However, I focus on positive illusions as a novel and particularly pervasive source of overconfidence. Positive illusions appear to be a broad and robust phenomenon precisely because a number of both "cognitive" and "motivational" psychological biases compound the effect in different but complementary ways. Cognitive biases, which result from constraints in the way the brain works, allow our decision-making to be skewed by such things as the familiarity of terms and concepts, availability of information stored in the brain, and the framing of decisions. A number of cognitive biases promote overconfidence. Motivational biases, which "protect" us emotionally from conflicting, unfamiliar, or unpleasant information, lead us to interpret new information to fit preconceived notions or to rationalize an already preferred course of action. "Group-think" and "denial" are well-known types of motivational bias. Many motivational biases also encourage overconfidence. Perhaps the most famous example is Stalin's refusal to believe the Germans were about to betray him and invade Russia in 1941, despite "no less than ninety separate, unequivocal warnings of an impending attack."[16]

That traits inherent to human biology and brain function influence decisionmaking is now well established. Systematic deviations from the predictions of traditional "rational choice theory" have been discovered in numerous contexts (mainly by experimental economists and psychologists). These biases are thought to have originated in the way evolution fashioned the brain's architectural mechanisms (our "hardware" constraints, as it were), and in the heuristic rules of thumb that people use to make decisions within these constraints (our "software").[17] Deviations from rationality are widespread across cultures, not just oddities of Western society. Many of these biases have been found to have clear origins in the processes of neurobiology and endocrinology.[18]

The evolutionary biologist Robert Trivers argues not only that we have such biases, but also that the process of evolution has hidden many of them from us via built-in mechanisms of self-deception. Indeed, he argues that self-deception plays a key role in their effectiveness in diverse aspects of human behavior and decisionmaking. Numerous examples of deception of self and others in nonhuman animals (especially in conflict situations) imply that it has an ancient origin in the evolution of the brain.[19] Humans are extremely sensitive to behavioral cues and facial expressions associated with lying and deception, indicating that this ability has been under significant selective pressure in our evolution.[20] As Trivers sees it, in order to subvert these ever-improving detection mechanisms, many aspects of our behavior have become *self*-deceptive, because this removes the possibility that we will betray our own lies through our behavior (so-called behavioral leakage). Self-deception may be highly adaptive if it increases the credibility of a bluff.

Positive illusions appear to be such a self-deceptive trait. A number of empirical studies suggest that accurate information is in fact available, but that it remains concealed in the subconscious. This implies that positive illusions represent a self-serving *bias* via self-deception rather than an *error* arising from some deficiency in mental processing. In other words, they must have been somehow adaptive in our evolution.[21]

Advantages of Positive Illusions

There is overwhelming empirical evidence that positive illusions serve useful functions. They enable individuals or groups to be more effective in striving for and achieving mental or physical goals, as if they are self-fulfilling prophecies. People with high self-perceptions—even if those views are exaggerated—are often more likely to succeed than those whose self-perceptions are modest. Shelley Taylor and Jonathon Brown have found that positive illusions lead to "higher motivation, greater persistence, more effective performance and ultimately, greater success."[22] And as Roy Baumeister suggested: "The lack of illusions may leave people reluctant to undertake certain ambitious, risky projects that often may yield the greatest successes and advances . . .

When actual performance is involved, the realist has to do without the benefits of confidence, such as the self-fulfilling prophecy effects of thinking that one can accomplish something terrific." The economist Robert Frank also recognized that "self-confidence enhances a person's performance, and that positive self-perceptions, even if somewhat illusory by objective standards, tend to serve people well in life." A U.S. National Institute of Mental Health report on the state of behavioral science noted: "Considerable evidence suggests positive psychological benefits for people who believe their future will be rosier than they have any right to expect. Such optimism keeps people in a positive mood, motivates them to work toward future goals, fosters creative, productive work, and gives them a sense of being in control of their destiny."[23]

Richard Wrangham has proposed that, over our long evolutionary history of intergroup conflict, positive illusions enhanced performance in warfare. Significant to this claim is the finding that positive illusions are exaggerated in threatening circumstances (see Chapter 2). If they improved fighting ability, positive illusions would improve survival and reproductive success and be favored by natural selection over the course of human evolution. This is especially salient given that warfare in hunter-gatherer societies appears to have had critical consequences for survival, access to materials and resources, and reproductive opportunities (wars were sometimes waged to capture women).[24] Wrangham's original warfare-based theory is, if anything, conservative, because it excludes the influence of interpersonal combat, one-on-one disputes, bargaining, attracting allies, and deterring rivals, all of which were presumably much more common than war, and in all of which positive illusions were likely to be advantageous.

Nevertheless, Wrangham argues that the degree of selection pressure on fighting ability has been unusually strong because warfare was frequent and severe throughout human evolution. Among hunter-gatherers, according to an extensive review by Lawrence Keeley, 8–59 percent of male deaths among tribal societies were due to warfare. This contrasts with a figure of less than 1 percent for the United States and Europe combined in the twentieth century, and that was considered a bloody century. Keeley's evidence combines archaeological data on prehistoric societies with data on hunter-gatherer societies that have been studied in recent times. Both strongly suggest that fighting was one of the most important selective pressures in our evolutionary history. As Wrangham puts it: "A selective regime lasting several million years, affecting a behavior responsible for a major source of mortality and reproductive success, is, of course, likely to have had substantial effects on psychological evolution."[25]

There are two distinct processes by which positive illusions might confer advantages in warfare and, thereby, increase what is known as "military effectiveness": either, in Wrangham's words, "by suppression of disadvantageous thoughts or feelings, or through an arms race of bluffing." These two complementary strategies have been labeled "performance enhancement" and "opponent deception."[26] (The word "bluff" implies *conscious* deception, but the positive illusions hypothesis suggests that the bluff occurs *subconsciously*—that one is not aware of overestimating oneself.) Both processes reduce the accuracy of mutual assessments, and thereby increase risk-taking. So while they may increase military effectiveness, they also tend to promote conflict. Let's look at the logic of these two strategies more closely.

An exaggerated assessment of one's own capability may enhance one's performance, and thus increase one's probability of winning, via *deception of oneself*. Positive illusions have been demonstrated to suppress thoughts or feelings that would interrupt progress toward a goal and thus to increase the chance of success: "Optimism leads to continued efforts to attain the goal, whereas pessimism leads to giving up." This is more effective if one genuinely believes the goal is attainable. As Shelley Taylor and Peter Gollwitzer explain, such self-deception "may enable people to strive longer and harder to reach their goals." According to this logic, positive illusions can increase one's probability of success by enhancing performance via strengthened resolve. The competitiveness and aggressive spirit of Marine platoons or fighter pilots capture the essence of the idea.[27]

An exaggerated self-assessment may also enhance one's probability of winning via *deception of the opponent*, since confident behavior increases one's chance of bluffing one's enemies into believing they are unlikely to win. If you yourself are not aware that you are only bluffing, there can be no "behavioral leakage" to give the game away, so the enemy is more likely to believe the bluff. That is, self-deception "reduces inadvertent signaling of weakness." This may affect the destructiveness as well as the occurrence of conflict: "Because self-deception reduces perceived opponent asymmetry, it should cause opponents to fight more intensely." The outcomes of such conflicts will also be less predictable as they become less dependent on material strength alone.[28]

These two mechanisms of positive illusions, performance enhancement and opponent deception, can of course be deliberate as well as subconscious. People may decide to feign confidence and exploit these strategies on purpose, whether or not they also experience some subconscious influence of positive illusions; both conscious and subconscious components may operate simultaneously. In international relations, an outward image of strong resolve and military capability is crucial to credible deterrence, for example. Negotiating positions, public support, and status in crises and wars can often be improved by confident statements, preparations, and commitments—without any actual action.[29]

However, the conscious and subconscious components should be distinguishable: if a strategy is conscious and deliberate it should be reflected in public but not in private. I make this distinction in my case studies by separating deliberate "showy" signals of resolve or bluffs, consciously intended to deceive others, from *beliefs* that were more optimistic than available information should have recommended. In reality, the line between conscious and unconscious behavior may sometimes be blurred. That is, positive illusions may reinforce one's own conviction about certain facts, even if the interpretation of those facts was largely skewed in the first place for political purposes. Before World War II Mussolini came to believe the very propaganda about Italian power that he himself had orchestrated to bluff others. More recently, the conviction of U.S. and U.K. leaders that Saddam

Hussein's Iraq possessed weapons of mass destruction may be another example.[30]

There are also indirect ways in which positive illusions may be helpful in conflict. First, resolve and bluffing may be observed by third parties, deterring potential future rivals: "Dominance need not be competitive. It can arise from strong personal characteristics that produce admiration and deference in others."[31] Second, third-party observation may attract potential allies hoping to benefit from an apparently strong partner. Third, a belief in one's superiority may encourage one to take preemptive action, which often lends a competitive edge: taking the initiative, surprise, faits accomplis, striking first, and an "offensive bias" are commonly cited advantages in military strategy and international relations. Fourth, if bluffing is advantageous but sometimes fails, then positive illusions that enhance performance may be crucial to fighting one's way out of a corner when one's bluff is called. Fifth, a tendency to take up challenges may allow one to exploit hidden weaknesses in rivals. Of course, one risks taking on more powerful opponents too, but as Daniel Nettle's work shows (see section 2 of the Appendix), the net gains of overestimates can exceed those of accuracy or underestimates. A rational assessment never to challenge equal or apparently stronger adversaries would therefore leave potential winnings untapped.

For positive illusions to be adaptive, the simple condition, as stated by Wrangham, is that over the long run those "with positive illusions tend to succeed sufficiently often that it pays to have such illusions. Miscalculations then result from a trade-off between successful and failed bluffs, rather than from an inherent inability to assess correctly." Despite the havoc sometimes caused by such miscalculations, positive illusions remain advantageous in conflict because without them an actor would be too cautious or outbluffed. This rings true in the real world: while war may be a scourge on society, there has rarely been a shortage of people ready to exploit others who shy away from it. As Clausewitz wrote: "Boldness in war . . . must be granted a certain power over and above successful calculations involving space, time, and magnitude of forces, for wherever it is superior, it will take advantage of its opponents' weakness. In other words, it is a genuinely creative force."[32]

The confidence of soldiers, commanders, statesmen, and nations has long been appreciated as an ingredient of success. Napoleon believed that, in war, morale was three times more valuable than physical strength. More than a century and a half later, writing about the Vietnam war, Leslie Gelb and Richard Betts suggested that high morale remained a key attribute: "Optimism is psychologically necessary for dedicated and energetic performance."[33] Indeed, differences in morale can turn the tide of wars. Low morale can lead to military coups or domestic revolutions that bring down the home government (as with Milosevic in Serbia); high morale can allow nations to keep fighting apparently hopeless battles for years without surrendering (as with the resistance against the Soviet invasion in Afghanistan).

Weaker sides sometimes win wars—even against superpowers—and this is often attributed to the higher resolve of the underdog. In extreme cases, the resolve of a weaker power can render even massive military coercion by the stronger side effectively useless.[34] The United States failed to break North Vietnamese resolve despite years of carnage and more tonnage of bombs dropped than during all of World War II. As Ho Chi Minh promised: "Kill ten of our men and we will kill one of yours. In the end, it is you who will tire." The U.S. army chief of staff, General Harold K. Johnson, suggested that there had been an "unexamined assumption that a display of American power would cause the enemy to run." The fact that it was "unexamined" suggests that assessments of wartime supremacy are not always made consciously; they arise from deeper beliefs that may be taken for granted.[35]

Many of the most immediate threats to international security feature much weaker states that simply make bold moves or take strong stands (Iraq's defiance of Western coalitions in 1991 and

2003, the Taliban's defiance in 2002, North Korea's nuclear ambitions). Terrorism, too, is characterized by individuals with such conviction that they are willing to fight and die in a war against powerful enemies. I argue that, by virtue of human psychology, we should fully expect a bias toward overconfidence by all sides in conflicts today, whether they are superpowers, small states, freedom fighters, or terrorists.

Still Adaptive Today?

Humans are fish out of water. Modern life is far removed from our "natural" environment of evolutionary adaptation, where our lineage spent 99 percent of its five to seven million years of independent evolution. Modern civilizations and large static populations are extremely recent, only around eight thousand years old. Our brains evolved to deal with the trials and tribulations of living in small groups of hunter-gatherers. Evolution works slowly to extinguish behavior that does not have a systematic selection pressure against it, so many human traits reflect our past rather than our present. Positive illusions may well persist today even if they have ceased to be adaptive.

For positive illusions to still be evolutionarily adaptive in modern life, there would have to be a systematic selection pressure favoring them because they promote reproductive success. Whether this is true or not is unknown, but it seems unlikely: Do people with higher positive illusions really have more offspring? On the other side of the coin, there is also little reason to expect any systematic selection pressure *against* positive illusions: people do not systematically die or fail to reproduce as a result of such illusions (some may, but it is probably not a widespread effect). I argue, therefore, that positive illusions are unlikely to be evolutionarily adaptive in today's world. Rather, they are an "adaptation"—a human trait which arose because it was adaptive at some point in our evolutionary past. If, today, we sometimes encounter situations in which positive illusions provide advantages, they may still be "adaptive" in the strategic or vernacular sense (as is often argued in the psychology literature), but not necessarily the evolutionary sense. To avoid this confusion in the following discussion, I will refer to positive illusions as being "advantageous" instead of "adaptive."

In many contexts positive illusions *are* advantageous in modern life. As we have seen, they promote positive attitude, persistence, and success in numerous challenges, and physical health (by, for example, reducing stress that can compromise the body's immune defenses). Studies have demonstrated that positive illusions enhance performance in sports, academic work, musical composition, cooperative tasks, and even relationships, which may last longer as a result of positive illusions about them.[36] To some extent, positive illusions "are self-fulfilling, creating the world that we believe already exists."[37]

But the evidence is sometimes conflicting. As Richard Robins and Jennifer Beer point out, "the question of whether positive illusions are adaptive [today] remains open to empirical enquiry." Daniel Goleman blames positive illusions for encouraging people to devalue or ignore environmental disaster, so that despite their "vital role in the psyche of the healthy individual," they are "toxic for us as a species." Goleman adds: "We fool ourselves so easily about the dangers to our species because our illusions work too well. While our emotional and physical well-being is based in part on artful denial and illusion, the state of the world is such that we can no longer afford that artifice."[38]

Roy Baumeister notes that many of the self-defeating behaviors found among humans involve misjudging the self or the social environment in some way: "Overestimating one's abilities and likelihood of success can lead one into various undertakings that consume time and energy and produce failure." He also recognizes that "military operations furnish perhaps the clearest illustration of the dangers of making decisions based on illusions, for the costs of failure are apparent and dramatic."[39]

However, whether positive illusions are advantageous or disadvantageous in modern war is a complex question. For the great majority of our evolution, combat would have occurred between small hunter-gatherer groups. One feature of "primitive" warfare is that warriors of the two sides often assemble and display to each other before a battle, seemingly to assess their relative power. The ability to intimidate may be a key determinant of success. In modern war, such visual factors are almost completely absent. The scale of modern war and the detachment of modern weapons make combat, command, and planning much more abstract and isolated from direct feedback.

For soldiers in combat, resolve and signaling confidence to the enemy may still have their traditional advantages. For middle-ranking bureaucrats in charge of military policy, far from the battlefield, overconfidence may lead to a misallocation of resources without any compensating bluff to the enemy. For those behind desks, therefore, an accurate assessment is more likely than over-optimism to increase the chance that their side will win (for them, positive illusions may merely create havoc). In the highest echelons of political power, the level of communication with the enemy is more similar to that of soldiers than to that of bureaucrats: shows of resolve and bluffing between national leaders are quintessential elements of international politics. Genuine conviction and confidence, over and above conscious strategizing, are signaled in public speeches, negotiations, political bargaining, diplomacy, alliance seeking, seeking treaties, development and deployment of military power, and even parliamentary infighting. And such signaling may carry crucial messages not only to rival nations but to one's own domestic audience as well. The potential impact of positive illusions among such leaders is therefore highly significant—for better or for worse. Resolve and bluffs may bolster national security, but they may also drive conflicts of interest into war.

Positive illusions, like many psychological responses, seem to have evolved to be "switched on" or altered by specific stimuli in the environment. This is a neat method of triggering a needed response—as long as the organism is in its native environment of evolutionary adaptation. Only then will the "proximate" stimuli reliably coincide with the "ultimate" advantage of the response.

Niko Tinbergen famously cautioned us to make this analytical distinction between proximate and ultimate causation if we wish to understand behavior.[40] Now that we humans are no longer in our native habitat, the same old proximate responses continue to be fired off in the brain in response to certain stimuli, even if the result is inappropriate behavior. We often can't help it. But the ultimate function is no longer necessarily served.

What is more, the triggers in today's world may be exaggerated versions of those in our natural environment, "super-stimuli" that elicit disproportionate responses. For example, seeing thousands of troops massed ready for war may switch on or multiply positive illusions that—regardless of rational logic—override any reports of enemy strengths and confer the feeling that one's army cannot possibly be beaten.[41] Prior to the 1967 Arab-Israeli war, President Nasser of Egypt was said to have become "intoxicated with the array of men and weapons he saw deployed during his tour of Egyptian positions in the Sinai." His military overconfidence, and the attendant bellicosity, is thought to have been an important cause of the war.[42]

Empirical Evidence of Positive Illusions

Individual Illusions

Positive illusions are widespread, pancultural, robust, and found in astonishingly diverse contexts. People consistently overrate various individual qualities such as their health, leadership ability, professional competence, sporting ability, and ethics.[43] People tend to see themselves as better than others with respect to intelligence, attractiveness, fairness, or skill.[44] They also believe they have higher than average morals, health, and managerial skills.[45] People tend to think they are more likely than others to have gifted children, get a good first job, and do well on future tasks, and that they will be happier, more confident, more hardworking, and less lonely in the future than their peers. One study even found that 94 percent of college professors believe that they do above-average work.[46] People are also overly optimistic about negative events, tending to believe they will live longer than average, will not be victims of car accidents, crime, or earthquakes, will not get ill, suffer depression, or have unwanted pregnancies.[47] A review of this literature back in 1994 reported: "Evidence for unrealistic optimism in normal samples is voluminous and continues to grow."[48]

People also overestimate their ability to control events, or other people's behavior.[49] For example, when playing Prisoner's Dilemma games, subjects act as if they can control the simultaneous decision of the other player. In bargaining situations, people tend to overweigh views that favor themselves, to be overly optimistic about what outcomes are achievable, and to be overconfident that they will attain them. After the event, people tend to attribute failures to uncooperative and unethical practices by the opponent, not to themselves.[50] Their self-serving evaluations also tend to increase the costs of conflict by preventing combined gains and delaying agreement, which leads to escalation. People also tend to "think they are tapping more sources of information than they are, overestimate the degree to which they combine evidence in complex ways, and flatter themselves by thinking that they search for subtle and elusive clues to others' behavior."[51]

Positive illusions vary among people and contexts (see Chapter 2), but "the evidence clearly indicates that most people anticipate that their future will be brighter than can reasonably be justified on statistical grounds."[52] Such effects are now so common in the literature that they have been combined to build a general theory for why positive illusions are essential to mental health and how they serve useful functions.[53]

The applicability of psychological biases to political phenomena is sometimes doubted because the biases are discovered in laboratory experiments involving relatively small sample sizes. However, in addition to the never-ending replications of positive illusions studies, a survey of a million high school students found similar effects: 70 percent rated themselves as above average in leadership ability (only 2 percent rated themselves below average), and 60 percent similarly overrated their athletic ability (only 6 percent below). In ability to get along with others, all of them rated themselves as at least average, 60 percent placed themselves in the top 10 percent, and a whopping 25 percent placed themselves in the top 1 percent.[54]

Another criticism is that laboratory experiments often use college students as subjects, who are then assumed to represent humans in general. Much of the evidence for positive illusions, however, has come from research on athletes and people with various illnesses, a much broader cross-section of personality types, education, ages, experience, and professions. Taken together, the numerous replications, large sample tests, and diverse subject groups suggest an unusually high degree of robustness and generalizability for the phenomenon of positive illusions.

Group Illusions

People not only overestimate themselves, they also overestimate the groups and societies to which they belong. People even judge others in their own group as better than the group's average, and still do so when their group members are anonymous strangers assigned to the group randomly. "A well-functioning group," in Daniel Goleman's words, "is bound together by a kind of group narcissism, one that subscribes to the familiar positive illusions: an unrealistically positive sense of itself, the somewhat grandiose sense of how much the group can make a difference . . . and an overly optimistic sense that things will turn out well."[55]

Such biases for one's in-group and against out-groups are well established in a paradigm of social psychology known as social identity theory, founded on the work of Henri Tajfel and John Turner. Social identity theory builds on a mass of empirical evidence demonstrating that people rapidly identify with even arbitrarily assigned groups and systematically overvalue their own group's performance and qualities. Tajfel argued that these tendencies result from people's deep-seated desire to maintain positive self-esteem, and that people invoke intergroup comparisons in an attempt, as Marco Cinnirella puts it, "to construe our own in-groups as both different from, and superior to, out-groups of which we are not members."[56] Experiments have also shown that people overestimate the ideological difference between their own and an opposing group, and see their opponents' viewpoints as more extreme than they in fact are.[57]

Group positive illusions appear to be related to group violence. Roy Baumeister's review of human aggression studies showed that "groups whose members demonstrate higher levels of self-esteem also demonstrate higher levels of hostility and violence" and that "collective violence tends to be linked to explicit beliefs in the superiority of the violent group." Another study found that nearly all tyrants in modern history, and many of their subjects, held strong beliefs in their own cultural superiority (the Nazis being the most obvious example).[58]

The psychologist Irving Janis argued that decisionmaking in groups is likely to exacerbate optimistic biases because "groupthink" results in reinforcing perceptions of superiority, including these:

- a shared illusion of invulnerability,
- an unquestioned belief in the group's inherent morality,
- collective attempts to maintain shaky but cherished assumptions,
- stereotyping out-groups as too evil for negotiation or too weak to be a threat,
- self-censorship of doubts or counterarguments to conform to the group,
- a collective illusion of unanimity in a majority viewpoint (based on the faulty assumption that silence means consent),
- direct pressure on dissenters to maintain group loyalty, and
- self-appointed mind guards to protect the group and the leader from information that might weaken resolve.

(According to the political scientist Karen Alter, all of these criteria could be identified in the Bush administration's assessments of

Iraq before the 2003 war; see Chapter 8.) Groupthink and positive illusions would reinforce each other dramatically. As Goleman noted, "the sense that whatever the group plans is bound to succeed" is "an illusion that is virtually the sum total of the three positive illusions" that have been described for individuals (overoptimism about oneself, one's control of events, and one's future).[59]

The impact of positive illusions on individuals and groups may be further compounded at the societal level. Positive illusions at this level appear to be particularly important in times of war. As Vladimir Volkan argues, "Anyone trying to deal with interethnic or international conflict must grasp the psychological cogency of man's need to have enemies as well as allies, and his stubborn adherence to identification with a group when undergoing hardship and danger." During World War II the psychologist Norman Meier observed: "Intensive nationalism, like excessive egotism, is inclined to lead toward attitudes of superiority, with corresponding ratings of inferiority for others . . . Most nations, being composed of fallible human beings, are guilty of some degree of this self-delusion."[60]

Decades of research have corroborated this finding: whole societies are likely to succumb to mutually reinforced positive illusions because of inherent differences in feedback from "in-group" and "out-group" interactions. *Within* a society, the inaccuracy of perceptions of other people is limited by overlapping interests, and by frequent interaction and corrective information. *Between* societies, however, individuals interact much less often, and misperceptions are challenged much less frequently and are often exacerbated by differences in ideologies and values. So negative views about the moral worth, physical strength, and bravery of "foreigners" remain unchecked by feedback or shared interest. Conflict is therefore more likely, because both sides hold constantly reinforced illusions that their society has superior morals, gods, national aspirations, or soldiers. Stephen Van Evera argues that such perceptions are systematically reinforced by "chauvinist mythmaking," a "hallmark of nationalism" that includes "self-glorifying, self-whitewashing and other-maligning" and that is accomplished via school curricula, popular history, literature, and the political elite. An example is the British complacency about enemy capabilities before Japan's invasion of Malaya during World War II. Defenses were left to the last minute, at least partly because senior commanders held the belief that Japanese soldiers were small, were physically weak, had poor eyesight, suffered from inferior leadership, and could not drive armor through the jungle. Of course, all this was quickly found to be false.[61]

Times of crisis significantly exacerbate in-group positive illusions and out-group derogation. Lawrence LeShan describes "a strong tendency in us humans to shift our method of appraising an international situation from a sensory reality to a mythic reality as tensions escalate." The mythic version of events is buoyed by many shared misperceptions: a reduction to an "us and them" or a "good and evil" mentality; a devaluation of the enemy; beliefs that "our" allies are virtuous, "theirs" are immoral; that God is on "our" side; that winning is crucial and losing unthinkable; that the enemy acts for evil motives whereas "we" are fighting out of self-defense, benevolence, or morality; that the enemy is prone to lying so communication is pointless; and that identical acts are good when done by "us" but evil when done by "them." Contrary opinions are suppressed, those who question accepted wisdom are branded as unpatriotic, and concerns for underlying causes fade against the importance of outcomes. As LeShan suggests, the "mythic evaluation of reality" may be the most effective way to fight a war once it is happening, "but the decision of whether to fight a war should be made in the sensory reality, without the contamination of mythical elements."[62] Unfortunately, aspects of positive illusions may already be built into a nation's institutions and psyche.

What about Leaders?

It is important enough to discover that normal people have systematic positive illusions. However, military and political leaders, particularly those who reach top decisionmaking positions, are not typical people—because of self-selection of people who *want to become* leaders, institutional and public selection of those who *become* leaders, and the nonrandom selection of henchmen by those who *are* leaders. It is conceivable that leaders' experience and sagacity may make them *less* prone to decisionmaking biases than the average citizen (for example, they may be more used to making complex choices), but there is no evidence for this. In the case of a bias toward optimism, I argue that leaders are, if anything, particularly likely to exhibit high levels. Unfortunately, there is little evidence for this either: experimental work comparing the positive illusions of leaders with those of the average person has yet to be done. Nevertheless, there are many reasons to expect positive illusions to be especially strong among those who wield the most power—and this possibility, though tentative, is important in a consideration of the effect of such illusions on war.

Recall what positive illusions comprise—exaggerated self-perceptions, illusions of control over events, and overly optimistic expectations about the future. Now consider the careers of leading politicians. The people who make it to the top of political hierarchies tend to be those who have especially pronounced self-esteem, confidence in their ability to change things, and optimism that they can make a difference. To get to such a position, they require a character that can shoulder major burdens, accept numerous setbacks, and withstand constant criticism, and yet still get up every day believing they are right. Few people attain power without the self-confidence to travel the long, strenuous, and unsympathetic road to get there.

In his book on U.S. presidents, Richard Shenkman reports that unrelenting ambition is a key character trait all the way from George Washington to Bill Clinton. Even odd examples like Lincoln, who started life uneducated and in poverty, appear to have begun their careers "full of optimism." Throughout U.S. history, the intense competition to attain power has meant that "in the struggle to win only the most ambitious survived." Shenkman concludes: "We like to pretend that normal people should be elected president. People, that is, with a normal amount of ambition. But normal people don't have what it takes—that extraordinary drive to succeed."[63]

Alan Ehrenhalt also noted the selection effect for ambitious personalities, describing the U.S. government as "increasingly dominated by a modern class of professional politicians, people who work full time at getting and holding office. In many cases, they have done little else in their entire adult lives." The result is that those in office, not just in the White House but across the government, "comprise a careerist elite whose lifetime political preoccupation has separated them from most people." The length, scale, and rigors of the presidential election are "merely a grotesque exaggeration of the job that confronts ambitious politicians at all levels of the system." Ehrenhalt labels this phenomenon "self-nomination": presidential candidates essentially nominate themselves by being unusually willing to make the enormous efforts and sacrifices required to seek office. Voters have to choose from among this subset of ambitious personalities.[64]

Selection effects are likely to be prevalent in both democratic and nondemocratic regimes. The public, parliamentary, and media scrutiny of the political process in democracies is well suited to weed out unconfident types, and one may imagine that in nondemocratic regimes leaders will tend to be even more confident personalities: it is commonly the ruthless and the battle-hardened who sweep others out of their way to attain power. Clausewitz suggested that such selection effects apply to military leaders as well: "A distinguished commander without boldness is unthinkable. No man who is not born bold can play such a role, and we consider this quality the first prerequisite of the great military leader." In addition, data show that rates of personality disorders and psychological problems are higher among leaders than in the population at large—and many such disorders are accompanied by strong positive illusions.[65]

Once a leader is in power, a number of reinforcing effects may kick in. Barbara Tuchman wrote of John F. Kennedy's team of advisors: "Power and status exhilarated these men and their fellows; they enjoyed the urgencies, even the exhaustion, of government."

Their successes, such as the Cuban missile crisis, strengthened their belief in their ability to accomplish great things. This kind of confidence may sometimes be justified—sometimes leaders can indeed accomplish great things—but there is also a danger that it will become overconfidence. "As people become more powerful," Roy Baumeister notes, "they may tend to hear increasing doses of flattery and agreement, which may impel them toward ever more favorable views of themselves." The old insight that power corrupts and leads to an increasing sense of omnipotence and invulnerability has often proved accurate in history, from Napoleon to Hitler.[66]

Although there will of course be exceptions, I argue that these selection processes, combined with the trappings of power, are likely to produce an overrepresentation of particularly confident people in the higher ranks of government. Furthermore, because the people who reach those positions are the ones who have the strongest influence on national policy, even if they are not *more* overconfident than ordinary citizens and soldiers, even if they merely have the same tendency toward optimistic bias as the general population, their overconfidence is likely to have momentous consequences.

Implications for Theory

The recognition of systematic and widespread positive illusions offers to vastly improve our understanding and theory building in international relations. There is a swelling tide of theory and empirical evidence (from both experimental and real-world studies) examining the role of various psychological biases in international relations.[67] What is not so common is to seek the *origins* of these biases. We often know that they *do* occur from experiments and case studies. But we don't often know *why*. Research on positive illusions offers not only a well-documented empirical phenomenon but also a well-developed and intuitive theory for its biological origin, adaptive function, and sources of variation. The empirical phenomenon of positive illusions leads us to expect that decisionmakers will *systematically* succumb to overconfident assessments, a revelation that has important implications for two fundamental branches of theory in international relations: rational choice theory and neorealism.

Rational Choice Theory

"Rationalist" approaches to understanding war hold that states—like the decisionmakers who run them—act *as if* they calculate the probabilities and utilities of all possible outcomes, and then choose the best available "utility-maximizing" option. Empirically observed phenomena such as positive illusions suggest that rationalist approaches are overly simplistic models of reality. Still, they remain a fundamental starting point for explaining state behavior. Unchecked positive illusions among individuals, groups, and nations foster underestimation of others as well as overestimation of oneself. This increases the chance that two opponents will both believe they can defeat the other, and thus that both will willingly go to war. Positive illusions therefore offer a solution to the War Puzzle—a reason why states are often unable to locate an alternative outcome that both would prefer to a fight.[68]

Note that even the winners, if they were rational, should prefer to negotiate to save the costs and risks of fighting. But a settlement can only be reached if both sides agree on the probable outcome of a war—and thus on how much each should concede in order to avoid fighting. The theory of positive illusions predicts that decisionmakers will not rationally calculate the correct outcomes; rather, they will tend to overestimate the probability and/ or the ease of their own victory and thus prefer war to any negotiated settlement that their adversary would accept.

Wars rely on uncertainty about success, and for war to be initiated, both sides generally need to believe they will gain from it (regardless of how easy they think actually winning may be). It is strategic to appear confident (to bluff strength that may deter rivals and win concessions), and to hide any evidence to the contrary. Consequently, James Fearon has argued that a central cause of war within the rational choice framework is that leaders have private information about their own sides' resolve or strength, plus "an incentive to exaggerate their true willingness or capability to fight."[69] Fearon suggests that this process is consciously enacted by state leaders (and reinforced by institutional practices). The positive illusions hypothesis suggests that precisely the same strategic advantage of exaggerating one's true willingness or ability to fight has selected for a *subconscious* psychological bias toward feigning confidence. Overconfidence may therefore result from conscious strategy and/or subconscious strategy. Positive illusions, however, offer explanatory power and have advantages that are missing in other explanations of war: concordance with human nature and specific sources of variation.[70]

The whole rational choice framework rests on the assumption that human brains and states are rational calculators, which accurately weigh the combined probabilities and utilities of all possible options. It is recognized as an "ideal," but one that has great relevance for understanding international relations. However, human behavior is now well known to deviate from this ideal.[71] Actual responses appear to originate from a combination of cognitive calculation, psychological biases, and emotions. Scholars from several disciplines, including neurology, economics, evolutionary biology, and psychology, are converging on the conclusion that our evolutionary legacy is essential to an understanding of observed human behavior.[72] What is more, many such traits pervade group, organizational, and national behavior as well.[73] In summary, then, Fearon's intuition about the strategic incentive to exaggerate one's willingness or ability to fight seems to be correct. But it may be promoted by evolutionary mechanisms such as positive illusions rather than solely from conscious strategizing.

Neorealism

Another central paradigm in international relations theory is "neorealism," which holds that the causes of war are to be found in the structure of the world's "anarchic international system." States must strive for power in order to protect themselves, because there is no overarching authority to police them and they do not know what other states intend. However, while anarchy and uncertainty about others' intentions are constant, wars sometimes occur and sometimes do not. So the key question is: What explains the *variation* in war and peace? Neorealism offers an account of the underlying or "permissive" causes of war. It does not, however, offer an account of the *proximate* causes—the sparks that ignite conflict. Neorealism can explain broad changes in the likelihood of war (since this may vary with changes in power among states, and with the "polarity" of the system—is it a unipolar, bipolar, or multipolar world?), but it cannot predict *when* wars will occur.[74]

While genuine power disparities sometimes offer unambiguous opportunities for powerful states to exploit their advantage—choosing war to gain power—neorealists (like rational choice theorists) tend to see war as very costly for both sides. They therefore usually invoke states' *misperceptions* or *mistakes* in evaluating power differences as the proximate causes of wars. Both neorealist and rational choice accounts are incomplete because they do not explain the *source* of these misperceptions. The theory of positive illusions offers two sources.

First, although misperceptions or mistakes may occur in either direction (inclining a state either toward or away from war), one factor that has been consistently invoked throughout the historiography of war is so-called false optimism. Several scholars examining the causes of war have found this to be a common theme, notably Geoffrey Blainey, John Stoessinger, Stephen Van Evera, and Sumit Ganguly. Each concluded that, while the desire for power may always be the underlying force, the actual outbreak of war is normally associated with overoptimism and overconfidence: states tend to *over*estimate themselves, their allies, or the benefits and swiftness of war, and to *under*estimate their opponents' capabilities, allies, or intentions, or the costs and duration of war.

Second, Van Evera has argued that wars result from actual or perceived differences in four specific aspects of relative power: the offense-defense balance between two states (or alliances); the size of a "first-mover advantage"; power fluctuations creating windows of opportunity; and the chance to cumulatively obtain more resources (when gaining one resource facilitates gaining a second). His key conclusion is that wars usually begin not when a state correctly identifies these opportunities, but rather when a state *exaggerates* them. That is to say, when a state wrongly perceives that conquest will be easy, that there is an advantage to being the one to initiate conflict (a first-mover advantage), that there is a window of opportunity to exploit, or that by going to war it will cumulatively gain more resources. The kindling for wars is prepared by the underlying structure of the system, but wars are ignited by a state's overconfidence in one or more of these four areas.[75]

Despite this recurring indictment of false optimism and mistaken opportunities as causes of war, no good explanations have been offered for *why* states systematically overrate their relative power. As Van Evera notes, a theory is not ultimately satisfying "if it leaves us wondering what causes the cause proposed by the theory."[76] The positive illusions hypothesis adds something that neorealism and rational choice approaches cannot tell us. It predicts that misperceptions will be systematically biased in a positive, self-serving direction, and thus it explains why misperceptions are so frequently associated with war. It also offers specific sources of variation (see Chapter 2), and an *origin* for such a bias, as stemming from an adaptive strategy in our evolutionary past (and perhaps a selective advantage in recent history as well). While the underlying causes of particular wars and crises, including those discussed later in this book, are already well established, an appreciation of positive illusions may enhance our understanding of why leaders chose to risk war, or to sue for peace, at the times that they did. I argue that the desire for security and power imposed by the anarchic international system forms much of the underlying cause, and that this is modified by domestic politics and organizational biases. Positive illusions help pull the trigger—they are a proximate explanation. As Richard Lebow noted: "Leaders who entertain expectations of easy victory may be willing to assume greater risks because the prospect of war exercises less of a restraining influence upon them. They may also conclude that the probability of war is low because they expect their adversaries to back away . . . rather than face certain defeat."[77]

Examples from History

According to Lebow, the 1904 Russo-Japanese war is a striking example "of the effects of unwarranted military confidence upon crisis decisionmaking." He continues: "The magnitude of Russia's defeat stood in sharp contrast to her leaders' expectations of victory. From the onset of the crisis the Russians were so certain of their superiority that they were convinced that Japan would never actually risk a test of arms." Their "racist delusions of superiority" allowed them to view the Japanese forces as "an army of ducklings" which "could not be compared to any major European army, least of all the Russian." One member of the Russian general staff declared: "We will only have to throw our caps at them and they will run away." A significant faction of the Russian decisionmakers and advisors were confident they could defeat the Japanese, even without help from allies, and even though Japan had a superior navy and an army that outnumbered theirs by three to one. Gordon Martel similarly attributed the war partly to Russia's "misplaced confidence in her strength in the far east." James Fearon noted that "on the eve of the war, Russian leaders believed that their military could almost certainly defeat Japan," while on the other side, the Japanese chief of staff "estimated a fifty-fifty chance of prevailing, if their attack began immediately. Thus Japanese and Russian leaders disagreed about relative power—their estimates of the likelihood of victory summed to greater than 1. Moreover, historical accounts implicate this disagreement as a major cause of the war."[78]

Sumit Ganguly identifies overoptimism as a root cause of the wars between India and Pakistan. Although differing ideologies and conflicting claims to Kashmir may explain the underlying hostility, they fail to explain the outbreak of the four India-Pakistan wars. Ganguly favors the explanation that the wars were sparked by perceived windows of opportunity "augmented by false optimism." Particularly in the wars of 1947–48, 1965, and 1999, "Pakistani decisionmakers grossly underestimated Indian military prowess and likely Indian responses to military challenges . . . The anti-Indian and chauvinistic ideology of the authoritarian Pakistani state repeatedly contributed to a flawed assessment of India's military capabilities and will." A powerful jingoism was evident in India as well, but there overconfidence was apparently constrained to some extent by open and democratic debate within the decisionmaking elite and the public as a whole.[79]

Of the Korean War, Max Hastings wrote: "At the root of American action lay a contempt, conscious or unconscious, for the capabilities of Mao Tse-tung's nation and armed forces." U.S. decisionmakers, as Lebow puts it, suffered from a "complacency engendered by racial stereotypes of the enemy." The American commander, General MacArthur, appeared to hold particularly positive estimates of his own capabilities relative to those of the adversary, and he strongly influenced the decision to send troops on the basis of what John Garofano calls a "bold but unrealistic assessment." The massive amphibious landings at Inchon were considered something of a masterpiece of daring, sweeping behind and trapping the North Korean army. But as the war progressed MacArthur paid a price for his great confidence and low regard for the "oriental military ability."[80]

The Chinese had made clear their intention to intervene if United Nations forces crossed the thirty-eighth parallel. Many U.S. decisionmakers doubted this intention, especially MacArthur, who "repeatedly and cavalierly dismissed Peking's ability to organize and coordinate an offensive in Korea." If they did intervene, MacArthur claimed, any support from their Russian allies would be useless: "Their incompetence would cause them to 'bomb the Chinese as often as they would bomb us'." As we now know, in November 1951, 180,000 Chinese soldiers attacked the coalition forces as they approached the Yalu River and ultimately drove them all the way back to the thirty-eighth parallel. The result (apart from the deaths of 450,000 South Koreans, 33,000 Americans, 3,000 allies from other nations, and around 1.5 million North Koreans and Chinese) was an armistice simply reestablishing the approximate prewar borders. As Saul David put it: "Such an outcome could have been achieved before Christmas 1950 if MacArthur and the U.S. government had not been so ready to underestimate the political will and fighting capability of the Chinese."[81]

Positive illusions were also evident prior to the 1973 Arab-Israeli Yom Kippur war. John Hughes-Wilson concluded that "at every level Israel underestimated her enemy." As mentioned earlier, the Israeli chief of staff commented ten days before the war: "We'll have one hundred tanks against their eight hundred . . . That ought to be enough." Israeli forces were indeed superior in combat to their enemies, according to later quantitative analyses by T. N. Dupuy—but by a factor of two, not eight. Baylis Thomas wrote of "Israel's complacency about its invincibility and a certain racist assumption about the inferiority of Arab soldiers."[82]

On the other side, there have been some interesting statements made about Arab self-confidence. Dupuy describes "an Arab cultural tendency to allow emotion and wishful thinking to influence planning, evaluation and operational leadership." In the words of one Palestinian Arab, "We are emotional rather than coldly analytical. Honor is exaggerated at the expense of real need. We would *like* to see certain things and we think they *are*." Dupuy reports that an Egyptian general also identified this tendency "in almost identical words." Leaving these anecdotal impressions aside, the Egyptian war aims themselves imply that Egyptian leaders had remarkable confidence, given that, as Baylis Thomas notes, "for Egypt to cross the Suez Canal to establish a beachhead on the east bank was considered impossible by all [outside] military observers."[83]

I do not suggest that positive illusions necessarily affected the outcome of these wars, but they may have played a part in the decision, by both sides, to fight. In these, and in my case studies, I am not arguing that positive illusions are the all-encompassing explanation for war—but that they offer a compelling extra piece of the War Puzzle.

Chapter 2

Looking for Illusions

Recurring optimism is a vital prelude to war. Anything which increases that optimism is a cause of war. Anything which dampens that optimism is a cause of peace.
— Geoffrey Blainey

Situational factors can explain 100 percent of the variance in the degree to which people demonstrate positive illusions . . . [such factors] can greatly enhance or virtually obliterate their existence.
— Shelley Taylor and David Armor

Positive illusions vary. First, they vary among individuals. Second, they vary with context: for example, they are greater when assessments are less verifiable or made in threatening circumstances. Third, I hypothesize that, over and above these sources of variation, the effects of positive illusions—the forms of overconfidence they engender—will be exacerbated in nondemocratic states and in states with closed decisionmaking processes. The prediction is that positive illusions are least likely to produce war in democratic governments with an open debate, and most likely to produce war in nondemocracies with a closed debate. This will be tested in my four case studies.

The Positive Illusions Theory of War

My central hypothesis is that positive illusions in states' decisionmakers increase the likelihood of war. This prime hypothesis, however, omits the chain of events that leads from individuals harboring positive illusions to the complex outcome of war. This chain of events is detailed in the explanatory hypotheses, which propose that, in certain contexts, positive illusions cause various types of overconfidence among decisionmakers, and that such overconfidence, in certain decisionmaking environments and institutions, promotes war (see Figure 2). The antecedent conditions are crucial because, given that war is a sporadic event, only a causal factor that is *variable* has the potential to explain why it occurs at some times and not at others. (For a summary presentation of my hypotheses and predictions in tabular form, see section 5 of the Appendix.)

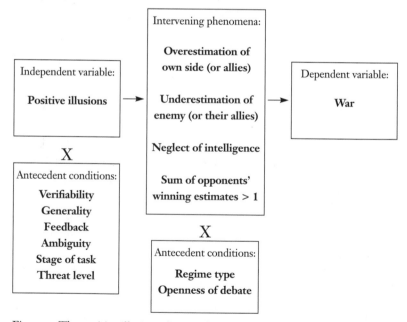

Figure 2. The positive illusions theory of war. Positive illusions, given certain antecedent conditions (a relationship denoted by X), engender four main intervening phenomena of overconfidence in state decisionmaking. These manifestations of overconfidence, given further antecedent conditions, may increase the probability of war (over and above any underlying rationale for a particular war).

Sources of Variation

Positive illusions, as mentioned earlier, vary among individuals and among contexts. (They also appear to vary among mental states, genders, and cultures; see section 3 of the Appendix.) Behavioral explanations of war are often ignored in international relations scholarship because human nature is seen as constant, while war is not.[1] But this view is outdated and wrong.[2] As David Welch has written, "To read the classic texts of international relations theory, one would never suspect that human beings have right brains as well as left; that in addition to being selfish, they also love, hate, hope, and despair; that they sometimes act not out of interest, but out of courage, politeness, or rage." Traits that make up human nature (such as anger) vary enormously among individuals (different people express different amounts and manifestations of anger) and among contexts (anger is differentially triggered or restrained depending on the situation). We do not expect some rigid behavioral "trait" to explain diverse political phenomena; but the *variable state of a trait* may indeed covary with variation in political phenomena (among other things), offering a potential causal explanation. In his review of research on optimism, Christopher Peterson warned that we "should not become so focused on optimism as a psychological characteristic that [we ignore] how it is influenced by external situations."[3] Research has shown that there are specific antecedent conditions that alter the strength of positive illusions (see Figure 2); I will outline these in a moment.

Even if these sources of variation were absent, however, any trait of "human nature" can still have different political effects depending on the different environments within which it is expressed. For Alexander the Great, anger could have immediate policy outcomes (such as razing a town to the ground), but there are numerous mechanisms to temper the impact on policy of an angry British prime minister or American president: the same trait in two different governments may lead to entirely different policies once squeezed through the local machinery of decisionmaking and approval. Therefore, there are also antecedent *structural* conditions that alter the impact of positive illusions on policy, or more specifically on the forms of overconfidence it engenders. I focus on two such conditions: regime type and openness of debate.

Positive illusions are "likely to vary as a function of the person, the situation, and their interaction."[4] I hypothesize that variation in positive illusions themselves, plus any variation imposed by the structures through which they are expressed, correlates with the probability of war. Of course, there is some probability of war even if there are no positive illusions (owing to a variety of other causes). But above whatever that probability is, increasing positive illusions increase the probability of war—so the theory of positive illusions can add to our understanding of why war breaks out when it does.

Individual Variation

Peterson stresses that "our human nature provides a baseline optimism, of which individuals show more versus less," because of, for example, differences in self-esteem or in experience. Given individual variation in optimism, we might expect a normal, bell-curved distribution of positive illusions in a population, just as people's height or IQ follows such a distribution (see Figure 3). As Lionel Tiger wrote in his book on the adaptive importance of optimism, "in dealing with natural systems the shortest analytical distance between two points is a normal curve." This curve is useful because, as well as illustrating the empirical phenomenon that the average person's expectations exceed realistic assessments, it also highlights the point that many people will exceed the average, and some by a lot.[5]

I argued in Chapter 1 that people at the high end of this distribution are likely to be overrepresented among leaders and decisionmakers. Furthermore, people at the extreme high end of the distribution are likely to be overrepresented among those infamous figures whose confidence is so extreme that it ultimately

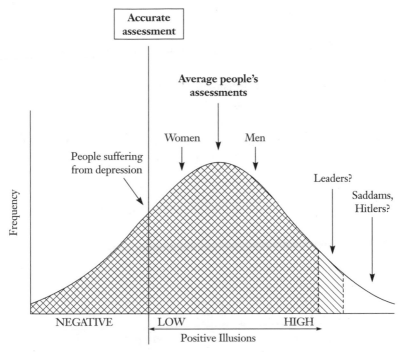

Figure 3. Conceptual scheme of variation in positive illusions among the population at large. Most people tend to overestimate their abilities, their control over events, and the future, so the population average exceeds a realistic assessment of these things.

brings about their own demise—the Napoleons, Hitlers, and Saddam Husseins of history. For the purposes of the case studies, it is enough to bear in mind that individuals vary in positive illusions so we do not expect all leaders to exhibit them in the same way.

Antecedent Conditions for Positive Illusions

As Shelley Taylor and her colleagues have noted, "positive illusions are most evident in the abstract when they hold the power to inspire and motivate but are less in evidence when they can be directly disconfirmed by the feedback of specific situations." By this logic, we may expect positive illusions to be particularly prevalent in the period immediately before a war, but then to decline as feedback on the war's costs accumulates. The same authors also give more precise predictions about when positive illusions will ebb and flow: "Positive illusions are lessened as verifiability increases . . . more evident at the general than at the specific level, more in evidence at the beginning of a project than the end of a project, more in evidence with respect to ambiguous personal qualities than with respect to concrete personal qualities with clear behavioral referents, and more in evidence when a course of action has been selected than when it is under debate."[6] Positive illusions are also expected to increase in times of threat. Let us examine each of these antecedent conditions in turn.

High versus Low Verifiability. Positive illusions are not wild deviations from reality—people do not normally believe things that are obviously incorrect.[7] Rather, people tend to put an optimistic spin on things. Moreover, positive illusions are responsive to information. As people receive feedback on their performance in a task, their illusions about that task will diminish. By contrast, assessments about which one never receives feedback will be prone to large positive illusions. The extent to which an assessment is "verifiable" will, thus, affect the degree of positive illusions.

In war, this is likely to be a particularly important variable. Politicians, for example, rarely receive *direct* feedback about their policies, because bad outcomes can be attributed to numerous other factors, people, and problems in the decisionmaking tree. This is especially the case with decisions to initiate or escalate conflict: a disastrous outcome need not implicate the policy itself but may imply only that for some reason it did not work out as intended.[8] By contrast, decisions made by military officers may expose the decisionmakers to immediate risks (task failure, loss of equipment, casualties). In such circumstances commanders are likely to receive more direct feedback, and also to be better able to attribute that feedback to the consequences of specific decisions. Therefore positive illusions should tend to decrease from politicians, to local decisionmakers, to military personnel on the ground, because of the increasing verifiability of decisions. The lower down in a hierarchy one travels the fewer steps there are in the decisionmaking process from conception to execution, and therefore the greater the likelihood that feedback will be directly attributable to specific decisions. The prediction is that positive illusions decline with the increasing verifiability of policy outcomes.

General versus Specific Attributes. Positive illusions are greater when they are formed at a general rather than at a specific level. Assessments of some very general notion, such as one's intentions or future plans, are likely to elicit positive illusions because people have little direct information to contradict them. Assessments of more specific things, such as whether or not one can play the piano, cannot be exaggerated so easily—both the assessor and anyone else can confirm them. In war, high-level strategic decisions are often very general, involving a number of assessments that do not, or cannot, draw on detailed information about each aspect (such as an enemy's intentions). Indeed, the strategic level necessarily remains general because it is only by cutting out all the specific details that one can appreciate the wider picture. Lower-level decisions necessarily involve more specific facts and figures, such as what resources would be needed to accomplish some local objective. Detailed facts about the area and personnel involved (and over a shorter time horizon) can also be gathered specifically for the task in hand. Here, the prediction is that positive illusions will be greater at the strategic level, when broad, general attributes are being assessed.

Feedback: Beginning versus End of Period. Undue optimism diminishes after negative events, or when people see that others are competing for the same goal or are trying to prevent them from achieving it.[9] Shelley Taylor argues that "illusions are able to respond to and make use of negative information when appropriate, while still maintaining positive beliefs overall." Negative information may come from direct experience of the environment, or from other people. In addition, when the objective results of a decision are scheduled to be revealed at a certain time in the future, optimistic expectations decrease as the time approaches (the date of exam results, for example).[10] In these cases, assessments start off optimistic, become more accurate, and sometimes end up negative. Assessments gradually become more realistic as information accumulates and concern about accountability increases (something like: "I got us into this war, we're losing it, and now I'm going to be made to pay for it").[11] As feedback becomes more imminent still, pessimistic concerns may overtake accuracy, as an incentive emerges to reduce expectations in order to avoid disappointment. This turn toward pessimism may be driven by increasing attention, anxiety, salience, or information processing, but anxiety seems to be the most important factor (it is known to have an inverse relationship with optimism). If anxiety is low (because of excessive self-assurance, false information, drugs, or alcohol), optimism will continue unabated.

All this suggests that overoptimism should decline with time (at least in cases where feedback is accumulated or anticipated). However, four factors may make the passage of time less likely to diminish the impact of positive illusions on war. First, before a war, there is no feedback, so initial assessments and the key decision to fight lack such regulation. Second, if feedback is far in the future, ignored, or not perceived to be relevant, optimistic predictions will prevail. Third, feedback in war may be qualitatively different from the topics in psychological experiments—all-or-nothing feedback is rarely expected at a particular moment (except perhaps anticipation of the general results of a specific event, such as the D-Day landings). Fourth, in experiments, the incremental lessening of optimism about specific events (such as the posting of exam scores) has been found to occur only in people with low self-esteem, not in those with high self-esteem. Thus, senior politicians and military leaders, who might be expected to have high self-esteem, may retain optimistic biases despite anticipated feedback. In fact, Roy Baumeister reports that individuals with high self-esteem tend to *increase* their positive illusions after a failure, despite the negative feedback.[12] So this form of variation may be somewhat dampened in the case of war—but even so, the prediction is that positive illusions generally decline with the increasing imminence or accumulation of feedback over time.

Ambiguous versus Clear Attributes. Positive illusions about self-assessments are exacerbated when the attribute being assessed is ambiguous. In such cases, people tend to create their own self-serving criteria and use those criteria to judge whether they are good at a particular task or not. For example, when asked to assess their own leadership ability, people may base their response on aspects of leadership they know they *do* excel at (such as time management), while ignoring aspects they are bad at (such as delegation of tasks).[13] Moreover, besides being inclined to focus on their own strengths, they are disinclined to focus on the strengths of others.

Experiments by David Dunning and his colleagues showed that as traits become more ambiguous, self-assessments become more overoptimistic, and that this variation is due to people using more idiosyncratic criteria. When required to use other people's criteria, subjects were less biased. The authors conclude:

> The above average effect by itself fails to serve as clear evidence of bias and distortion in social judgment. In effect, when people consider their own definition, and perhaps the one most relevant to the daily tasks they face, they may be largely accurate. However, even if this is the case, we can still conjecture that the above average effect, and the self-serving use of trait ambiguity, may have alarming social costs. These costs occur when one individual considers his or her peculiar definition as the only one worthy of consideration and fails to recognize when other plausible definitions are relevant . . . To the extent that people fail to recognize when other definitions of ability are relevant for success and achievement, estimates of their future well-being will be exaggerated.[14]

Dunning also found that, when judging others, people do not invent criteria favorably tailored to those others, as they do for themselves. If they did, others would be perceived as above average. Instead, people seem to impose their own self-criteria on other people, so that they perceive others as worse than they actually are. Thus there is a double-whammy effect that reinforces people's perceptions of their own superiority.[15]

In the complexity of war, the traits to be assessed and the appropriate criteria of judgment are likely to be ambiguous, all the more so because opposing sides have incentives to conceal them from each other. Like the blind men in the Indian parable, each describing an elephant (a "snake," a "tree," a "broom," a "wall"), even experts are likely to disagree on the adversaries' relative capabilities because they will give more or less weight to different factors in making an overall assessment.[16] As Michael Handel implies, this variable may most afflict a political leader, "who often deals with an adversary's [more ambiguous] intentions and long-range policies rather than with air photographs, tank and troop concentrations and other 'hard' evidence."[17] The prediction is that positive illusions will increase with the increasing ambiguity of the thing being assessed.

Stage of Task: Deliberation versus Implementation. Shelley Taylor and Peter Gollwitzer showed experimentally that, when people are engaged in *setting* goals, positive illusions are dampened (allowing them to set more feasible objectives). In contrast, when they are *planning* or *implementing* goals, positive illusions are exacerbated (which under normal circumstances allows more effective action). This was only a relative change: even subjects who were setting goals—as well as control subjects who were neither setting nor implementing goals—exhibited positively biased self-perceptions. The point is that the *level* of positive illusions varied among groups. When deliberating about how to solve problems people seem more likely to consider pros and cons in an even-handed way. When deliberation gives way to a focus on intended projects, evenhandedness disappears. People in the implementation stage of a task—both those still planning the implementation and those already engaged in it—did not attempt to find clarity, were distracted by irrelevant thoughts, reflected less on pros and cons (and preferentially considered pros when they did), and focused exclusively on getting the task done. They also showed a strong resistance to going back and reconsidering decisions they had already made. Thus, "implementation of a course of action appears to be a time when positive illusions are mustered, even exaggerated, in service of an explicit goal."[18]

The most drastic difference was in perceived invulnerability to risk. Although this did not differ between the deliberation and control groups (that is, deliberation did not *reduce* this type of positive illusion), it was strongly *exaggerated* in the implementation groups, suggesting that "implementation may especially blind people to risk." "Such perceptions," the researchers add, "may be adaptive in helping people to further the goals they have chosen to implement by keeping them from being sidetracked or concerned about potential risks."[19]

These findings suggest that positive illusions are selectively engaged when they are most useful: when "people attempt to implement the chosen goals (intended projects) as efficiently as possible . . . the vacillation of the predecisional phase is replaced by determination." Windows of more realistic thinking do occur, when "feedback is used to determine courses of action at choice points," but the danger is that "people who turn an unresolved problem into an unintended project by making a decision may close their minds to this window, as postdecisional individuals do not possess easy access to impartial deliberative thinking." Considering only a limited number of options and then prematurely selecting one of them may make for a disastrous closing of minds. Follow-up experiments have shown that deliberative and implemental thinking have different effects on behavior as well as on cognition, and that people in an implemental mindset outperform those in a deliberative one. Optimistic biases during implementation "appear to act as an insurance policy that goals will be aggressively pursued once deliberation is over."[20]

Thus positive illusions are likely to be amplified in wars that have already been decided upon. However, deliberation may not always dampen positive illusions about whether or not to go to war, because the mindset of implementation may arise even *before* this decision is made. It is difficult to judge whether foreign policy, specifically, is deliberative or implemental. If a state's national interest is, say, the pursuit of security and prosperity, then this may already be an implicit goal, and all subsequent foreign policy decisions may more closely resemble implementation (planning how to achieve it, getting on with achieving it). Whether each such step poses a fresh deliberative task, rather than continued implementation, is unclear.

As an example, once the United States was committed to preventing the spread of communism in Southeast Asia during the Cold War, the question then became, *How?* Eisenhower may have deliberated over whether or not to invest the initial support for the war in Vietnam, but Johnson's decisions about whether to escalate were, perhaps, more of an implementation problem—he had to carry out the predefined task of fighting and winning. America was already committed politically, the goal already well established. This could help to explain Eisenhower's relative reluctance to commit and Johnson's massive escalations. Nevertheless, the prediction is that positive illusions will increase significantly from the deliberation stage to the planning and implementation stage of a task.

Threat Level: Danger versus No Danger. While positive illusions are common even in peaceful and secure times, they are more likely to be engaged, and to become extreme, in threatening circumstances. As Daniel Goleman wrote, "we seem most likely to fall back on our illusions in the face of an overwhelming threat." For example, positive illusions are widespread among people with life-threatening illnesses. More specific to conflict, Richard Wrangham argues that when there is a threat of violence, and during fighting itself, positive illusions may be triggered or amplified as an adaptive response (and may therefore have a tendency to exacerbate crises and wars once people are already in them). Roy Baumeister suggests that it is specifically when inflated self-perceptions are threatened that aggression is triggered. And Lawrence LeShan details how societies switch from realistic perceptions to self-serving misperceptions in times of war: when a nation is threatened, its people devalue adversaries, assume the adversaries have evil intentions, band together, and claim higher morals and virtues.[21]

Positive illusions are different from defensive psychological mechanisms such as denial or repression, which increase *in defiance of* an increasing threat: "Highly threatening but probable events are recognized for what they are, namely probable threats, and their likelihood, though distorted in [a] falsely optimistic manner, is nonetheless perceived realistically relative to less probable threats."[22] Thus, while positive illusions may arise in response to danger, they do not necessarily become ever more overblown as the threat intensifies. The prediction is that positive illusions will increase in times of threat.

Antecedent Conditions for Overconfidence

Overconfidence is the intervening variable that I propose lies between positive illusions and war. It incorporates four main intervening phenomena engendered by positive illusions: overestimation of one's own side (and allies); underestimation of enemies (and their allies); neglect of intelligence; and overestimation of the chances of success, so that the two sides' estimates of their own chances sum to greater than 1 (see Figure 2). These forms of overconfidence are predicted to make war more likely—provided that they do not undergo corrective assessment before they influence policy.[23]

I suggest that the two key antecedent conditions affecting whether overconfidence leads to war are "regime type" (the official checks and balances on decisionmaking, which vary among states and are better in democracies) and "openness of debate" (the unofficial checks and balances imposed on decisionmaking, which vary among states and are better when more open). Regardless of initial levels of positive illusions, different combinations of these two variables will yield different predicted risks of war by allowing different amounts of overconfidence to survive in the system and influence policy.

Regime Type. I classify regimes as "democratic" or "nondemocratic" according to whether the governments took power with or without a free vote. In modern democracies, scrutiny by the public, the media, elected representatives, and cabinet members should more easily detect, oppose, and prevent poor or biased assessment by leaders. A tyrant's beliefs and wishes, in contrast, can be translated into policy largely unchallenged. Indeed, many of a tyrant's senior aides and military commanders are likely to be favored supporters or relatives, who lack incentive or even difference of opinion to question their benefactor's judgment. Furthermore, overconfidence among leaders is less likely to be contested in tyrannies than in democracies because propaganda is less challenged by feedback from rival sources, which may be scarce or even censored. If it is contested, the perpetrators may be punished.[24]

The prediction is that leaders' overconfidence is more easily counteracted in democracies. The U.S. government *ought* to be particularly good at blocking unfounded confidence because it is designed to maximize checks and balances and to encourage a divided government.[25]

Openness of Debate. I classify debate as "open" or "closed" according to the degree to which leaders encourage diverse and nonpartisan opinions, consider multiple options, exploit intelligence analysis, stimulate further intelligence gathering, cooperate with intelligence services, and heed advice. (This variable presupposes that relevant information is available—it focuses on the *use* of this information. Although information will never be perfect, decisionmaking units can be classified roughly by their relative openness in dealing with information.) Information is useless if it is false, irrelevant, misunderstood, or ignored. Thus the way in which information and advisors are *used* is at least as important as the intelligence itself. As Paul Kowert wrote: "Merely acquiring knowledge . . . does not in itself constitute proof of learning. One must also ask whether leaders use this information to reassess their policy options, even when doing so might challenge cherished assumptions about the world."[26]

More open debate should better scrutinize, provide alternative options, and uncover weaknesses of biased assessment by leaders. More closed debate is likely to consider only limited options, unlikely to challenge the efficacy or judgment of a chosen policy, and likely to ignore or fail to seek outside advice. Openness of debate can be independent of regime type, since even tyrants may have very effective decisionmaking processes, advisors, and treatment of intelligence. However, as Ernest May pointed out in his classification of "collegial" (more open) versus "centralized" (more closed) decisionmaking groups, in the latter, strategic assessment "is at the mercy of the person in control."[27] The prediction is that overconfidence will be more easily dispelled where decisionmaking is *inclusive* (open and nonpartisan) and *expansive* (considering many options and viewpoints).

Testing the Theory

States often teeter on the brink of war but then find a way to avoid it. Thus if I looked for evidence of factors promoting war only in the very situations they are hypothesized to account for, namely wars, I would not be able to falsify the reverse claim that wars are less likely if decisionmakers do *not* have positive illusions. In order to avoid this potential bias, I analyze not only wars but also crises that were resolved peacefully, a procedure that allows me to test whether a *reduction* of positive illusions contributed to their peaceful resolution.[28] Crises provide particularly good tests because they are situations in which war could easily break out— so that avoidance of war in a crisis is more telling than avoidance of war in calmer times. With respect to positive illusions, crises are of special interest because they are events that force on decisionmakers an urgent reassessment of their state's interests, of the relative capabilities of the two sides, and of the probability of winning or gaining from any impending conflict.

The Case Studies

I deliberately selected cases according to two separate but reinforcing selection criteria: first, cases where the *hypothesized effect should be unlikely* to occur; and second, cases where the hypothesized effect is apparently not needed because there are *good existing explanations* for the events (though not necessarily with a consensus among historians). This combination means that such cases provide particularly tough challenges to a novel hypothesis.[29] In each case study, I test my novel hypothesis against the null hypothesis that there is no causal relationship. However, I go beyond simply eliminating the null hypothesis to test whether my theory offers additional explanatory power over and above the dominant existing explanations for each case.

I also selected cases on the basis of data richness; extreme values of the dependent variable (crises that led to war *and* crises that led to peace); extreme values of antecedent conditions (widely different regime types and openness of debate); and large within-case changes in the study variables (permitting multiple observations, *within* similar conditions, of whether variables of interest were related to each other as predicted). I intentionally chose two cases involving the United States because of the significance of current U.S. foreign policy and military engagement around the globe. Finally, I selected cases that represent key turning points in twentieth-century history, which are therefore key proving grounds for the novel hypothesis of positive illusions.

Accordingly, I apply the theory of positive illusions to two wars and two crises: World War I, the Vietnam war, the Munich crisis of 1938, and the Cuban missile crisis of 1962. At the end of the book, I look speculatively at an informal case study: the invasion of Iraq in 2003.

Eliminating Alternative Proximate Factors

For each case, I initially ensure that three alternative proximate factors for the decisions taken (that is, factors independent of the underlying sources of conflict) can be rejected. These factors offer hypotheses that, if accurate, would render my theory unnecessary, since there would be no need for additional explanatory power to complete our understanding of why war did or did not break out. They are not competing theories as such; rather, they suggest that the spark for war or crisis, irrespective of *motive*, occurred as a result of fundamental constraints on available time, available options, or available information.

Insufficient Time for Assessment. For each case, I ascertain that the time for assessment was long enough to eliminate the possibility that decisions were simply based on "knee-jerk" reactions. Wars may be fought because decisionmakers do not have enough time to adequately assess their options—in which case overoptimistic decisions may just represent imperfect decisionmaking rather than overconfidence as such. Former U.S. secretary of defense Robert McNamara wrote that, in both the Kennedy and Johnson administrations, "we often did not have time to think straight." He noted that this problem is common to all administrations, countries, and times, but that he had "never seen a thoughtful examination of the problem. It existed then, it exists today, and it ought to be recognized and planned for when organizing government."[30]

No Other Options. For each case, I also ascertain that war was not the only possible course of action. Wars may occur, for example, because a state is backed into a corner from which it can do nothing but fight (at the extreme, a state is hardly expected to do anything other than fight if it is under invasion). A problem here is that what constitutes a viable alternative option is often subjective. Some decisionmakers may see war as necessary, given their preferences and sensitivities to the costs of fighting (or not fighting), while others may argue that the constraints are not really that limiting. Both may seem right from within their respective framings of the choice. The best we can do is strive to examine the choices as the decisionmakers apparently saw them at the time.

Insufficient Information. For each case I also ascertain that available information was at least *good enough* to eliminate the possibility that decisions were actually good ones given only poor information. How this information was actually used is another—much more important—matter, which is discussed in the next section.

Evidence for Positive Illusions

This is the key stage of analysis of the case studies: Did decisions reflect more optimistic expectations than the available information warranted despite adequate time for assessment and the existence of alternative options? If those criteria are met, then positive illusions are implicated. The challenge is determining on what basis expectations were overoptimistic. My analysis of evidence for positive illusions includes two main tasks to meet this challenge. The first task in each case study is to examine what I label "information and reaction." This establishes whether relevant information—according to actors at the time and later historical analyses—was available and conveyed to decisionmakers, and how they reacted to it. The second task is to ask: In the light of this information, did decisionmakers exhibit overly optimistic expectations?

Information and Reaction. The theory assumes that decisionmakers act poorly despite good and available information. For each case, therefore, I ascertain that in addition to information being at least *good enough* to eliminate the "good decisions based on poor information" possibility, the information is actually used effectively. I only attribute to positive illusions instances in which information was good and available and yet the decisionmakers neglected it or made decisions inconsistent with it.

To do this, I examine decisionmakers' reactions to incoming information. Do they have a tendency to disregard it? If not, do they actually absorb it? Do they actively seek new information? This part of the analysis is crucial, because the simple fact of apparently bad decisions coinciding with contradictory information does not go far enough in testing the positive illusions theory. One has to determine that the decisionmakers actually *believed* their policy would succeed, even *in spite of* objective evidence against it. Therefore, I also test whether decisionmakers *change* or *update* their beliefs as they receive corrective information. Updating would imply that positive illusions were gradually reduced through the working of a balanced decisionmaking process. Positive illusions do not make us immune to eventually perceiving reality. However, we may be resistant and slow to change because "people are capable of explaining away, compartmentalizing, or otherwise dismissing or minimizing negative feedback."[31]

Factors Implicating Positive Illusions. Positive illusions comprise exaggerated self-perceptions, exaggerated sense of control over events, and overoptimistic expectations of the future. As noted earlier, I hypothesize that such illusions engender specific types of overconfidence: overestimation of one's own side (and allies); underestimation of enemies (and their allies); neglect of intelligence; and the two sides' estimates of winning probability summing to greater than 1 (see Figure 2). Such overconfidence might be revealed by four measures:

- The judgments of other actors at the time and what historians and political scientists have concluded should have been clear at the time (that is, controlling for the benefit of hindsight).

- Statements by decisionmakers that express overconfident beliefs (ideally in private, not in public, since public statements may be partly propaganda).
- Facts that betray overconfident beliefs (actual policies, decisions, commitments, or actions).
- Comparison of expectations to actual outcomes (were expectations overoptimistic in comparison to what was actually attained?).

With a small number of cases, this last measure suffers from being judgmental after the fact. However, one can take multiple observations within a case to improve validity (and also to ask whether sequential decisions reflect new information), and it nevertheless stands that "if the predicted performance exceeds the actual performance, then the prediction can be regarded as optimistic."[32] Ideally, we want to see evidence of all four measures.

Politics is, very often, a series of displays and bluffs designed to disguise true intent. In other words, an analysis of what decisionmakers say (especially in public, but also sometimes in private) may in fact demonstrate very little because they may have vested interests in pretending to believe one thing while, in reality, pursuing another. Ideally, one needs to know what the decisionmakers *really* thought and believed. I have tried to identify this, where possible, by favoring private statements over public ones and by aiming for sources such as diaries and internal documents, which in theory reflect personal beliefs. Even these are problematic because people often write their diaries in the knowledge that they may be judged on them by later historians. Clearly, looking for illusions is tricky.

A better method of searching for overoptimism is looking at decisions actually made, rather than just what decisionmakers *said* they expected or would do. These can be argued to represent much more honest signals of intent, expectations, or hopes, given that actions (such as sending troops to war) are a costly way to demonstrate one's intentions and cannot easily be faked. Of course, even such extreme actions (such as mobilizing reserve forces) can be carried out in spite of the costs, and even without an intention to fight, as a conscious and deliberate signal to other actors. Even so, major policy decisions, such as the continuing and massive U.S. escalation in Vietnam, betray underlying beliefs and expectations better than do mere *statements* about beliefs and expectations.

The Tests

All four case studies allow tests of predictions of the prime hypothesis, the explanatory hypotheses, and antecedent conditions. My analysis makes use of the three major case study methods: controlled comparison, congruence analysis, and process tracing.

In *controlled comparison*, the "method of difference" compares cases with similar general characteristics but different variable values to look for correlations between positive illusions and war (for example, where the United States was a constant actor across cases, but the outcome was different). The "method of agreement" compares cases with different general characteristics and the same variable values (as where the country varied among cases, but the outcome was the same). I also conducted these paired comparisons using opposing sides of the same war or crisis (in which each side again has different general characteristics but the outcome is the same).

In *congruence analysis*, "Type I" compares values of the study variables to a base rate. In my study, the base rate is that of no war (that is, peace). I then test whether a high value (above the base rate) of the dependent variable, war, is associated with a high value of the independent variable, positive illusions (are they also above the norm?). "Type II congruence analysis" tests whether the independent and dependent variables covary across different circumstances within the same case. I am able to do this in all cases to some extent, and especially for Germany during 1938–1939 and the United States during the Vietnam war.

Process tracing examines the precise chain of events in the decisionmaking process leading from the initial conditions to the outcome. It fully exploits the case study advantage of using detailed written and oral testimony by decisionmakers and actors both at the time and in retrospect. This method provides exact links between cause and effect, so, while they may always be open to interpretation, in principle the predictions are strong and unique. The case studies are not intended, of course, to offer comprehensive historical accounts of the events; rather, they focus on those aspects relevant to the theory of positive illusions.

Where possible in the case studies, I test predictions of the six antecedent conditions for positive illusions. However, formal examination of the influence of all six antecedent conditions on positive illusions is not the central focus of the analysis: much more important is how, *over and above any initial levels of positive illusions*, regime type and openness of debate filter out the overconfidence caused by positive illusions to prevent those illusions from influencing decisionmaking and policy outcomes.

To examine whether regime type and openness of debate can explain variance in when overconfidence contributes to war, I conduct a controlled comparison of cases to compare each of these two antecedent conditions with outcomes of war versus peace. I also use congruence analysis to assess whether, overall, extreme cases of each variable exacerbate overconfidence and war. I can also examine this *within* cases to test whether variation in regime type and openness, despite perhaps no variation in the underlying level of overconfidence, is related to changes in the dependent variable (escalation, or changes from peace to war). Here, too, I use process tracing, to identify whether antecedent conditions cause the study variables to covary in the way predicted by the theory.

While analyzing the case studies I kept in mind several potential pitfalls, and to avoid them I took care to do the following: differentiate apparent positive illusions from alternative explanations of events (in particular from simultaneously operating international, domestic, institutional, and bureaucratic constraints);

evaluate decisions from the perspective of the policy options actually considered, as opposed to all those potentially available—a difference that can have dramatic consequences for policy;[33] consider confirmatory and contradictory evidence equally and avoid any tendency to "pick and choose" evidence to confirm the hypothesis under test; and avoid a reliance on hindsight that might support *a priori* positions and lead to undue focus on examples of incompetence.

Chapter 3

World War I

Both the Triple Entente (Britain, France, and Russia) and the Central Powers (Germany and Austria-Hungary) expected a quick victory in 1914.

—Stephen Van Evera

The optimism on the eve of the First World War belonged to a long but unnoticed tradition. In one sense only was it unusual. That was probably the first war since 1803 to involve, from its very commencement, more than two major powers, and so the fighting was expected to be serious and destructive. As expectations of that war therefore carried a pessimistic thread, the optimistic threads must have been far thicker in order to weave the prevailing mood.

—Geoffrey Blainey

Positive illusions should not have played a large part in World War I. Both sides had considerable time for assessment of their potential enemies (precluding the hypothesis that decisions were simply knee-jerk reactions); options other than war were available, even though they were somewhat constrained by perceived military imperatives (precluding the hypothesis that decisions simply represented the only possible course of action); and intelligence information was reasonable (precluding the hypothesis that decisions were good ones given poor information). (See Table 1.) World War I is also a tough test case because it is one of the most intensely studied conflicts in history, and has a plethora of existing explanations. Various economic, social, diplomatic, and military factors predisposed the various powers to armed conflict. Furthermore, people were not oblivious to the danger. Any opti-

Table 1. World War I: elimination of basic alternative explanations and overview of conclusions.		
	Central Powers	Triple Entente
Assessment opportunity	Long (though a perceived window of opportunity)	Long
Alternative options	Yes (though some perceived constraints)	Yes (though some perceived constraints)
Information availability	Reasonable	Reasonable
Positive illusions?	Yes	Yes
Main factor	Expectation of quick war and victory	Expectation of quick war and victory

mism would have to be especially significant to outweigh the expected devastation and horror of "modern" war.

Nevertheless, available information was not adequately used to form realistic expectations. On both sides, key decisionmakers, the military, and the public exhibited positive illusions about winning. Both sides thought that the war would be short, that they would win, and that they would benefit from it. The Germans also seriously underestimated the likelihood that other states would ally against them, and the strength of those potential foes. Overall, there was an extraordinary popular enthusiasm for war.

Background

The causes of World War I have been hotly debated ever since the day it began. Even now, there is no consensus on which factors were most important in causing a clash that would wipe out or mangle a generation of young men.[1] The only consensus, perhaps, is that diverse economic, social, diplomatic, and military circumstances conspired in an unfortunate coincidence to drag all of Europe's Great Powers into war. As the July Crisis spiraled out of control in 1914 following the assassination of Austria-Hungary's Archduke Ferdinand by a Serbian nationalist, a widely accepted idea that striking first was a military imperative in modern warfare began to favor war whether the key decisionmakers liked it or not. The tangle of alliances among states began to oblige them to take action, and "by 28–30 July the generals had taken over from the politicians and the nature of their plans made a general war among the great powers a virtual certainty."[2]

However, this focus on the war being somehow inadvertent wholly overlooks an extraordinary atmosphere of bellicosity and martial enthusiasm throughout Europe in the years before 1914. The Germans were particularly confident of victory, and had for years been developing the revered Schlieffen plan that would allow them to smash France, whose army, German military authorities argued, was "not prepared for a fight." But positive illusions were widespread: "The Russians too had parallel dreams of quick triumph, talking of victory in two or three months. Some Russian officers even boasted that they would reach Berlin in six weeks. French leaders expected a swift victory, and a British officer declared Germany would be 'easy prey' for Britain and France. Austria and Russia each expected to defeat the other. Even the Turks caught the mood: In later 1914 the Turkish war minister confided that after victory in the Caucasus, Turkey might march through Afghanistan to India."[3]

Traditional Explanations

Many historians see World War I as a result of a concatenation of unfortunate circumstances, and those circumstances are as diverse as they are numerous. The German historian Fritz Fischer, and the "Fischer School" that followed his line of argument, suggested that the main cause was Austro-German expansionism, that Germany had long planned an ambitious preventive war, and that Germany's tactics in the Balkans deliberately pushed the other powers over the edge (this claim created a storm of debate in the 1960s). Fischer argued that there had been a "conscious and deliberate grasp at world power, based on overconfidence on the part of Germany's rulers."[4] Other authors focus on the intricate system of alliances among the Great Powers, which meant that eventually the crisis in the Balkans would ensnare all the major European states. Furthermore, there were long-running arms races that predisposed states to suspect one another of intending to use their growing arsenals. There was also the problem of inflexible military doctrines, as well as Russia's and Germany's war plans that called for attacks on multiple fronts to deliver knockout blows to anyone who threatened them (thereby drawing in additional states).

The plans for prewar mobilization (regardless of actual war plans) also had drastic consequences. Some authors argue that Russia's provocative mobilizations threatened both Austria and Germany to such an extent that they had no choice but to react. Russian civilian leaders initially wanted to mobilize in the south only, which would have been less alarming to Germany, but logistical constraints meant that mobilization had to occur either fully or not at all. Russia then tried to keep the general mobilization secret, but it was discovered by Germany two days later. Germany's own mobilization sparked war directly, because it triggered an immediate attack on Liège in Belgium to seize the fortresses and rail junctions, objectives that Germany decided had to be taken *before* the Belgians learned that Germany was mobilizing (which would take several days). This was part of the famous Schlieffen plan to outflank the French defenses by lunging through Belgium into France.

Some also blame the war on the British failure to deter Germany or to restrain Russia. Had Britain made it clear that it would retaliate for an invasion of Belgium, Germany (particularly the kaiser) might have had second thoughts, and Russia would not have felt so isolated under the Austro-Germanic threat. Unfortunately, the British did not realize that German mobilization meant certain war, and so did not recognize the need to prevent the Russian mobilization that would spark Germany's.

There were also social and ideological pressures underlying these complex organizational entwinements. Nationalism, militarism, and imperialism were important contributory factors leading to the establishment of the provocative alliances and military arrangements outlined above. Although these factors are less talked about, the historian Gordon Martel calls them "issues that will not go away."[5]

Together, these explanations might suggest that World War I was basically an accident. But the path to war was not paved with inadvertent blundering as much as with misperceptions of potential opponents and their intentions. In her recent survey of theories on the origins of World War I, Annika Mombauer found no consensus on the causes of the war, but she did find "some consensus" that a majority of historians today "would no longer support Lloyd George's dictum of the European nations slithering into war accidentally."[6]

The Cult of the Offensive

Perhaps the most pervasive theory of World War I today is the so-called cult of the offensive, a phenomenon that is widely recognized to have existed among all the European states of the time. Simply put, offensive military action was seen as the only method of achieving quick victory and preventing others from gaining the upper hand. This view had gained strength rapidly after 1890 and reached a peak by 1914. The apparent advantages of offense were based on the expectation that modern armies, which were massive and could for the first time be moved around at high speed by rail, would be able to deliver a devastating and rapid blow against which defense would be futile. "Strategists had committed themselves to the view that standing on the defensive would lead to ruin." Hence, even if one side did not want to fight, the perception was that to avert disaster under such circumstances it must nevertheless attack in order to preempt an enemy from doing the same.[7]

The effect is argued to have been compounded by poor relationships between political and military decisionmakers in various European states:

> On balance, offense tends to suit the needs of military organizations better than defense does, and militaries normally exhibit at least a moderate preference for offensive strategies and doctrines for that reason. What was special about the period before World War I was that the state of civil-military relations in each of the major powers tended to exacerbate that normal offensive bias, either because the lack of civilian control allowed it to grow unchecked or because an abnormal degree of civil-military conflict heightened the need for a self-protective ideology.[8]

Such civil-military conflicts appear to be a common cause of faulty assessments, both then and now. The perception in 1914 may have been further reinforced, according to Michael Howard, because military organizations were "not likely to admit that the problems which faced them were insoluble, and that they would be incapable in the future of conducting wars so effectively and decisively as they had in the past."[9]

Whatever its origins, the perception that taking the offensive was the way to gain the advantage is thought to have directly and powerfully contributed to war in 1914. In reality, when the offensive strategy came up against the huge *defensive* advantage that actually existed (as a result of rapid-loading and accurate rifles, machine guns, barbed wire, entrenchments, and colossal artillery barrages), what occurred was a carnage unprecedented in the history of war. Even railroads, which were initially thought to favor the offense, turned out to be a mixed blessing: defenders could sabotage them while retreating, and different countries had different track-gauges so one country's trains could not always enter another's home territory. The perceived offensive-defensive imbalance was not apparent in all aspects and at all times, but it stands as a dominant explanation for the war, and provides an underlying logic that helps to explain many of the other phenomena that are well established to have contributed to the war.[10]

The Remaining Puzzle

Even if the cult of the offensive accounts for much of the war, however, it has three limitations. First, it does not predict why all sides (including civilians, the military, and politicians) were enthusiastic about the war. We know that the advantage of offense was a widely held perception among leaders and civilians in Europe, especially in Germany and France. But if people believed that taking the offensive was a winning strategy, they should also have feared it—easy conquest was an opportunity, but also a dreadful threat to all states and their citizens because it could be turned against them. So why did they welcome war?[11]

Second, it does not explain why states thought they were superior to others and thought they would win (we might expect them to do so if they believed they would succeed in striking first and outwitting everyone else, but this begs the question—why would they believe that?). Even many German planners, who were worried that the rising power of rivals would leave them only a brief window of opportunity to take action, nevertheless believed that they would win a war launched in 1914.

Third, this explanation is a fairly narrow one, limited to wars that break out when a cult of the offensive exists. It does not explain why wars occur at other times. Stephen Van Evera found considerable support for the theory that a belief in the advantage of taking the offensive leads to war in his study of Europe, the United States, and ancient China, but he does not assert that it accounts for all wars.[12]

Van Evera also points out that that theory "cannot explain every factor at work in 1914. Other important causes likely include: the rabid nationalist mythmaking that infected European societies after 1870; the bizarre false optimism with which all belligerents entered the war, which cannot be fully explained by concealments stemming from the cult of the offensive; the strange general belief that war was a positive and healthy activity."[13] Positive illusions may help provide an explanation, because while they are concordant with a belief in the advantage of offense (at least for one's own side), they also account for these other factors and the concurrent belief in victory. Positive illusions predict Van Evera's "other important causes": intergroup beliefs of superiority, false optimism, and an optimistic outlook on war.

The very difficulty of pinpointing the causes of World War I suggests, first, that many factors were simultaneously at work (and therefore any existing single explanation is insufficient) and, second, that there remains room for additional explanations that might help to tie these diverse factors together. The enormous literature on this topic has fueled, rather than resolved, the debate: "Hundreds of books and articles have been published on the subject over the decades, thousands of documents have been unearthed in archives and made available to historians—but nonetheless key issues are still far from resolved, and publications on the First World War and its origins continue in abundance."[14] Given the continuing and unfinished puzzle, it is interesting to consider positive illusions as a contributory factor.

As I will show, there is good evidence that positive illusions played a significant role. Geoffrey Blainey found overoptimism to be a major factor: "On the eve of a war that was to kill more soldiers and involve more nations than any other previous war one consolation was believed. The coming war, it was predicted, would be short . . . There was an even greater consolation to leaders who realized that the war, though short, would be terrifying. That consolation was victory. Both alliances expected victory." A quarter of a century later, Van Evera concluded the same thing: "Both the Triple Entente (Britain, France, and Russia) and the Central Powers (Germany and Austria-Hungary) expected a quick victory in 1914."[15]

Significantly, this expectation was held by the military, many politicians, and civilians alike. Alfred Vagts noted that victory was "the belief of the soldiers and sailors of *all* the Powers and of the statesmen acting on their advice," and John Merriman concurred: "In Berlin and Paris during early August 1914, hundreds of thousands of people enthusiastically celebrated the outbreak of the war that many had begun to see as inevitable. On both sides, virtually everyone expected a short, victorious war. Their troops, heading off to the fighting in early August, would be 'home before the leaves fall,' and then there would be more cheering and celebrations." It is hard to imagine how pervasive this atmosphere was: "There was dancing in the streets and spontaneous demonstrations of support for governments throughout Europe. Men flocked to recruiting offices, fearful that the war might end before they had the opportunity to fight. There was a spirit of festival and a sense of community in all European cities as old class divisions and political rivalries were replaced by patriotic fervour." All this optimism would be ruthlessly scythed down in the months and years to come. By Christmas of 1914, Germany and France had lost 300,000 of their young men killed in action, with a further 600,000 wounded. And the war would drag on four more years.[16]

The Triple Entente

Many Frenchmen relished the opportunity to take revenge on their archenemy that they'd last encountered parading along the Champs d'Elysées after the Franco-Prussian War in 1871. Despite that defeat, in 1914 "French military leaders were confident of victory." Some even talked of a "beautiful war," and General Castelnau (deputy to the chief of staff, General Joseph Joffre) announced: "Give me 700,000 men and I will conquer Europe." There are numerous examples and anecdotes of such over-optimistic expectations of victory. Their prevalence and diverse sources reflect a widespread optimism in the military, political circles, the media, and the public. Moreover, the apparent overconfidence matches the facts and commitments evident in military and political planning.[17]

According to Blainey: "The higher soldiers of France seemed confident in facing the same enemy which had humiliated them in 1870. In February 1914 they secretly issued Plan 17, which envisaged strong French thrusts into Germany should war arise.

While German generals predicted that within six weeks of the outbreak of war their vanguard would be near Paris, many French generals predicted that their soldiers would be at or across the Rhine." There was a significant concern that Germany might invade through Belgium (as indeed it would do), but Joffre "rejected all these warnings." His "obstinacy" was deemed to arise from his "full confidence in Plan 17. He believed that an all-out immediate offensive, one that was oblivious to the enemy's intentions, location, and firepower, was the best strategy to pursue." John Merriman corroborates this interpretation:

> The French high command, which had known the basics of the Schlieffen Plan for years, did not believe the German army could move rapidly through Belgium, in part because the attacking forces would have to overcome the imposing fortress at Liège. The French also knew that the plan called for the incorporation of reserves into the main German army, and doubted they could quickly become an able fighting force . . . The French high command had its own plan for war. It, too, envisioned a rapid attack based on the *élan*, or patriotic energy, of the troops . . . But having miscalculated the size of the effective German fighting force, the French also underestimated the speed with which their enemy could mobilize for war and attack.[18]

The French commander Marshal Foch "believed that morale was stronger than firepower," and the French army "went to war in 1914 believing that charges by massed ranks of infantry with artillery support could overwhelm the defensive power of magazine rifles and machine guns." Both the French and the British military held that "higher morale on the attacking side could overcome superior defensive firepower, and that higher morale could be achieved by assuming the role of attackers, since attacking would lift the soldiers' spirits. One French officer contended that 'the offensive doubles the energy of the troops.'" Even some Belgians, despite their tiny military force and the prospect of their entire country becoming a war zone, were optimistic about the war. On hearing Germany's ultimatum, one Belgian officer exclaimed, "War, what an exalting thing!"[19]

The French exhibited remarkable positive illusions about their supremacy over the Germans, in claims like this one: "We, the French, possess a fighter, a soldier, undeniably superior to the one beyond the Vosges in his racial qualities, activity, intelligence, spirit, power of exaltations, devotion, patriotism." Even French schoolbooks asserted that "one Frenchman is worth ten Germans," and as Van Evera notes, the "wide currency of such nationalist chest-pounding in prewar Europe goes far to explain the rosy optimism that infected both sides as they rode to war in 1914."[20]

The Russians, though fearful of Germany, were also confident. They too underestimated the carnage that would result, which is all the more extraordinary given their relatively recent defeat by Japan in 1904–1905, a conflict that had given Russia harsh experience of the reality of modern warfare. Of all the Great Powers in 1914, perhaps Russia should have had the least illusions of victory. And yet the war minister, General Soukhomlinov, was "confident" in private as well as in public, and "believed that victory would be achieved in a few months, and most of the Russian ministers agreed." A Russian diplomat in St. Petersburg during Russia's mobilization "was one of many who observed in senior military circles the faith in a glorious victory." This optimism is evident in the facts of Russian planning as well. Russia settled on "an extremely ambitious strategy" that would involve a three-pronged attack on Germany and Austria simultaneously.[21]

In Britain, "most ministers also expected a short war," and according to Gordon Martel, the British even "rated themselves more highly than the Germans did." Paul Kennedy found that "qualitative assessments by British generals were all too obviously influenced by cultural and political prejudices," and that "no real effort was made . . . to debate or to challenge statements about the quality of potential enemies', or allies', forces." This feeling of superiority diffused widely among British civilians. Viscount Esher noted that British high society "mostly look upon the war as a sort of picnic." One writer called wars "bracing tonics to the national health," and Lord Lansdowne suggested that war was useful for "strengthening the moral fibre of a nation." The young men of Europe were not, initially, forced to the front against their will in 1914, and scenes of men flocking to volunteer are among the pervading images of the war. Martel suggests that "the popular tide of warlike enthusiasm among the peoples of Europe" could conceivably have "overwhelmed the statesmen who were unable to stem the tide of the forces that they had unleashed."[22]

Overall, despite certain problems, British assessments are considered to have been relatively good. However, the British seriously underestimated the chance and the likely success of a German push into Belgium. The British expeditionary force, although its creation revealed a certain foresight that such a force would be needed, was far too small for the task at hand—blocking the onslaught of the German army. (French and British forces also misjudged the place of the main attack.) Military leaders were partly to blame for letting organizational preferences dictate planning, but political leaders misread the strategic situation in a "naive belief that only a limited amount of support would be necessary." The general staff also "underrated many of the physical and technical aspects of modern warfare. Not only did they fail to appreciate the German capacity to crush fortified redoubts with the enormous Krupp and Skoda siege guns, but they also had not realized the value of machine guns." Like the French, British officers believed that "modern [war] conditions have enormously increased the value of moral quality," and that "moral attributes [are] the primary causes of all great success." Disastrously, therefore, the prevailing view was that "mind would prevail over matter; morale would triumph over machine guns."[23]

The Triple Entente exhibited a systematic tendency to underestimate its foes and overestimate its allies. The British director of military operations, General Henry Wilson, often backed the French, and extolled their virtues and their experience from the French colonial wars. As for Russia, the British recognized its weaknesses (such as a supposed lack of sufficiently trained officers), but still managed to estimate its power as high enough to "reinforce the cozy assumption of some political figures that any 'continental commitment' might be limited and temporary." Russia's vast manpower resources were expected to crush Germany from the east. Viscount Esher, "no mean military observer," declared on 5 August 1914: "Unless the Kaiser possessed the talents of Napoleon, 'he is done a month hence when Russia advances.'"[24]

Positive illusions are also evident in the way the British based their planning on their own military doctrines, which they considered superior, and assumed the Germans would simply let them work within those doctrines. "The power of prejudice and preconception appears in Admiralty estimates of German naval strategy. Since British doctrine required a decisive clash of battle fleets, German plans had to be construed as leading to such an outcome." But this was totally unrealistic, and, most important, should have been clear at the time given Britain's own intelligence reports. The Royal Navy expected naval engagements to occur away from the dangers of the German coast, and "with such a favourable scenario envisaged by the Admiralty and with no perception of the German superiority in armor, torpedoes, shells and mines, it is not surprising that British officers looked forward to fighting a modern-day Trafalgar in the middle of the North Sea. All that was needed was for the other side to oblige!" Senior commanders in the navy also thought submarines would be relatively useless, but in reality the German U-boats would "undermine both the Royal Navy's strategy of offensive sweeps into the North Sea and its cozy assumptions about the security of seaborne traffic."[25]

The army suffered from optimistic assumptions as well. It too "developed a net assessment which was largely a function of preconceptions as to how a war ought to be fought." Part of the failure to assess the situation accurately appeared to be due to "the struggle for the strategic leadership within British defense policy and to the corresponding competition for budget shares." However, military commanders did believe that their own strategies were superior to those of their enemies, as well as superior to rival proposals from their compatriots. Paul Kennedy, in his study of British prewar assessment, concluded:

> The British, while reasonably well prepared at the tactical and technical level for a short conflict, had failed—along with everyone else—to anticipate the grand-strategical aspects of a war involving all the great powers. This may seem a somewhat ungenerous summary at first sight. After all, the German naval threat on the high seas was contained; the military threat westward by the German army was checked in the fields of Belgium and northern France; as an additional bonus, Germany's colonies and overseas trade were virtually eliminated; and, ultimately, the Allies did win the war! But the point is that almost no aspect of that eventual victory had been correctly assessed by the British prior to 1914.[26]

The first contingent of infantry was the British seventh division, which "arrived in France in October with 400 officers and 12,000 soldiers: after eighteen days of fighting around Ypres, it had 44 officers and 2,336 men left." The British, "like the other belligerents, fought a war which they had failed to imagine." And, as with the other belligerents, their expectations had erred in the positive, overconfident direction. This overconfidence led not only to the outbreak of the war, but also to its persistence, its severity, and the failure of its combatants to adapt.[27]

The Central Powers

Great confidence and enthusiasm were also evident on the other side of the impending war. As German troops left for the field of battle in August 1914, Kaiser Wilhelm II appeared in shining armor before them to give a rousing address, declaring: "You will be home before the leaves have fallen from the trees." His optimism was "matched by similar expressions of overconfidence and military splendor in Austria, Russia, and the other nations on the brink of war." The German general staff "expected to crush France in four weeks and finish off the rest of the Triple Entente in four months. Other Germans talked of victory in eight or ten weeks. A German officer expressed the typical view: 'The chances of achieving a speedy victory in a major European war are . . . very favorable for Germany.'" A certain Count Haeseler announced that he "expected to breakfast at the Café de la Paix in Paris on Sedan Day (September 2)," and Count Hochberg "told a colleague in early August: 'You and I will be meeting again in England.'" Van Evera summarizes one German general's assessment as a "forecast that the German army would sweep through Europe like a bus full of tourists." The general declared: "In two weeks we shall defeat France, then we shall turn round, defeat Russia and then we shall march to the Balkans and establish order there."[28]

And this optimism was not just a quirk of particular people. The whole German population did not necessarily expect an easy victory, but during the July Crisis overconfidence was widespread in the institutions where it mattered: "A British observer noted the mood of 'supreme confidence' in Berlin military circles, and a German observer reported that the German general staff 'looks ahead to war with France with great confidence, expects to defeat France within four weeks'." Some military planners did foresee the advantage that defenders would hold on the battlefield, but "most German officers and civilians thought they could win a spectacular, decisive victory if they struck at the right moment . . . Victory, moreover, would be decisive and final."[29]

Positive illusions were not confined to assessments of military performance. The optimism that pervaded their thinking led the Germans to "underrate both the dangers that war posed and the risk that German-Austrian belligerence would cause it." German planners also tended to overestimate the roll call and resilience of their allies, while simultaneously underestimating those of their potential enemies. It was hugely optimistic to expect, as "many

Germans" did, that "the Entente powers would peacefully accept Austria's crushing of Serbia." On 26 July the German foreign minister, Gottlieb von Jagow, was "sure of England's neutrality."[30]

This was a vital assumption. Once the war was under way, the kaiser lamented: "If only someone had told me beforehand that England would take up arms against us." Even in the event that Britain did try to intervene, German planners thought the German army would be able to defeat France before the British had a chance to gain a foothold. They "believed that the small, volunteer British army posed little threat." If anything, the British troops would just be swept aside along with the French. General von Moltke, chief of the general staff, "was convinced that, even if the British did enter the war . . . the French could still be beaten quickly and decisively; the 150,000 men of the British expeditionary force would make no difference." The threat from Britain was, at the time, ambiguous, and "no one, not the Russians, not the French, not the Central Powers, knew what Britain's response to the crisis would be."[31] Given the uncertainty of whether Britain would fight, Germany was astonishingly optimistic in assuming that it would not. An enormous burden hung on this optimistic assessment, because the whole German war plan was grounded on being able to destroy France in the few weeks before Russia was fully capable, when Germany would have to switch its main forces to the eastern front.

The German chancellor, Theobald von Bethmann-Hollweg, after sending his ultimatum to Russia and France, uttered the immortal pronouncement: "If the iron dice are now to be rolled, may God help us." But as Blainey observes, "while warfare was a game of dice, it was also a game of chess, and in that game the German leaders believed they were masters." Bethmann-Hollweg himself "believed that the war should be over, at the most in four months." Moltke predicted the defeat of France in six weeks. Count von Lerchenfeld reported that the general staff expected to defeat France in four weeks, and he later noted that "military circles in Berlin were utterly confident, even though Germany and Austria 'will be facing the whole world.'"[32]

Not all the European states expressed wildly unrealistic over-confidence. Austria-Hungary, while it certainly did not expect defeat, did not expect any quick victory either. Austria-Hungary's military force was inferior to those of the other Great Powers, and it rightly expected the war to be a difficult struggle. Germany continued its exuberance, however. Even once the war was into its first month, German troops were expected home by Christmas and German diplomats did not bother to try to obtain Italy's support, as they didn't think they would need it. In a few short weeks, the army ground to a bloody halt at a vast front line stretching from Belgium to Switzerland. As John Merriman put it, these "two long, thin lines of trenches" finally "punctured the dreams of rapid victory based upon a mastery of offensive tactics."[33]

In the German navy, too, there was an almost complacent over-confidence. Admiral Bachmann was "so sure of the ability of submarines to sink the merchant vessels on which Britain relied that he predicted panic in Britain and surrender within six weeks." He made this comment at a time when Germany itself was already short of raw materials and food, and "had not prepared adequately for a war that had now lasted half a year, let alone a war eight times that long."[34]

The enemies of the Central Powers were concurrently exhibiting identical overconfidence. In London there had been a remarkable "absence of investigation of how Britain herself might be damaged economically by cessation of Anglo-German trade" (not to mention by a naval blockade). Britain relied on Germany for a significant portion of its exports and imports, and despite recognition of this, a Board of Trade report "offered cheery assumptions about the losses the Germans would endure if they could no longer import vast amounts from the British Empire, and it made the outcome seem even desirable by detailing the areas in which British producers would benefit from the elimination of German competition."[35] Before the war the British Admiralty had claimed that "the enemy would be grievously hurt by a [British] blockade"—and this assumption went unchallenged, even after reports on the "relative invulnerability of the German economy" were corroborated by a German study, forwarded by the British naval attaché in Berlin, "demonstrating how nearly self-sufficient Germany could be."

Germans also nurtured significant positive illusions about the superiority of their culture: "Wilhelmine-era German nationalists proclaimed that Germans were 'the greatest civilized people known to history' and that 'the German should feel himself raised above all the peoples who surround him and whom he sees at an immeasurable depth below him.' Germans were assured that 'the French army lacks the . . . united spirit which characterizes the German army, the tenacious strength of the German race, and the esprit de corps of the officers.'"[36] Even intellectuals such as Rainer Maria Rilke and Thomas Mann

> viewed the war as an essential defense against hostile forces representing cultures less rich and technologies less advanced. In "Fünf Gesänge" Rilke, the leading lyric poet in the language celebrated the resurrection of the god of war rather than a symbol of weak-minded peace. In defense of *Kultur,* Mann went to occupied Belgium to observe the future. To be excoriated as Hun barbarians when Germans allegedly represented the higher civilization appeared to him an absurd inversion of values, a feeling shared by educated young officers at the front who came out of professional life.[37]

Both sides also displayed extraordinary positive illusions about the costs and benefits of war. As Van Evera describes, many Europeans believed that "a great war would be a beneficial, healthy exercise for society":

> German publicists stressed "the inevitableness, the idealism, and the blessing of war," and declared that war was a "savior and a healer," "the periodically indispensable solution" to national problems, which brought "uprise and adventure, heroism and excess, cold deliberation and glowing idealism." A German newspaper called for a "brisk and merry war" . . . A leading Ger-

man historian wrote of "the grandeur of war." German youths were told that "war is beautiful." A German officer argued that war is a "powerful promoter of civilization" and is "fought in the interest of biological, social, and moral progress." When war broke out, the German crown prince summoned his compatriots to a "bright and jolly war."[38]

To summarize, a large proportion of the population from all levels and roles in society, and on both sides of the conflict, looked forward to war and expected nothing less than victory. I argue that this overconfidence was a significant factor in triggering the outbreak of war (remember, I am arguing that positive illusions offer an *additional* factor in explaining the war, not that they are the *only* factor).

Did Positive Illusions Contribute?

Annika Mombauer writes in her survey of the historiography of World War I: "It might seem as if historians have analyzed every possible angle and have advanced every plausible, and indeed some implausible, theories regarding the origins of the war. Can there be anything left to argue about? Surely, historians have arrived at a consensus which most can accept?" But in fact, as she continues, the opposite may be true. She cites "an international trend of intensified discussion of the First World War as a whole, while key questions, particularly in view of the war's origins, remain unresolved despite all efforts."[39]

Geoffrey Blainey, writing in the 1970s, pointed to overoptimism as a key cause of World War I, and also of many other wars. The "war-eve optimism of 1914," he wrote, "was not exceptional . . . An analysis of the hopes and fears held on the eve of earlier wars reveals a similar optimism." In 1914, he argued, "both sides were confident of victory. Even Russia, France and Austria, each of which had lost its last major war, expected victory. Underlying the optimism of European leaders in 1914 was something more powerful than their knowledge of recent military and financial history."[40]

Stephen Van Evera, writing twenty-five years later, also identified a "bizarre" optimism that accompanied many wars throughout history, and again particularly in 1914.[41] The "cult of the offensive" theory, while compelling, does not entirely account for the extent of overconfidence on all sides. Perhaps, then, it is no coincidence that Mombauer can conclude that the causes of this war are still unresolved, while at the same time Blainey's and Van Evera's insight remains consistent and yet largely unexplained— why did people exhibit this undue optimism? One parsimonious way to fill in the gaps in current explanations of the origins of World War I is to find a theory that predicts a link between overconfidence and war. Positive illusions is such a theory.

Overconfidence was evident not only in prewar strategic assessment but also in the war itself. Stories of incredible overconfidence and apocalyptic slaughter are commonplace from the western front, where "year after year," as Winston Churchill wrote, the generals "conducted with obstinacy and serene confidence offensives which we now know to have been as hopeless as they were disastrous." The invasion of Turkey at Gallipoli in April 1915 also suffered from severe overconfidence. As Eliot Cohen and John Gooch describe it, there was a

mood of buoyant optimism that predominated at all levels before the first landings took place, a mood that owed much to a failure to consider exactly what an amphibious operation might entail and not a little to a deeply entrenched attitude of racist superiority toward the Turkish people in general and the Turkish army in particular. The notion that British troops—any British troops—must be superior to their Turkish opponents . . . was widespread throughout all levels of British society, and the expedition's commander was deeply impregnated with it. "Let me bring my lads face to face with Turks in the open field," he begged his diary some three weeks before Suvla Bay. "We must beat them every time because British volunteer soldiers are su-

perior individuals to Anatolians, Syrians or Arabs [and] are ani-
mated with a superior ideal and an equal joy in battle." [He] val-
ued each British soldier as worth several dozen Turks; at Suvla
Bay the cold statistics suggest that every Turk was the equal of
ten Britons.[42]

The plan of assault had been strongly advised against by the
commander of British naval forces in the Mediterranean, who instead recommended a much "longer-drawn-out operation" fea-
turing heavier bombardment of Turkish defenses and thorough
minesweeping. Field Marshall Lord Kitchener initially estimated
that 150,000 troops would be necessary for such an operation, but
only 70,000 could be spared from the western front. Meanwhile
their allotted task expanded dramatically because "as the weeks
passed the excessive hopes placed in the efficacy of naval bombardment were revealed to be far too overoptimistic."[43] The
army's role in the operation consequently had to change from
simply supporting the navy (by destroying artillery batteries
along the coast) to seizing the peninsula in a ground assault—and
all this with fewer than half the troops initially considered necessary for the original, smaller task.

Overconfidence caused operational problems for all sides. Germany committed itself to "a wildly over ambitious offensive strategy," and Russia's strategy was also "extremely ambitious."[44] According to Jack Snyder, on both the western and eastern fronts
"each offensive failed to achieve its ambitious goals and, in doing
so, created major disadvantages for the state that launched it":

> None of these disasters was unpredictable or unpredicted. It
> was not only seers like Ivan Block [whose early forecast of the
> horrors to come was ignored] who anticipated the stalemated
> positional warfare. General Staff strategists themselves, in their
> more lucid moments, foresaw these outcomes with astonishing
> accuracy . . . This is not to say that European war planners fully
> appreciated the overwhelming advantages of the defender;
> partly they underrated those advantages, partly they defied

them. The point is that our own 20/20 hindsight is not qualitatively different from the understanding that was achievable by the historical protagonists.[45]

This is of key importance to the theory of positive illusions—we can, to some extent, rule out the possibility that events only seem overoptimistic with the benefit of hindsight. On the contrary, as illustrated in the many examples above and by Snyder's analysis, prewar assumptions and the first clashes of the war were not the result of intelligence failures or lack of information. The information was available; expectations simply did not reflect it. Even where information was absent on particular issues, initial assessments were systematically biased in a positive direction. Given all this, Snyder asks, "Why then were these self-defeating, war-causing strategies adopted?" Again, positive illusions provide one potential solution.[46]

Willingness to Risk War

It might be argued that a more important reason for the war was that each state had no other option but to fight: that inaction was not seen as an option. As Martel suggests, maybe it was "not the alliance 'system' that drew the great powers into war in 1914, but the belief that it was more dangerous to stay out of a war than enter into one." He continues: "Had they anticipated the extent of the carnage, the duration of the war, the political and social chaos that it caused, they might have made different decisions. But even this is doubtful. By and large the men who made the decisions . . . believed it better to die honourably than to survive in disgrace—and this applied to their states as well as to themselves."[47]

Other factors also constrained political choices. For example, the Russian government could have expected to be "severely shaken by opposition had it failed to respond forcefully to Austria-Hungary's ultimatum." One can also argue that whether Germany invaded Belgium or not, Britain "would have intervened in any case, believing that this was essential to preserve the balance of power and prevent the German domination of Europe." Thus decisionmakers may have preferred to risk war rather than to risk the consequences of not fighting. Overall, therefore, July 1914 might be seen as "a brinksmanship crisis, resulting in a war that everyone was willing to risk but that no one truly wanted."[48]

However, this argument fails to account for each side's enthusiasm and expectations for the war. Furthermore, if states believed they had no option but to go to war, this presupposes that they believed they would gain more by fighting than by remaining at peace. Martel himself argues that even if war seemed the only alternative, states also "hoped and assumed" that they would win it. Therefore, war was never seen as such a bad choice after all. This is illustrated by the German reasoning for war:

> While most political and military decisionmakers in Berlin did not actually want a *European* war [that is, they hoped it would not spread after they attacked France and Russia], they were certainly willing to risk it. They had been encouraged to do so by Germany's leading military advisers, who had advocated war "the sooner the better" on many occasions and had assured the politicians that Germany stood a good chance of defeating its enemies. Germany's military leaders had been conjuring up the image of a Russia that could still be defeated by Germany at this time, but that in future would be too strong to be taken on successfully.

The fact that they were willing to risk war in 1914 conforms to, if not actually requires, the notion that even states that felt they were being backed into a corner were optimistic that they would win at that time. Otto von Bismarck called such wars "suicide from fear of death."[49]

Unbridled Overconfidence

The question of why war erupted in 1914 and not during the various other crises among the same European powers in preceding years (the first and second Moroccan crises and the first and second Balkan wars) implies that factors unique to July 1914 were instrumental in causing war. One factor that seems to have pushed positive illusions to particularly high levels at this time is each state's lack of open debate on the war. In the years leading up to 1914, military plans were often not known even to their country's own minister of foreign affairs or diplomats. In Germany, the chancellor, the secretary of state, Admiral Tirpitz, and "probably" even the kaiser were unaware that German mobilization would trigger an immediate offensive against Liège. The Schlieffen plan itself was a "flawed scheme" that might have been modified in Germany's favor had it been better debated, but its "illogic was hidden by secrecy."[50]

Even in democratic Britain, which had specific systems in place to foster political-military consultation, strategic assessment was hampered by several instances of exclusive decisionmaking. Before the war, Britain's foreign secretary, Sir Edward Grey, "kept those members of the cabinet who were known to be opposed to any British armed intervention in the dark concerning the details of the crisis and the expectations of support in France and Russia." At the same time, Grey himself did not know about the British and French militaries' plans for cooperation. In Austria and Russia, too, there were several instances of military officials withholding "crucial data from civilians." This created a tragic farce in which diplomats were vying for peaceful settlements without realizing that their own military establishments had already tripwired the continent for war.[51]

As we shall also see in later case studies, openness of debate often seems to be crucial in reining in precisely the kind of overconfident assessments that were allowed to run unchecked in 1914. The relevant information may have existed, the inherent caution of the diplomats may have been in play, but key actors subverted the system by restricting debate and screening out dissenting opinions, so that decisionmakers' baseline overconfidence was not effectively challenged. Ernest May found that faulty assumptions failed to be corrected, or even to be scrutinized, in Britain, Germany, and Russia alike. The amount of damage this caused appears to have increased with the degree of exclusivity in deci-sionmaking:

> For all their muddle, the British understood how the various powers were aligned. And while each Russian may have used his own particular map of the external world, each used more or less the same map most of the time. The Kaiser, by contrast, could go in a matter of hours from conceiving Germany the center of a United States of Europe to seeing it encircled and besieged by enemies. And the structure of government provided little or no safeguard against having the wholly wrong percep-tion govern national policy. Everything depended on the wis-dom of the man at the top.[52]

Within the militaries as well, institutional biases often elimi-nated any prospects for correcting overconfidence or adapting to circumstances. Cohen and Gooch present a striking example in the British army: "The personalized promotion system . . . en-sured that middle-ranking officers undertook offensives of no tac-tical or strategical use whether they believed in them or not: If they obeyed orders, they could hope for promotion, but if they did anything else they faced the certainty of removal and disgrace. The way Haig [commander in chief of the British expeditionary force] ran his headquarters, preserving an Olympian detachment, tolerating no criticism, and accepting precious little advice, rein-forced the rigidity of the system."[53]

Shattered Illusions

With hindsight it is difficult to imagine why people held the ex-traordinary views that they did in 1914. Blainey suggests that the "complicated trellis of hope—a criss-cross of military and finan-cial fact and fantasy—tempered the horror of the coming war." Forgetting or failing to imagine the suffering inflicted by war seems to be a recurrent theme of the human experience. Before the outbreak of war there is often a general willingness to fight.

But once people begin to be killed in large numbers, the original enthusiasm gives way. The outbreak of World War I is commonly attributed, in part, to a lack of understanding of what would happen when densely packed men attacked trenches filled with machine guns. And yet, that same disastrous form of combat had occurred in the war between Russia and Japan only ten years before. It was well documented, and the Russians at least (having lost that war) should have learned from the experience. In fact they did change their policy for a time: "Russian planners returned to a more defensive approach after Russia's defeat in the 1904–1905 Russo-Japanese war, and they adhered to a defensive doctrine until 1912." But it wasn't long before buoyant enthusiasm arose once again, just in time to repeat the carnage in World War I.[54]

The "picnic" that many Britons envisaged rapidly changed into a bloodbath that would haunt a generation. But it took the death of millions to remind the opposing populations and their leaders of the horrors of war. The excruciating slowness to adapt to changes in warfare during the course of the fighting testifies to the optimism and simplistic expectations that had launched the war in the first place:

> Once the surface naval war had assumed the shape of a stalemate, once the campaigns on the western front had lost their mobility, and once the first shocks to the international credit and transport system had been overcome, Britain's prewar assessments and planning were shown to be inadequate. The changed conditions of land warfare had not been anticipated by the General Staff, with the dual consequence that it did not possess the reserves of materiel for that type of war and that it had not given thought to how such physical obstacles could be overcome, except by putting pressure upon the enemy's trenches by deploying ever more men and guns.[55]

The psychologist Yechiel Klar, who has studied positive illusions under the threat of terrorism in Israel, suggests that these illusions vary dramatically *before* a person experiences a danger versus *while* that danger is taking a direct toll: "People are optimistically inclined mainly when the negative events under study are hypothetical and 'psychologically unreal.' In contrast, when the group to which people belong is the target of some significant ongoing calamity, even when the participants themselves are currently not the direct victims, the unreality of the event dissolves and optimism (both absolute and comparative) decreases or vanishes altogether."[56] Even this corrective effect may be short-lived, however. Some types of positive illusions seem to kick in just when the going gets tough—perhaps on account of their original function of improving our sticking power in times of struggle. John Stoessinger wrote: "Old people to whom I spoke about the war remembered its outbreak as a time of glory and rejoicing. Distance had romanticized their memories, muted the anguish, and subdued the horror." So it seems to be with war. We forget the last war thoroughly enough to become optimistic about the next. This may well be another legacy from our evolutionary history—the blocking out of negative information is a well-known phenomenon with potentially important adaptive functions—but it can have deadly consequences. Even the extreme lessons of World War I are often forgotten, but its unexpected horrors did go some way toward what John Merriman called the "shattering of illusions that war could be short and glorious."[57]

Chapter 4

The Munich Crisis

The Prime Minister, Sir Thomas Inskip, Sir John Simon . . .
they are blind to what seems to others the most obvious aspects
of the contemporary world. These simply do not reach them. In
the case of the Prime Minister this blindness is an essential ele-
ment in his strength. If he could see even a little, if he became
even faintly cognisant of the turmoil of ideas and projects and
schemes to save the country which are tormenting the rest of us,
his superbly brazen self-confidence would be fatally impaired.
— John Maynard Keynes

Hitler's belligerent speech of September 26 and their own
boldness frightened the British and French majority into back-
ing down; their warning had been a bluff.
— Glenn Snyder and Paul Diesing

My two crisis case studies serve to test my reverse hypothesis—
that, while positive illusions may propel states into a crisis in
which war becomes particularly likely, a subsequent *reduction* of
positive illusions leads to peace, not war. The Munich crisis, like
World War I, provides a challenging test case because positive illusions are not expected: both the Allies and Hitler had a long period in which to assess each other's motivations and capabilities
(precluding the hypothesis that decisions were simply knee-jerk
reactions); alternative options were available (precluding the hypothesis that decisions simply represented the only possible
course of action); and intelligence information was, though
flawed in some key aspects, sufficient to allow decisionmakers to
appreciate the general asymmetries (precluding the hypothesis
that decisions were good ones, given poor information). (See Ta-

Table 2. The Munich crisis: elimination of basic alternative explanations and overview of conclusions.

	Britain	Germany
Assessment opportunity	Long	Long
Alternative options	Yes	Yes
Information availability	Partly flawed	Reasonable
Positive illusions?	Some* (but not at end)	Yes (but not at end)
Main factor	Expectation of diplomatic peace (at end: fear of war)	Enormous ambitions (at end: fear of defeat in a premature war)

*Chamberlain did have illusions about Hitler's intentions, but not about his military capabilities.

ble 2.) The Munich crisis is also a challenging test case because it is one of the most intensively studied crises in history, and thus has well-established and widely accepted explanations.

I argue that Britain's prime minister, Neville Chamberlain, held positive illusions about Hitler's *intentions*, if not his *capabilities* (the latter were, if anything, overestimated). This meant that although unduly optimistic views influenced Chamberlain's dogged pursuit of an unlikely peace, there were no positive illusions that the Allies would win a war at that time. On the other side, while Hitler's bold strategic ambitions caused the crisis, the German rearmament program was still in progress, and Hitler's advisors successfully dampened any expectations that he could easily win a war at that time. Thus I argue that this crisis did *not* develop into war at least in part because the initially overoptimistic strategies that led to the crisis were successfully dispelled.

Background

On 16 September 1938 Hitler addressed the Nazi Party Congress, demanding self-determination for the German-speaking peoples living in the Sudetenland (then within Czechoslovakia). This was the latest in a series of aggressive German moves, and Europe was slowly shoring up resolve to halt Hitler's apparently relentless ambition. The Czech government asked the Russians to confirm that they would honor the Russian-Czech Pact in the event of a German invasion. The Russians responded that they would, but that this was conditional upon prior French action. The French also claimed that they would honor their Treaty of Alliance with Czechoslovakia but that their military response would hinge on Britain guaranteeing an attack force, since the French prime minister, Daladier, believed that the French army was only capable of playing a defensive role. Thus there was a passing down of responsibility from the Russians to the French to the British, as ultimate guarantors of the defense of Czechoslovakia.[1]

Despite the threat of multinational opposition, Hitler remained intent on attaining his goals, and the possibility of imminent war hung over Europe throughout the crisis. Conflict was finally averted by the Four Power Agreement, signed on 30 September by Britain, France, Italy, and Germany, which brought peace at the expense of the Czechs, who were not part of the agreement and yet were forced to accept its terms (the main demand being the annexation of the industrially rich Sudetenland by Germany). Although both sides consciously bluffed strength, the Allies did not stand up to Hitler militarily in 1938, and Hitler also preferred diplomatic rather than military means at that stage. Only a year later, however, the situation would have changed sufficiently for Hitler to choose war.

Britain

Information and Reaction

The story of British intelligence before World War II is commonly presented as a catalogue of flaws and errors. The various intelligence gathering services and intelligence assessments were not well coordinated in the period between the two world wars.

A new organization founded in 1936 to centralize intelligence analysis—the Joint Intelligence Committee (JIC)—was "virtually boycotted by the Foreign Office until July 1939 and achieved little until after the war began. During the final years of peace and the early months of war Whitehall received a remarkable mixture of good and dreadful intelligence and was frequently incapable of distinguishing the two." This led to some important errors in assessment of German capabilities. However, if anything, these errors *exaggerated* German military strength and the speed of its rearmament program, giving the Allies the impression that they were not likely to win if war broke out. Hitler had been bluffing, and had largely succeeded:

> In 1936, for instance, the best guesses of British Intelligence were about 100 per cent too great. In 1940, when the German army was supposed to have been overwhelming and to have defeated the French by a mass of metal, the French in fact had more tanks than the Germans. And by 1940, Great Britain was producing more tanks, more aeroplanes—in fact, more of everything except rifles—than Germany, and kept ahead all through the war. It was not so much that Germany had more armaments, but that from quite an early stage, Hitler said she had.[2]

What was actually more important in the prewar diplomacy was assessing German aims and intentions rather than their military strength: military capabilities were irrelevant if Germany was not going to fight. Assessments of intentions are so difficult that, according to Robert Jervis, states often resort to "an approach that, were it suggested by an academic, would be seen as an example of how out of touch scholars are with international realities. On several occasions, states directly ask their adversaries what it is they want. The British frequently discussed directing such an inquiry to Hitler."[3] Such was their uncertainty. In the end, Chamberlain did ask him, and bought Hitler's bluff wholesale.

Despite a concordance of various sources of intelligence confirming the rapid German rearmament, British officials were split on how to act upon this information. On one side were the appeasers (led by Chamberlain), who believed that Germany need not be a threat to Britain and that peace could be sought. On the other were those opposed to appeasement (notably Churchill), who expected war or at least the need for a credible deterrent threat and therefore clamored for a major armaments buildup. Chamberlain clung to the hope that it would be possible to negotiate peace and, most important, maintained the view that Hitler's intentions were limited—believing the claim that the Germans simply wanted to redress the injustices imposed upon them in the Treaty of Versailles and unite the German-speaking peoples. For him "it was better to gain German friendship by generosity than to incur enmity by a firmness that was essentially a bluff, given British military weakness." Mussolini was also threatening the peace with his ambitions for Italy. Given the inflammatory circumstances, Chamberlain felt that "in order to avert the risk of war, it was essential to take the initiative to improve relations with Germany and Italy, and only thus could Britain's potential commitments be brought into balance with its military aims." Although Chamberlain's policy had some support, it also received significant disapproval. Anthony Eden, the foreign secretary, resigned in February 1938 over the appeasement policy and was replaced by Lord Halifax, a supporter of Chamberlain's views. Meanwhile Germany continued to arm.[4]

Leaders in France also seemed to pursue an optimistic policy that contrasted with intelligence about Hitler's aims. According to James Richardson, during the crisis the long-serving French ambassador to Berlin, André François-Poncet, "provided ample evidence" that Hitler's "immediate objective went beyond self-determination. However, there is no indication that his penetrating observations had the least influence on French policy."[5]

Chamberlain's rather particular views were apparent in a number of areas. He strongly resisted entering into negotiations with Russia, which he distrusted, and which he saw as weak after Stalin's purges of the Red Army. But it would become essential to cooperate with Russia to construct a credible alliance against Germany. Chamberlain became totally isolated within the cabinet on this issue. He eventually gave in, but the belated negotiations failed to forestall the Nazi-Soviet nonaggression pact, signed on 23 August 1939, which would shock the world. More important, perhaps, was that Chamberlain saw it as something of a personal goal to prevent another war from happening on his watch. He had been deeply affected by World War I and was determined that such a calamity should not happen again.

When German-Czech talks failed in the summer of 1938, Chamberlain took it upon himself in "a dramatic personal initiative" to go to Germany to meet with Hitler.[6] This decision was made without consulting the cabinet. At the meeting he and Hitler arranged for the potential separation of the Sudetenland. On 22 September the prime minister traveled to Germany again, supposedly to simply confirm details. But Hitler now demanded more: a military occupation of the German-speaking region. Chamberlain considered granting even this, but the British cabinet rejected any such terms. Conflict now seemed likely, and much of Europe expected it. However, at the brink of war, Mussolini prompted Hitler to invite Chamberlain and Daladier to a new conference, at Munich. At this now famous meeting, Chamberlain was able to claim a triumph because he attained some minor concessions from Hitler. He also got Hitler to sign a legendary piece of white paper—a declaration that Britain and Germany would never go to war.

Just six months later—on 14–15 March 1939—German forces invaded Czechoslovakia proper. The Czech president, Benes, notified his government not to resist the invasion, seeing only disaster should they do so. He was painfully aware that they could not prevent the German occupation without Allied assistance. Churchill, though not yet in power, contemplated sending Benes a telegram saying, "Fire your cannons, and all will be well." We will never know for sure whether the Allies really would have intervened at that stage if Czechoslovakia had put up resistance. Either way, Chamberlain became a symbol of the world's lesson never to appease aggression.[7]

Positive Illusions?

Earlier in the 1930s, there had been some evidence of military optimism in Britain. Much of the debate centered on the economic and production capacities of the potential opponents in a European war, rather than on the military balance as such. Even after the rigors of World War I, the British Empire remained an economic giant, and many thought this would ensure its superior might. Until 1937 at least, the leading British economist, John Maynard Keynes, was fairly confident that Britain would maintain superiority: "At present, perhaps, and in two or three years most certainly, Great Britain will possess a far greater preponderance of sea power in European waters than she has ever possessed in her history. I believe that our navy is not afraid of attack from the air. Germany has no navy at all, and, practically speaking, Italy has none." At that stage, Keynes also estimated that, should it come to war, "Czecho-Slovakia could give a pretty good account of herself, even if she is left entirely unsupported."[8]

By the time of the Munich crisis, however, Germany had significantly rearmed, and the relative weakness of the British military was fully recognized by key decisionmakers. The armed services chiefs of staff warned Chamberlain just before the Munich conference that "to take offensive action" before they had a chance to organize "would be to place ourselves in the position of a man who attacks a tiger before he has loaded his gun." Chamberlain himself warned: "We must not precipitate a conflict now —we shall be smashed." This information was acted upon in subsequent policy preferences for peace: "British interests with respect to Czechoslovakia were examined systematically by the Cabinet Foreign Policy Committee shortly after the *Anschluss* [with Austria]. This followed a series of earlier assessments which emphasized the constraints of Britain's limited military power. Even fully rearmed, Britain could not secure the Empire against three major powers, and until 1939 there was no adequate air defense. There was no confidence in any potential ally, but Britain would have to support France against attack by Germany."[9]

If anything, British decisionmakers underrated the degree to which their own power might deter Hitler. Indeed, in the years before World War II, Britain may have "deterred itself" by an erroneous fear that the Germans would want, and be able, to use air power to "wipe out London at the start of a world war." The potential bomb damage was overestimated on the basis of incorrect data. Such pessimistic views corroborated existing beliefs, and these beliefs were never reviewed. Chamberlain said: "We cannot expose ourselves now to a German attack. We simply commit suicide if we do. At no time could we stand up against German air bombing." British leaders were mistaken in thinking that Germany had either the intention or the capability to bomb British cities. Neither was true: the Luftwaffe had been developed primarily to support ground forces, and there were no plans for air raids (the aerial onslaught during the Battle of Britain in 1940 had not featured in initial German war plans, and the force used to accomplish it "was an improvised one").[10]

If these misinterpretations of German intentions were not bad enough, the British also exaggerated German air strength. This misperception seemed to become fixed because it fitted the preconceived notions of both appeasers and nonappeasers. For the former it demonstrated that war would be very costly and should therefore be avoided; for the latter a larger Luftwaffe demonstrated that Germany had become more aggressive and therefore that the RAF must be built up to oppose it. This reinforcement of both opposing beliefs amplified and sustained the misperception. As a result, the British "did much of Hitler's work for him. While he did seek to deter Britain, the British perceptions cannot be completely explained by the German behavior. British fantasies, developed by different groups for different reasons, inhibited accurate analysis of the German air threat and led decisionmakers to accept pessimistic views."[11] Overall, these bizarre circumstances led to an elimination (or prevention) of any positive illusions.

By the time of the Munich conference, therefore, while it cannot be said that Chamberlain or other key decisionmakers harbored any positive illusions about British capabilities (if anything their assessments falsely inflated the threat), they severely underestimated Hitler's wider intentions. Chamberlain maintained the unduly rosy view that Hitler had only limited aims in spite of mounting evidence against it. "Throughout the crisis and after it Chamberlain continued to believe that his strategy of appeasement was succeeding. He did this by interpreting evidence to fit his preconceptions and by either ignoring directly negative evidence or discrediting its source." Following Munich, Chamberlain's public statements became "increasingly optimistic." Even after Hitler marched into Prague on 15 March 1939, demonstrating beyond doubt that he was not solely righting the wrongs of Versailles or seeking self-determination for German-speaking peoples, Chamberlain "seemed at first unwilling to accept that his policy of 'appeasement' had run its course and failed." Halifax, who had by and large supported him up to now, began to diverge from Chamberlain's views at this point.[12]

Is it fair to Chamberlain to characterize his appeasement policy as overoptimistic? The bulk of the historical evidence and the significant resistance at the time suggests that it was unrealistic, but there were some arguments for pursuing it. James Richardson points out that, at the time, appeasement could be argued to be a worthwhile gamble if it might avoid war. Rather than British decisionmakers misperceiving Hitler's "larger intentions," Richardson suggests that their policy was "premised on uncertainty," and that as long as the uncertainty remained, "they would refrain from any step which they believed would heighten the risk of an otherwise avoidable war." Even so, Richardson notes that "neither side correctly perceived the other's specific intentions." Chamberlain was "satisfied that Herr Hitler would not go back on his word once he had given it," and remained confident that Hitler's objective was "racial unity, and not the domination of Europe."[13]

John Mearsheimer, who generally sees appeasement as a disastrous strategy, calls the Munich crisis "the only case I know" in which appeasement may have been justified—to buy time to arm —"in part because British policymakers believed that the balance of power favored the Third Reich but that it would shift in favor of the United Kingdom and France over time." Hence Chamberlain may have been right to use appeasement as a stalling tactic. However, Stephen Walker's in-depth analyses of Chamberlain's and other decisionmakers' beliefs demonstrate that the faith in appeasement was real, not staged to buy time. According to other authors too, this "breathing space" argument was "not one used by Chamberlain at the time . . . because Chamberlain was convinced that an understanding with Germany *was* possible. He continued to believe this until March 1939 and even beyond it."[14]

Germany

Information and Reaction

Before the outbreak of World War II, Germany's military intelligence was among the best in the world. Hitler received "abundant, if not necessarily correct, information from the cumulative effects of the routine information flow as well as from digests of the foreign press and excerpts from wire services. 'There has probably never been a head of government,' his press chief wrote later, 'who was so swiftly informed on public opinion throughout the world as Hitler'." There were problems in Hitler's idiosyncratic use of this intelligence and his authoritarian decisionmaking process, and competition among intelligence agencies for his attention was counterproductive. But enough good information filtered through to permit assessments of grand strategic decisions such as whether or not to initiate a war. Indeed, the available information was good enough to stimulate vigorous opposition from many of Hitler's own advisors and generals. This is all the more significant given that the nature of his regime, and of his intelligence agencies, selected for information that would please him.[15]

The main problem was that Hitler did not know who his eventual opponents would be. The Allies were not yet bound to one another, and the status of Britain, Russia, and the United States was unclear. Thus, even if intelligence was relatively good, there remained a fundamental problem of evaluating the as yet undeclared enemies that Germany would have to fight.

Crucial to my argument in this chapter is that, at least before the war began, Hitler acted rather rationally. Even though his overall strategy was hugely ambitious throughout, his prewar diplomacy constantly adapted to changing circumstances and was updated on the basis of new information. For example, on one weekend in May 1938, Britain and France issued warnings to Germany in response to reports of large-scale troop movements near the Czech border in Saxony. In fact these were just military exercises, and Hitler was apparently surprised at the challenge. At that time the German military was still the weaker side; "the Wehrmacht was not yet ready to meet the British-French-Czech challenge." Hitler recognized this threat and withdrew German forces from the area.[16]

Later that year, Hitler wanted to launch a military offensive against Czechoslovakia—partly to avenge his humiliation at the "weekend crisis" in May. However, his advisors argued against an invasion because of the continued likelihood of a German defeat. In a meeting on 20 June 1938 a secretary to the foreign ministry told Hitler that "if they were to immediately attack Czechoslovakia, they would possibly invite a conflict with the British and the French that the German army could not withstand." This assessment appears to have been taken seriously. Over the ensuing months, too, evaluations of a likely German defeat clearly entered into Hitler's decisions. Later that summer, in the run-up to Munich, "it seemed that Hitler was hesitating himself about the course of action to follow, because on 30 August the same state secretary . . . again stated that an invasion of Czechoslovakia would make the western powers their enemies and would consequently lead to a European war, which would sooner or later lead to German capitulation."[17] Thus in 1938 German decisionmaking was adequately updated.

Positive Illusions?

It is clear that Hitler's ambitions led to the Munich crisis in the first place. However, Germany's and Italy's claims of military superiority were largely propaganda to bluff strength in a deliberate display of military hardware without having invested enough in ammunition, parts, or replacements. Mussolini was well aware of Italy's weakness: "For all his public boastings, he knew the military and political fragility of Italy better than anyone. He was willing to talk about a war in 1942, if Germany would give him the munitions; but in 1939—No!" But Mussolini seems to have held inflated views of Italian capabilities in spite of his awareness of his country's weakness, and the historian A. J. P. Taylor suggested that the conscious bluffing strategy, deliberate at first, eventually began to deceive Mussolini himself.[18]

Hitler's public self-confidence at this stage also appears to have developed an element of self-delusion later on: "The German military machinery, which emphasized rearmament in 'width' rather than 'depth,' was adequate in the prewar period to further Hitler's coercive diplomacy. But Hitler's obsession with this type of showy rearmament was to have negative results once war began. As late as 1939, when informed that ammunition stocks were extremely low, Hitler replied, 'Nobody inquires whether I have any bombs or ammo, it is the number of aircraft and guns that counts.'" During the crisis over the Sudetenland, however, "while the German economy was geared *to* war, it was not geared *for* war," and Hitler was aware of this.[19] Whether or not their bluffs worked as threats to other states, both fascist leaders, for all their later extremes, at the time of Munich were aware—or were made aware—of the Great Powers that would oppose them, and at this stage there were limited positive illusions that they could defeat them. Hence it seems that the absence of military confidence was crucial to peace. Indeed, it was Mussolini who persuaded Hitler to invite Chamberlain and Daladier to Munich to negotiate.

Hitler's planning was, at least initially, conducted with his generals and advisors, and the principal intelligence information was openly discussed. At these times the German decisionmaking process benefited from other individuals' views on the available intelligence, and Hitler's plans were often not supported by his own staff. This rules out the possibility that Hitler's early actions were simply good decisions based on poor information: on the contrary, the same information was interpreted by other key figures as reasons to hold back. This strongly implies that Hitler's own views were toward the overoptimistic end of the spectrum. But before the war and certainly at the time of the Munich crisis, Hitler's foreign policy was by no means a reflection of his expectations alone: a relatively open debate ensured a realistic assessment of the chances of military action, even if many shared his ultimate goals. According to Taylor, his goals were also those "of his predecessors, of the professional diplomats at the foreign ministry, and indeed of virtually all Germans . . . to free Germany from the restrictions of the peace treaty, to restore a great German army, and then to make Germany the greatest power in Europe from her natural weight."[20]

Did Positive Illusions Contribute?

British Restraint

As we have seen, the British had an initial confidence in their superior might. By 1939, however, this view had been significantly updated on the basis of Hitler's changed behavior, his openly expanded intentions, and his much more powerful military. Churchill lambasted Britain's failure to arm fast enough. Keynes, who complained that British preparations were "ludicrously feeble," blamed the country's leaders for the impending disaster and, notably, implied that their confidence in their ability to attain peace was based on illusory beliefs. He accused Chamberlain and others of being "blind to what seems to others the most obvious aspects of the contemporary world." This corresponds to the notion that positive illusions are effective precisely because they are *self-deceptive*.[21]

It appears that Chamberlain's positive illusions about Hitler's intentions did indeed contribute to exacerbating the Munich crisis in 1938, but that a fear of German military strength stopped the Allies short of risking war at that point. Chamberlain himself recognized that "if we now possessed a superior force to Germany, we should probably be considering these proposals in a very different spirit." Between Munich and the outbreak of war in 1939, Chamberlain continued to seek his illusive negotiated solution. After Hitler invaded Czechoslovakia, German forces were strengthened by the seized Czech industry and materiel, and they no longer had to maintain strong defenses on their southern border. While Hitler's previous moves in Europe could be argued to have represented only ambiguous feedback against the appeasement strategy, this takeover shattered the agreement set out at Munich.[22]

"Even for Chamberlain," John Merriman wrote, "this marked the end of illusions." In fact, some illusions did survive beyond that, as Chamberlain's beliefs persisted despite the "strong and very incongruous stimulus" (Hitler's invasion of Czechoslovakia) that caused others to change their beliefs. Even after Germany invaded Poland on 1 September 1939, Chamberlain spent the following day trying to arrange a separate peace with Germany. By this time few people could twist the evidence to support such optimistic hopes. Joseph Goebbels wrote in his diary on the day of the invasion: "Still the foreign press talk of a settlement. But that is just illusory." Chamberlain had persisted in his appeasement strategy despite repeated evidence that it was failing.[23]

Chamberlain, who was sixty-eight at the time of the Munich crisis, was one of the oldest prime ministers in recent times, and he declared in 1919 that he was "not looking forward to a parliamentary life; somehow I seem to have got too old for much in the way of personal ambition."[24] His premiership was largely accidental; the sudden fall of the Lloyd George coalition in October 1922 left an open field for Chamberlain's party in which its leader, Andrew Bonar Law, was bound "to promote a number of figures from the ranks of obscurity." In other words, Chamberlain was unusual in being relatively old, not greatly ambitious, and not subject to the usual selection processes that grind out leaders from the rest. It is possible, therefore, that he did not hold the confidence typical of other leaders, and that this contributed to his pacific policies and unwillingness to provoke conflict.

German Restraint

Hitler's great strategic ambitions and bellicose posturing contributed to pushing the stakes as far as a crisis in the first place—both he and others held a belief that this aggressive tactic would be successful. According to Richardson, in the course of the Munich crisis there was "a measure of wishful thinking in long-term expectations both of Hitler and his critics." But while this optimism may have led to the crisis, any German illusions stopped short of believing in an easy military success. Most of those around Hitler, many of whom did not share his views, agreed that Germany would lose an armed confrontation fought in 1938. Hitler was thus relatively well advised at this point, and he listened to and acted on this advice.[25]

Positive illusions on both sides may have contributed to the European powers careering into the 1938 crisis. The leaders were not alone in their views, but the evidence did argue against their policies to many factions in both countries. Hitler's "bold foreign policy gambles—the remilitarization of the Rhineland in 1936, *Anschluss* with Austria, Munich and the destruction of Czechoslovakia—were consistently opposed by his generals and greeted with apprehension by the German people." Indeed, factions of the German military even attempted to warn the British of Hitler's wider intentions, twice in 1938 and again in 1939, in the hope that diplomacy could forestall an overambitious war. Despite considerable domestic opposition on the British side as well, Chamberlain allowed Hitler to become significantly emboldened and to appropriate important material resources. "Advice on the relative advantages of fighting now or later was sought very late and was little discussed."[26]

However, once these risky strategies by both Hitler and Chamberlain had pushed their countries to the brink of war, a sharp reassessment of military capabilities left each side fearful of the other, and war was avoided. Hitler did not hold positive illusions that the Allies would be easy to defeat at this stage (or if he did, his advisors managed to prevent this illusion from being translated into policy). Neither did British decisionmakers entertain positive illusions that they could, at that time, fight a successful war against Germany. "Germany was not yet prepared for major war and Britain, having undertaken a systematic assessment of its interests and options, made a sustained effort to *avoid* a confrontation."[27]

The most compelling evidence of positive illusions in this case was not in estimates of military strength or probability of winning, but rather in assessments of the opponent's *intentions*. This is a theme that recurs in the other case studies. Richardson, who studied seven Great Power crises since the mid-nineteenth century, concluded that misperceptions of military capability were responsible for only one of these (Russia opting for war with Japan in 1903), but that *misperception of intentions* was a factor in exacerbating all of them, and a very significant factor in three.[28]

Why War in 1939?

Having concluded that at the time of the Munich crisis an absence of positive illusions led to peace rather than war, I can now examine the prediction that positive illusions *were* in evidence when war did eventually break out in 1939. I will show that this is the case. In the intervening period Hitler became significantly emboldened by his series of successes, and he increasingly mistrusted his own intelligence agencies and advisors—thereby gradually removing constraints on his level of confidence. Most of all, he underestimated the Allies' will to fight, and overestimated his ability to defeat them if they did. Hitler said in August 1939: "Any political or military success involves taking risks . . . The men of Munich will not take the risk."[29]

Allies

Some possible positive illusions on the Allied side may have contributed to the decision for war. For example, France harbored a certain complacency about its ability to defend itself against a German invasion. The Maginot line was not expected to fall, certainly not as quickly as it did, and the French discounted the possibility that the Germans would be able to launch an attack through the Ardennes, which is exactly what happened. But overall the Allies cannot be said to have been overly overoptimistic about victory. In September 1939 any lingering Allied illusions about Hitler's intentions were shattered, and Britain was left with little choice but to act on its ultimatum to Germany. But in terms of military capabilities the Allies were, in many respects, overly pessimistic, not knowing "the deep anxieties which rent [the German] High Command."[30] However, if anything, this fact makes the Allied decision to go to war in 1939 all the more significant. Despite perceiving the odds against them as even greater than they actually were, the Allies were willing to fight and, if one is to believe Churchill and many others, expected that they would eventually win.

Churchill believed in victory from the first day of the war until the last. His recollections of the House of Commons debate at the outbreak of the war indicate a deep optimism about what was to come, and suggest that his optimism was at odds with the current assessments of Britain's capabilities: "As I sat in my place, listening to the speeches, a very strong sense of calm came over me, after the intense passions and excitements of the last few days. I felt a serenity of mind and was conscious of a kind of uplifted detachment from human and personal affairs. The glory of Old England, peace-loving and ill-prepared as she was, but instant and fearless at the call of honour, thrilled my being and seemed to lift our fate to those spheres far removed from earthly facts and physical sensation." The point at which Britain did display a certain optimism was when it decided not to yield or seek peace in 1940 after the fall of France. At that point, neither the United States nor Russia had entered the war. Britain, alone in Europe, remained determined to fight a protracted war with a formidable enemy, despite a risk of invasion should it do so, and fought ferociously from its knees in the Battle of Britain.[31]

Germany

Hitler's chain of successes before the war (remilitarizing the Rhineland, *Anschluss* with Austria, Munich, the seizure of Czechoslovakia), often in the face of considerable domestic opposition, appears to have influenced his subsequent behavior. "With each victory he saw even less reason to heed advice or admit mistakes," and a growing sense of omniscience made him "increasingly resistant to new or contrary information." All this was in spite of the considerable intelligence capability that surrounded him, or even perhaps because of it (Hitler mistrusted his own intelligence agencies). David Jablonsky argues that Hitler "was not generally inclined to relate his own calculations to the probable intentions and capabilities of the enemy, since he was convinced that his will would always be triumphant in the end."[32]

Decreasing Openness. The fact that these flaws increased as time went on is significant for my theory linking positive illusions and war, because it supports the prediction that the debate became progressively closed, such that Hitler's overconfidence, while restrained by advice in 1938, was much less impeded by 1939. Several problems in the Reich's processing of information "enhanced the likelihood of unrealistic intelligence and threat assessments." First, Hitler eliminated important positions in his government whose role was to scrutinize plans or confirm consensus. For example, in 1938 he abolished the post of war minister, whose incumbent, until then, had made all major strategic decisions, and made himself the head of all three services.[33]

Second, Hitler's method of government created a system in which various organizations had incentives to compete for his attention: "Co-operation in the field of intelligence among Nazi decisionmakers was virtually non-existent, since control of intelligence assessments meant access to Hitler, and such access meant power . . . The consequence of all this was a perversion of the meaning of intelligence." Hitler also created significant motives to provide assessments that told him what he wanted to hear. At the beginning of the campaign in Russia, for instance, his belief in victory was bolstered by an intelligence organization "confident of its own ability and anxious not to repeat the pessimistic enemy over-estimations of previous years that had brought Hitler's wrath down on the General Staff."[34]

Third, Hitler surrounded himself with an "ever-narrowing inner staff circle" which "protected him from unwelcome information." Field Marshall Keitel in particular "set new standards for obsequious servility" (and came to be known as the "nodding ass"). Hitler rejected later attempts to remove Keitel on the grounds that he was as "loyal as a dog." And fourth, even when good information got through these barriers, "Hitler's character, working habits, and experience combined to make him the worst possible intelligence consumer. His sense of infallibility made him completely unreceptive to different, let alone contradictory, ideas . . . Belief in his own superiority left no room to learn anything from experience."[35]

In summary, positive illusions were increasingly left unchallenged, and therefore largely uncorrected: "When Hitler finally unleashed his forces on Poland on the morning of September 1, 1939, there was no celebration in the streets of Berlin, only the stony silence of fear and uncertainty. Hitler was popular, but war was not. A leader who took the counsel of others or who paid heed to public opinion would not have conducted policy in quite the same way."[36]

Increasing Positive Illusions. In the decision to risk war in 1939, Hitler was certainly overoptimistic about how the Allies would respond. In the run-up to the invasion of Poland, General Halder wrote that Hitler "reckons with the possibility that the French and British might adopt a passive attitude in the face of our invasion." Even if they were not passive, Hitler expected that Britain and France would "fight in September 1939 but doubted that they would continue to do so after Poland was defeated. Britain especially, he believed, had sufficient common interest with Germany to conclude a peace treaty after limited hostilities." These expectations were further evident following the war in Poland. "Hitler seems to have assumed that the British and French—who had done nothing to help Poland, could not do anything to help her—would fold up." Even after France had also fallen, most remarkably, "it never crossed Hitler's mind that Great Britain would continue the war." Shortly before the outbreak of war in 1939, Hitler drew together his chiefs of staff to inform them of his plans to invade Poland. "After the Führer's speech, only Minister Goering seemed to have applauded this decision enthusiastically. The other members of the meeting preferred to keep silent . . . On September 3 Britain and France declared war on Germany, a possibility that Hitler had severely underestimated."[37]

Hitler himself, who once "confessed to a compulsion to go against the odds and court disaster," was certainly encouraged to spark the war in 1939 because he underestimated the resolve of the Allied powers to fight and severely overestimated the German capability to defeat them. He had enormous positive illusions about the ease of defeating what were, to him, inherently inferior foes. He believed that the Slavs and other "mongrelized" groups would not fight well, and this view underlay "a consistent underestimation of his most powerful adversaries, the United States and the Soviet Union." In 1941 Hitler would "confidently assert that if the United States were to work feverishly for four years, it could not replace the materiel that the Russian Army had lost thus far. This underestimation was not limited to production and supply capability. 'I'll never believe,' Hitler stated shortly after Pearl Harbor, 'that an American soldier can fight like a hero'." Such convictions were contrary to clear evidence indicating otherwise, and contrary to the advice of many of his own generals and advisors. Both this and his decision to invade Russia in 1941 represent hugely optimistic decisions—as judged by others at the time (on both sides), by historians of the period, and by history.[38]

Hitler's aggression and boldness paid off earlier on, as his remarkable victories in France, Norway, Crete, and Gibraltar showed. But at the strategic level his optimism failed him. With fighting on several fronts simultaneously, his rapid victories were undermined by major commitments leading in all directions from Germany. In the end, his overconfidence brought disaster. "Because Hitler's strategic ends were infinitely expansive, no military doctrine . . . could keep up with his policy in the end."[39]

It is worth noting that great confidence was not limited to Hitler. Rommel, for instance, gained his formidable reputation in North Africa for daring attacks with sometimes vastly inferior forces. General von Manstein later suggested: "The German method is really rooted in the German character, which—contrary to all the nonsense about 'blind obedience'—has a strong streak of individuality and—possibly as part of its Germanic heritage—finds certain pleasure in taking risks." After the rapid successes in the invasion of France in 1940, it was Hitler who proved to be reluctant to take further risks and decided to "pull the reins" on his generals—who advocated a rapid onward push to consolidate the success and exploit the confusion. Once the invasion of France was under way, General Halder wrote in his diary on 17 May 1940: "On top there isn't a spark of spirit that would dare to put high stakes on a single throw."[40]

What is most striking is the difference in Hitler's beliefs between the time of the campaign in France and that in Russia. Each event illustrates his increasing positive illusions and a decreasing ability of the system to counter the attendant manifestations of overconfidence. Hitler's proposal to launch the invasion of France as early as 12 November 1939 was successfully postponed because "there was such strong opposition by nearly all the senior army generals." But increasingly Hitler "insisted over his generals' objections in the fall of 1939 that the *drôle de guerre* [phony war] must be broken by offensive action." Eventually he cajoled them to "agree" to the invasion. After the enormous initial successes of the campaign, however, he was able to make plans for future action even "against the wishes of most military leaders who wished to wait until the enemy reaction could be gauged."[41]

Hitler's subsequent decision to invade Russia illustrates a newly elevated level of confidence. His generals had managed to convince him in 1940 that the weather conditions and the vast logistical requirements made an attack on Russia totally impractical. But after the victory over France, Hitler told Keitel that "a campaign against Russia would be like a child's game in a sandbox by comparison." Thus in 1941 Hitler launched his "suicidal assault" against Russia, "counting blindly on an early victory." A. J. P. Taylor believes that Hitler's staggering success in France was the reason his generals did not oppose his move into the east and instead "accepted he could do something similar against Russia." But again it was not solely Hitler who entertained this optimism. Many German generals "grossly underestimated Russia's resources, manpower and fighting capacity. They agreed with Hitler that Russia would collapse within a month of the invasion." Their overconfidence is indicated by the fact that, "whereas against France the generals made detailed plans, no defined plans were made of what they would do when they got into Russia. They were confident that they would simply break through in one place after another, and the Russian armies would all surrender; in July the war would be over."[42]

German overconfidence was also betrayed by many aspects of the campaign strategy and planning. For example, winter supplies were not even given to the troops. Once winter set in and the German forces came to a standstill, Hitler seems to have been surprised how poorly equipped they were and what a disastrous state they were in. Taylor wrote: "The whole German invasion was conducted in such a slapdash way that, when the time came, in June 1941, a great deal of it was not ready. Slightly over half the German invading forces had to be supplied from French captured equipment."[43]

Even by the time of the devastating Russian winter offensive of 1942, Hitler maintained extraordinary positive illusions about the predicament of the German army, dismissing negative reports and bullying his subordinates to push on regardless. He complained that his generals "always overestimate the strength of the Russians . . . They are weakened . . . besides, how badly Russian officers are trained! . . . In the short or long run the Russians will simply come to a halt. They'll run down. Meanwhile we shall throw in a few fresh divisions; that will put things right."[44]

In the Munich crisis and the buildup to World War II, there was evidence of positive illusions about both intentions and capabilities. Both types of illusions may lead to war, but their causal mechanisms are different. My central thesis was supported: assessments of capabilities in 1938 were realistic (or even pessimistic), and hence neither side was willing to risk war. But positive illusions about intentions, though they aggravated the crisis, did not directly increase the probability of war. Here is why. Positive illusions about intentions were arguably evident on both sides at the time of Munich *and* at the time of the crisis over Poland in 1939, yet while the first crisis resulted in peace, the second resulted in war. Thus illusions about intentions are ruled out as a causal determinant of war. Instead, the implication is that positive illusions about *capabilities* were the more significant factor influencing the probability of war. Of the factors considered here, only that changed from 1938 to 1939 (on Hitler's side). This means that the core theory is strengthened—it is positive illusions about one's own *power* that lead to war. Also, this case illustrates clearly that positive illusions can arise on one side only and still have a causal impact on war. The more realistic opponent may not choose war, but may be forced to fight.

Chapter 5

The Cuban Missile Crisis

No student of Soviet affairs has suggested that Khrushchev was a prudent man. He was attracted to grand gestures and acted impulsively. He gambled, often with little apparent chance of success. Cuba fits this pattern of behavior.
                                                    —Richard Ned Lebow

I'm a pessimist, Mr. President . . . We've changed our evaluations.
                                                    —General Maxwell D. Taylor

The Cuban missile crisis offers another demanding test of the positive illusions hypothesis. On the Soviet side, the opportunity for assessment of the situation was long; options other than deploying missiles in Cuba were available; and the likely U.S. reaction to the deployment should have been clear. On the U.S. side, although the opportunity for assessment was short, the intense debate within the specially formed executive committee (ExComm) was a high-quality decisionmaking process; a number of options were available to President Kennedy; and U.S. intelligence information, though later found to have been flawed in certain important respects, was good enough for the decisionmakers to rank the stakes of the key available options. (See Table 3.) Also, the Cuban missile crisis is perhaps the most deeply studied crisis in international politics, with numerous explanations already offered for the moves made on each side.

I argue that the Soviet premier, Nikita Khrushchev, exhibited positive illusions in deciding to install missiles in Cuba against clear evidence that doing so would not be tolerated by the United States. Any positive illusions on the U.S. side, by contrast, appear

Table 3. The Cuban missile crisis: elimination of basic alternative explanations and overview of conclusions.

	Soviet Union (missile deployment to Cuba)	United States (response to discovery of missiles)
Assessment opportunity	Long	Short but intense
Alternative options	Yes	Yes (within constraints)
Information availability	Reasonable	Reasonable
Positive illusions?	Yes (but not at end)	No*
Main factor	Huge gamble (at end: fear of nuclear war)	ExComm deliberation and caution

*Some possible positive illusions about the effectiveness of U.S. deterrence strategy and efficacy of a military strike.

to have been dispelled by the thorough ExComm decisionmaking process. Proponents of military action were pacified—enough at least to seek a peaceful solution—in the course of extensive debate about options and their likely ramifications. Those who still preferred military action were overruled. As nuclear holocaust became a real possibility, any illusions Khrushchev had also seem to have disappeared and he sought peace, even at the considerable price of being seen to back down.

Background

On 15 October 1962 a U.S. reconnaissance aircraft revealed Soviet medium-range ballistic missile installations in Cuba.[1] President Kennedy was briefed the following morning. These missiles, which could carry nuclear warheads and had a range of around 1,000 miles, could easily have reached Washington. A few days later, intercontinental-range ballistic missiles were also discovered, with a range of around 2,000 miles, enough to threaten nearly every major U.S. city. By installing missiles in Cuba, Khrushchev broke a public commitment as well as several official agreements that he would do no such thing.

The now famous ExComm of key U.S. policymakers and advisors was quickly assembled to deal with the crisis. On 22 October Kennedy announced the discovery of the missiles in an address to the nation, along with the ExComm's resolved course of action: a "quarantine" on all shipments of offensive weapons to Cuba—essentially a naval blockade that would stop and search all Russian ships. After thirteen days of extreme tension in which the world reached its closest-ever point to nuclear war, Khrushchev declared on 28 October that he would remove the missiles. Kennedy, in turn, pledged that the United States would not invade Cuba (a long-expected possibility). In addition, in secret talks between Robert Kennedy and the Soviet ambassador to Washington, Anatoly Dobrynin, it was agreed that American nuclear missiles in Turkey would be removed within five months.[2]

The Soviet Union

Information and Reaction

There were two critical pieces of information that Khrushchev needed in order to decide whether to install missiles in Cuba. First, he needed to know the relative nuclear capabilities of the United States and the USSR, to assess whether sneaking extra missiles into America's back yard was worth the risk. Second, he needed to know the likely U.S. response. Both types of information were available to the Soviet Union at the time.

The supposed superiority of Soviet strategic forces that Khrushchev had been publicizing was false. In 1962 the United States had seventeen times as many nuclear warheads, and the decisionmakers in Moscow were well aware of it. With hindsight, "we know today that Khrushchev's bellicose posturing was primarily designed to mask Soviet inferiority." But U.S. decisionmakers were not initially aware that it was a bluff. "When Khrushchev took the offensive in Southeast Asia and Berlin, Kennedy assumed that it was the result of his belief in Soviet strategic superiority and his lack of respect for Kennedy's resolve. Khrushchev's repeated assertions that the 'correlation of forces' increasingly favored the Soviet Union appeared to confirm the first of these assumptions." In fact, Kennedy had exploited the supposed "missile gap" in favor of the USSR in his election campaign, a gap that the Democrats promised to close (even though it was shown to be imaginary soon after Kennedy took office). First, then, the Soviets were aware of the actual relative strengths of the two strategic forces. The United States was far more powerful, so missiles in Cuba with a first-strike advantage might serve as a "quick means to strategic parity." At the same time, however, Khrushchev knew that if it came to a crisis, as the far weaker power he would not be in a strong bargaining position—so it was an especially risky option.[3]

As for the likely U.S. response, several sources available to the Soviet leaders indicated that the United States would never tolerate the deployment of missiles in Cuba, and Kennedy had made this clear in public. Soviet missiles in Cuba were unlikely to be regarded by the United States or other nations as a simple mirror image of NATO missile deployments in Europe. It should also have been clear from a consideration of U.S. domestic politics, not just of Kennedy's administration, that such a move would be resisted—even at high cost. The Soviet foreign minister, Andrei Gromyko, warned Khrushchev: "Putting our nuclear missiles in Cuba would cause a political explosion in the United States."[4]

Khrushchev's decisions did not seem to reflect an accurate use of this information. If his aim had been simply to use the missiles as a bargaining chip, then the decision to deploy them might have been rational (because "having to" eventually remove them might have been part of the plan). But this was not the case. His principal aims were to create a defensive deterrent against an attack on Cuba (the United States had supported an unsuccessful attack in 1961 at the Bay of Pigs, and another invasion was considered very likely), and to redress Soviet nuclear inferiority. The fact that both of these aims required *permanent* missile bases in Cuba betray his actions to have been exceptionally optimistic.[5]

Khrushchev also appears to have been overoptimistic in imagining the missiles would not be discovered (he intended to announce them as a fait accompli once they were operational). Overall, he overestimated the chances that his plan would succeed, in spite of considerable information to the contrary. Richard Lebow argues that Khrushchev clearly underestimated the rapidity and firmness of the U.S. response: "When deciding to go ahead with the deployment, Khrushchev had not considered the domestic political pressures that would make the missiles intolerable to Kennedy. Nor is there any evidence that he considered the important differences between [the United States] openly deploying missiles in Turkey and [the Soviet Union] secretly installing them in Cuba after giving assurances to the contrary . . . Khrushchev's failure to grasp these realities and their implications was the result of anger and wishful thinking."[6]

Positive Illusions?

Kennedy was particularly concerned by the threatening behavior in "Khrushchev's bullying speeches, boasts of superiority, and crude displays of force." This conscious bragging seemed to spill over into a genuine overconfidence about sending missiles to Cuba. Khrushchev's "emotional arousal clouded his judgment and made empathy with President Kennedy and the constraints under which he operated all but impossible. It also ruled out a thorough and dispassionate evaluation of the likely repercussions of a Cuban missile deployment." The alternative possibility that Khrushchev was unwillingly following an agenda pushed by a hard-line Soviet Presidium is discounted by new research in Soviet archives showing that the decision to install missiles in Cuba was largely Khrushchev's own: "To interpret Soviet decisions is to interpret Khrushchev. He alone decided on policy." We can also reject the claim that Khrushchev viewed Kennedy as a pushover. Soviet documents indicate that Khrushchev's provocations "were neither opportunity driven nor prompted by a lack of respect for Kennedy's resolve." Rather, it appears that, in the face of available evidence, Khrushchev simply overestimated the probability that the United States would tolerate Soviet nuclear missiles in Cuba (and would fail to discover their installation). This claim is not particularly controversial; my point here is that it is consistent with the theory of positive illusions.[7]

A closed decisionmaking process appears to have allowed Khrushchev's positive illusions to go unchallenged. The Soviet leader, according to Stephen Van Evera, "underrated the risk of a firm U.S. response partly because he made his policy in dark secrecy, excluding advisors who could have predicted Kennedy's tough reaction . . . States tend to miscalculate because they make policy in a secret setting that excludes analysts who might correct their false premises." In this case it was an exceptionally secretive move: "Not even all members of the Central Committee or the cabinet ministers were involved. It was only possible to discuss it within a circle of about ten or maybe fifteen people, not more."[8] It is unclear how many of those ten or fifteen people may have held positive illusions, but Khrushchev appears to have been particularly prone to them, and to have been the key decisionmaker.

The United States

Information and Reaction

U.S. intelligence resources and transmission of information to the White House were generally excellent at the time of the crisis. After Pearl Harbor, the United States had determined to establish the world's best and biggest intelligence network, and had achieved this very rapidly. Indeed, it was routine high-altitude U-2 photography and scrutiny that revealed the missiles in the first place. However, we now know that during the Cuban missile crisis the "intelligence provided to U.S. decisionmakers was substantially imperfect, whatever the intelligence community may have known."[9]

There were intelligence failures with respect to two important facts relevant to U.S. response options. First, the CIA estimated around 20,000 Soviet troops in Cuba, but it was later revealed that there were actually more than twice that number: 42,000. Second, much more important was the fact, only discovered some years later, that Soviet short-range tactical nuclear weapons (on surface-to-surface missiles) had already been installed in Cuba specifically as a defense against a U.S. ground invasion. Had the Americans attacked, it has been reasonably established that these could have been used.[10] In addition, there was considerable uncertainty about what the wider Soviet response would be to any attack on Cuba. This uncertainty derived not so much from a lack of relevant information as from the intrinsic difficulty of second-guessing another state's actions. Where would the Soviets respond? How? With conventional or nuclear forces? The most commonly cited potential responses were a Soviet invasion or blockade of West Berlin and a retaliatory strike against NATO missile bases in Turkey—but the Americans could not know for sure what the Soviets would do.

These three key pieces of information would have had a significant impact on which options the United States perceived to be realistically available. Of course, all three unknowns soon became irrelevant, since the United States, for a number of other reasons, did not invade Cuba. Therefore, for the purposes of the main U.S. strategy, the information that reached the ExComm was apparently good enough to reveal major disadvantages of a military attack, and thus good enough for the policymakers to make informed decisions.[11] Having all the facts at the time would only have reinforced the decision to avoid military action, so my conclusions in this chapter would be unchanged.

Likewise, the fact that the United States grossly overestimated the number of ICBMs deployed at the time on *Soviet* soil (the supposed "missile gap") is irrelevant. U.S. decisionmakers were becoming aware of the reality in 1961–1962 (and said as much), but either way the decision to act militarily or peacefully over Cuba was not related to the number of missiles in the USSR.

Equally, the fact that the Soviet missile deployment in Cuba was not predicted or discovered until very late can be argued to be a further failure of U.S. intelligence, but that failure in itself did not affect the decision about whether or not to wage war once the discovery had been made.

Intelligence problems later on during the crisis itself were more significant, and several crucial developments and events were not conveyed to decisionmakers. Perhaps the most critical such event was when a U-2 was shot down over Cuba at the height of the crisis, on 27 October. The United States believed senior Soviet leaders had authorized the firing of surface-to-air missiles (which were Russian made and operated by Russian troops). But this was not true. In reality, Khrushchev had been outraged when he learned that Soviet forces had shot the aircraft down. U.S. leaders did not adequately consider potential misperceptions of their own actions by the Soviet side either. As the crisis unfolded, "there does not seem to have been much in the way of an ongoing intelligence assessment of what the Soviets would know about U.S. actions and intentions." For example, "the U.S. government had already developed plans and issued orders that, if a U-2 was shot down, a retaliatory air strike would be launched against offending air defense sites within minutes."[12] When the U-2 actually was shot down, White House decisionmakers had to intervene to forestall what could otherwise have been an automatic escalation. McNamara pushed for a retaliatory strike at dawn the next day, but Kennedy resisted. Despite these near misses, information problems were gradually sorted out, and special links were set up to allow direct communication between U.S. political and military leaders.

Apart from problems with intelligence information itself, the analysis of information during the crisis is generally seen as having been excellent, especially considering the time pressure, the enormous responsibility, and the high degree of uncertainty. Given the extensive research that has been conducted on the taped conversations and other documents of the ExComm discussions, it is not surprising that some inconsistencies and errors have been found. For example, Irmtraud Gallhofer and Willem Saris found that despite at least seven "distinct strategies" being floated, decisionmakers tended to consider only two at a time. But in general, the quality of expertise and debate within the ExComm was unprecedented in the history of foreign policy, and is "widely regarded as being of high quality."[13]

Compared with the typical decisionmaking tier in the U.S. government (within a similar time frame), the ExComm was significantly more diverse and more thorough. Moreover, the group was essentially apolitical. Although the final decisions were Kennedy's, domestic politics are not likely to have seriously affected the ExComm's deliberations because it "consisted of national security officials and advisers, not politicians." Such factors didn't disappear altogether, of course, but nevertheless, the ExComm "was hardly the forum for Kennedy to air his domestic political concerns. It seems more likely that he would have deliberately refrained from doing so to encourage his advisers to speak their minds freely and to evaluate their options solely with regard to their security implications." Furthermore, ExComm members felt a shared duty to get the missiles out of Cuba, and "this sense of responsibility, the resulting heightened sensitivity to the risks of inadvertence, and the associated fear seem to have reinforced each other and to have had a powerful cautionary effect on the ExComm's choices of action throughout the crisis."[14]

Positive Illusions?

Initially, all the U.S. decisionmakers "held one and only one opinion—that immediate military action was necessary." As the debate continued, some would become more dovish, while others would remain ardent hawks, but what is critical here is the expectation that a military option could succeed. Certain members of the ExComm were confident that a hard military response, in particular air strikes, would succeed, possibly even without any Soviet retaliation. General Curtis LeMay, the air force chief of staff, was a proponent of this view. It was shared by several political leaders:

for example, the secretary of the treasury, Douglas Dillon, was "certain that the weapons could be eliminated"; his greater concern was the potential "difficulties with public opinion." A number of other members of the ExComm, including Maxwell Taylor (chairman of the joint chiefs of staff), Dean Acheson (former secretary of state), John McCone (the CIA director), and Paul Nitze (assistant secretary of defense), also held the optimistic belief "from the start of the crisis that military action against the Soviet bases in Cuba carried little risk of retaliation." In fact, they believed "the United States held all the cards; the only question in their minds was how great was the fall that the Soviets were bound to take."[15]

Kennedy himself was initially disposed to military action as well. Some contemporaries (such as LeMay), as well as analysts since, have suggested that with a tougher policy, Kennedy could have got rid of Castro and the missiles at the same time. Such confidence is remarkable given that the military leaders were not prepared to offer any guarantees of success. They estimated that only 90 percent of *known* targets could be destroyed in a single air strike, after which further strikes would be necessary to concentrate on any (known) remaining ones. This may seem a pretty good success rate, but missing a few nuclear missiles is a big problem. Taylor had made these expectations clear from the beginning. On 18 October he told the ExComm: "There'll never be a guarantee of 100 percent."[16] The ExComm didn't know how many missiles had warheads either, but they had to assume that some did.

The important point for my argument is that, although the option of a military attack on Cuba was initially popular, in the course of the ExComm deliberations support for such aggressive action declined over time. Though it periodically reappeared, in the end, hawkish confidence in a military solution seems to have been stamped out, or overruled. The ExComm contained both hawks and doves throughout (and perhaps "owls," who preferred to take an intermediate strategy and garner information from the adversary's next move while keeping both hawkish and dovish options in reserve). While some hawkish committee members had staunch views that remained inflexible, the decisionmaking process did appear to cause some others to change their opinions. During the ExComm meeting of 19 October, for example, "a tentative consensus was already reached to advise the president to set up a blockade, although the military advisors were not yet convinced. In the course of further meetings on this day, however, proponents of the air strike also began to shift their support to the blockade option."[17]

It seems that focused reasoning—in the shadow of nuclear holocaust—gradually dispelled any initial optimism that military action could take place without invoking an intolerable escalation toward war. The many hours of debate and analysis by this remarkable collection of men tended to lead to a pacification of initial responses. Had they had less time, such a process might not have occurred, with the consequence that the initial and widespread optimism about air strikes might have been more prominent. As Stuart Thorson and Donald Sylvan have argued, "a shorter perceived crisis time might well have led to the selection by the United States of more severe military options."[18] It should be noted that on Monday, 29 October, or at the latest by Tuesday, the United States would have launched air strikes anyway—the diplomatic route had an expiration date. Thus it was largely Khrushchev's realization that the gamble had gone too far, rather than Kennedy's or the ExComm's, that ultimately averted war.

Did Positive Illusions Contribute?

Khrushchev overestimated the chances that his missile deployment would be successful (and also be undetected until after it was completed). It was this misplaced conviction that led to the crisis. The United States was partly responsible, too, in failing to predict that such a move was possible (because of the mistaken belief that the existing U.S. deterrent threat was working). Nevertheless, once the crisis broke, U.S. decisionmakers who were optimistic about the success of a rapid military strike were eventually convinced otherwise, or if not they were overruled. The ExComm phenomenon may, therefore, have been responsible for extinguishing any U.S. overoptimism about a military solution.

This is significant for my theory: positive illusions, especially the illusion of one's control over events, become less pronounced with more intensive deliberation (see Chapter 2). Lebow notes that both leaders progressively recognized that they could not control events as well as they had thought. In addition, credit is due to Kennedy, who, with the safety of much of the world's population in jeopardy, remained patient, resisted military bellicosity, constantly challenged assumptions, and consulted widely. Shortly before the crisis he had read Barbara Tuchman's book *The Guns of August*, which "captured the false optimism and the aggressive day-dreaming in Europe in the summer of 1914." A number of people have suggested that for Kennedy and other decisionmakers at the time, "the book could have been a rein on any tendency to indulge in wishful thinking."[19]

Khrushchev, once the crisis was in full swing, appears to have gambled a second time—holding out on a settlement to maximize potential U.S. concessions. This may have paid off in winning a U.S. pledge not to invade Cuba and a secret agreement to remove U.S. missiles from Turkey. But for their own ends, both Kennedy and Khrushchev prolonged the crisis, and therefore extended the period in which minor events could have made the delicate situation erupt into war, as several—such as the straying of an Alaska-based U-2 surveillance plane into Soviet airspace—nearly did.[20] Thus positive illusions may have contributed to causing the crisis, and to drawing it out, but they were not strong enough, or did not persist long enough, to push the decisionmakers all the way to war.

U.S. Restraint

I argued above that the ExComm environment tended to pacify bellicose posturing. But positive illusions may have left a mark on policy nevertheless. The initial U.S. reactions to the discovery of

Soviet missiles in Cuba, before there had been much feedback or reflection, were quite emotional (both President Kennedy and his brother Robert, for example, were incensed by the Soviet deception and were eager to strike back). Those bellicose tendencies exerted a crucial influence in ruling out—at the early stages—any attempt to rely on purely diplomatic channels to negotiate a solution. Doing so was never discussed (Kennedy tasked the ExComm with how to remove the missiles, not how to resolve the crisis). Hawkish views influenced policy later on as well. While the thorough debates about consequences of military action may have had an overall softening effect, at the same time the ExComm's hawks shifted the range of possible responses toward the more aggressive end of the spectrum. This led to the selection of a middle-of-the-road decision, a quarantine with a threat of force in reserve, to ensure an acceptable compromise amid the diverse views within the ExComm.[21]

After the crisis, Robert Kennedy drew specific lessons from the experience that amount to methods for stamping out positive illusions (or indeed any premature bias): "Maximize time for decisions and adversary responses; inhibit initial response tendencies; preserve diversity of opinion in one's own decision process; use expertise on the adversary; ensure civilian control of the military; give the adversary a face-saving way to comply with your requirements; and safeguard against inadvertent escalation." Ted Sorensen also suggested that the principal lessons included watertight decisionmaking, to ensure coherent signals to the enemy, and information-rich and detailed evaluation of available options. These all sound rather obvious after the event, but they delineate precisely the criteria that, when absent, may leave positive illusions unchecked and war more likely as a result.[22]

I would argue that, while the hawks may have presented rational arguments in favor of air strikes, they were being highly optimistic about both the chances of success and the likelihood of meeting a silent response. The military could not (and did not) guarantee that they would hit all the missiles, yet there was much talk of "surgical" air strikes and "removing" the missiles.[23] In the days before guided weapons, this was asking a great deal of the air force, especially given that the United States could not know whether intelligence sources had located all missile sites, or how many missiles were operational. Moreover, most of the decision-makers recognized the likelihood that a follow-up invasion by ground forces would be required, a massive undertaking that Maxwell Taylor had warned at the outset would require 250,000 men. The actual chances that the Soviets would fail to respond must have been somewhere close to zero.

If these were positive illusions, they were eventually eliminated or prevented from influencing decisionmaking. It seems that the remarkable phenomenon of the ExComm was largely responsible for defusing overconfidence in a military solution. Kennedy himself seemed to have had a particularly high awareness of the danger. He constantly demanded that the ExComm seek other options before resorting to air strikes. This conclusion is supported by Irving Janis's study of group decisionmaking biases that sometimes lead to policy failure. Janis concluded that, although various "groupthink" biases were responsible for the failed Bay of Pigs invasion in 1961, they were *absent* in the case of U.S. decisionmaking in the Cuban missile crisis. In the end, Kennedy's clarity of appreciation of the situation seems to have allowed him to avoid many potential mistakes, and to have been relatively sensitive to both U.S. and Soviet perceptions. Although the Kennedy administration carefully tailored an image of success, Robert Kennedy noted: "After it was finished, he [the president] made no statement attempting to take credit for himself or for the Administration for what had occurred. He instructed all members of the Ex Comm and government that no interview should be given, no statement made, which would claim any kind of victory. He respected Khrushchev for properly determining what was in his own country's interest and what was in the interest of mankind."[24]

Soviet Restraint

While I argued that Khrushchev's positive illusions that the United States would tolerate missiles in Cuba sparked the crisis, later on it was clear that any such illusions had disappeared on the

Soviet side too. By the end, it seems, Khrushchev had become extremely anxious and wanted an escape route. Some suggest that he deliberately proposed the Turkish missile deal in order to offer the United States a face-saving mechanism by which they could both exit the crisis. One U.S. commentator noted: "It was the behavior of a man begging our help to get off the hook."[25]

It is possible that the idea for a deal involving the Turkish missiles came from elsewhere.[26] But regardless of the origin of this proposal, it is clear that Khrushchev by this point was extremely concerned about the possibility of nuclear war, which might have happened as a result of either continuing escalation or another accident. His last letter to Kennedy suggests a desperation to put all other aims aside and end the crisis at all costs. And this was not just what he was telling Kennedy. On 28 October Khrushchev addressed the Presidium, telling them that they were facing the possibility of nuclear holocaust, and that "in order to save the world, we must retreat."[27] In the final stages of the crisis, Khrushchev had no positive illusions about victory.

During the Cuban missile crisis, it seems that the Americans perceived themselves to be in a game of "chicken," while the Soviets perceived themselves in a game of "prisoner's dilemma." These differing social dilemma games would predict that the United States needed to hold out as long as possible without conceding, while the Soviets needed to search for a way to ensure American compliance, and if they found none, to defect from cooperation. Such contrasting perceptions would mean that the two sides were vying for different goals, and would therefore have different criteria for evaluating what was possible to achieve. However, Christian Schmidt argues that the direct contact between Kennedy and Khrushchev once the crisis had begun permitted a reassessment of the situation. In effect, the leaders reformulated what sort of game they were in, a change that led to new preferences and to the possibility of a mutually advantageous settlement. Possibly the best model for this reformulation was a "coordination game," in which agreement could be reached provided there was mutual trust.[28]

But, while Kennedy and Khrushchev may have revised their positions, the mindsets of the initial games pervaded the thinking of other observers, who later passed judgment from within those invalidated frameworks. Those who emphasized the "blinking first" idea apparently retained the "chicken" model—as in Secretary of State Dean Rusk's triumphant comment "We're eyeball to eyeball and I think the other fellow just blinked."[29] On the basis of such a simplistic model, the United States can be argued to have "won" the Cuban missile crisis simply because it was not the one to back down. But this perspective does not necessarily reflect resounding moral virtue or good judgment, since it implies that the United States was more willing to risk nuclear war than was the Soviet Union.

While many scholars applaud the U.S. decisionmaking of October 1962 as a model for how to resolve a crisis, the fact that the crisis arose in the first place is evidence of a major failure in U.S. foreign policy and intelligence. Before the crisis, Kennedy's administration firmly believed the Soviets would not put nuclear missiles on Cuba.[30] On 16 October Kennedy lamented to the ExComm: "Maybe our mistake was not saying, sometime before this summer, that if they do this we're going to act." The U.S. administration had wrongly assumed that this was already explicit: "American leaders were taken by surprise in October 1962 because they thought it was clear to the Soviet Union that placing missiles in Cuba would not be tolerated."[31] But even if the U.S. decisionmakers were guilty of overestimating their deterrent threat (in which case a critic could argue that Khrushchev's attempt to put missiles in Cuba was rational after all), it would still be very difficult to defend the idea that the United States would ever have accepted missiles in Cuba. No U.S. president could have weathered the political storm sparked by such appeasement. Given this, the U.S. leaders may have misjudged their own deterrent, but Khrushchev misjudged their willingness to act. It can therefore be argued that Khrushchev demonstrated positive illusions about the feasibility of installing nuclear missiles in Cuba—an argument that holds whether or not his gamble represented a failure of U.S. deterrence.

The Cuban missile crisis can be interpreted as a manifestation of what has been called the "potentially fatal paradox behind American strategic policy: that the country might have to go to war to affirm the very credibility that is supposed to make war unnecessary." Deterrence failed in 1962 in the face of daring behavior elicited by positive illusions. As Davis Bobrow put it: "The crisis shows . . . that an opponent's leadership may take enormous risks without believing in the likelihood of commensurate gains, or on the basis of wishful thinking about those gains." Deterrence will fail if an opponent acts on positive illusions counter to the available evidence.[32] Saddam Hussein's extraordinary willingness to defy the United States and the United Nations, thus sparking the war that would destroy him, may be another example.

The final result of the Cuban missile crisis was a chilling realization that nuclear holocaust really was imminent—the shooting down of the U-2 without Soviet authority; the straying of another U-2 into Soviet airspace; the military escalations that were automatically enacted as a result of the elevated alert status. Once they were staring into the abyss of mutually assured destruction, both Khrushchev and Kennedy lost any positive illusions they may initially have had. As Kennedy said: "Unconditional war can no longer lead to unconditional victory. Mankind must put an end to war or war will put an end to mankind."[33]

Chapter 6

Vietnam

We have the power to knock any society out of the twentieth century.

— Robert McNamara

American intervention was not a progress sucked step by step into an unsuspected quagmire. At no time were policy-makers unaware of the hazards, obstacles and negative developments. American intelligence was adequate, informed observation flowed steadily from the field to the capital, special investigative missions were repeatedly sent out, independent reportage to balance professional optimism—when that prevailed—was never lacking. The folly consisted not in pursuit of a goal in ignorance of the obstacles but in persistence in the pursuit despite accumulating evidence that the goal was unattainable.

— Barbara Tuchman

The Vietnam war provides another tough test of the theory of positive illusions because faulty assessments should have been minimal. Investment in the war was so prolonged that there was ample opportunity for reassessment of progress (precluding the hypothesis that decisions were simply knee-jerk reactions); recent research suggests that the United States did have some other options that offered face-saving exit routes, options that, though they may not have been easy or desirable, were viable (precluding the hypothesis that decisions simply represented the only possible course of action); and intelligence information was voluminous and intensive (precluding the hypothesis that decisions were good, given poor information). (See Table 4.) Also, as with my

Table 4. The Vietnam war: elimination of basic alternative explanations and overview of conclusions.

	United States	North Vietnam
Assessment opportunity	Very long	Very long
Alternative options	Yes (though constrained)	Yes
Information availability	Reasonable (some flaws)	Reasonable
Positive illusions?	Some	No*
Main factor	Belief in eventual success or at least favorable bargaining position	Inexhaustible support and resolve

*Some possible positive illusions about the Tet offensive, but not overall.

other case studies, the Vietnam war has been the subject of innumerable studies and already has well-established explanations.

Nevertheless, there is significant evidence of an expectation that U.S. might would ultimately prevail. Policy did not change in line with accumulating information about its flaws. Key figures, including presidents, cabinet members, and military leaders, underestimated the opponent and overestimated their own ability to achieve their goals.

Background

From the aftermath of World War II until 1972, five presidents (Truman, Eisenhower, Kennedy, Johnson, and Nixon) steadily committed the United States to war in Vietnam. The myth that the United States stumbled into the "quagmire" of Vietnam in small steps without realizing the potential dangers was disproved by the "Pentagon Papers"—a collection of government documents, leaked to the press, that confirmed a clear appreciation of the risks. The intelligence effort was enormous (if anything, there was too much information to handle). Thus there should have been no illusions. Even the U.S. army was against a land war in Asia, having learned in Korea of the difficulty of fighting a determined native population and the danger of provoking the Soviet Union and China. U.S. military leaders also feared having to fight another limited war, being expected to win "with one hand tied behind their back" for political reasons. The Joint Chiefs of Staff advised accordingly against U.S. involvement. Before and throughout the conflict, evidence against the utility or likely effectiveness of U.S. involvement in Vietnam accumulated from the intelligence community, Congress, the presidents' own administrations, and specially appointed envoys (not to mention nongovernmental sources). Given this feedback, even accounting for the various political pressures constraining the perceived options, U.S. policy displayed an astoundingly die-hard optimism.[1]

The Vietnam war offers an opportunity to identify what common factor led the five presidents to believe that war was a worthwhile investment. It allows me to examine whether and why expectations varied while holding constant the general characteristics of the conflict over the period, thereby ruling out a number of potentially confounding factors. I focus mainly on Kennedy and Johnson, because they made the key decisions to intervene militarily and to commit U.S. combat troops.

David Kaiser and Fredrik Logevall have argued that it should have been clear to U.S. policymakers that withdrawal offered a better option than escalation. Many of the negative assessments of U.S. prospects came from research commissioned by the administrations themselves; as Barbara Tuchman wrote, "with hindsight, it is impossible to avoid asking why the American government ignored the advice of the persons appointed to give it . . . throughout the long folly of Vietnam, Americans kept foretelling the outcome and acting without reference to their own foresight." Tuchman may have exaggerated this effect somewhat, but the fact that the United States systematically escalated the war, despite considerable evidence advising against it, certainly implies that U.S. hopes and expectations outweighed the perceived risks and costs.[2]

The man who leaked the Pentagon Papers, Daniel Ellsberg, argued that the U.S. presidents had no particular expectation of actually winning the war, but were simply buying time for political reasons, resulting in what he called a "stalemate machine." New evidence shows that this view is false, but even Ellsberg, who held that policymakers were fairly realistic, noted unexplained "self-deception" and "over-optimistic expectations" in the later Johnson administration. Irving Janis found that "unrealistic hopes" remained important in 1964 and 1965 as well—the time of the crucial decisions for massive military escalation. Contrasting with this view, Leslie Gelb and Richard Betts argue that "virtually all views and recommendations were considered and virtually all important decisions were made without illusions about the odds of success" (though noting that of all things this is, "with hindsight, the hardest to believe"). However, while rejecting the notion that widespread overoptimism among decisionmakers was a constant cause of continued U.S. involvement, even Gelb and Betts agree that "*whether and when* these leaders were optimistic or pessimistic about the war is the only route to answering some of the pivotal issues and puzzles of Vietnam."[3]

I will examine the hypothesis that key U.S. decisionmakers held positive illusions about the costs of war in Vietnam, its risks, and the likelihood of eventual victory. But first I will present other explanations that have been adduced to account for U.S. involvement, factors that need to be borne in mind throughout my analyses of the individual U.S. administrations. I agree that those factors explain much of the underlying cause of the war, but I argue that they do not satisfactorily solve the whole puzzle.

One such factor was the determination to contain the spread of communism. The U.S. government was exceptionally sensitive to the "red menace" of communism in the period following World War II. There was a rising tide of communist movements around the world, and the U.S. role in counteracting it was a major influence on foreign policy for both Republican and Democratic governments throughout the Cold War. Although it may seem obsessive from today's standpoint, the political currency behind this fear in the United States of the time should not be underestimated. The Joint Chiefs even warned President Kennedy in 1963 that "the military and political effort of Communist China in South Vietnam . . . is, in fact, a planned phase in the communist timetable for world domination." People like Kennedy and John Foster Dulles (Eisenhower's secretary of state) felt a great responsibility for halting communism. The ghost of Munich weighed heavily on any suggestions of appeasement, especially with Kennedy. And the so-called domino theory—that if Vietnam fell to communism, so would the rest of Southeast Asia—was widely accepted and became a significant influence on policy.[4]

Another factor was the Cold War. Apart from worrying about communism itself, U.S. administrations tended, as Ernest May wrote, to see "all countries not allied with either the Soviet Union or the United States as battlegrounds in a global struggle between the two." During the Berlin crisis of 1961 (and following the difficult Vienna conference with Khrushchev), Kennedy remarked: "Now we have a problem in making our power credible, and Vietnam looks like the place." Thus Vietnam can be seen not just as one move of many within the larger game of Cold War chess, but as a key demonstration of U.S. resolve. To withdraw, wrote Secretary of State Dean Rusk, would mean "a drastic loss of confidence in the will and capacity of the free world to oppose aggression." U.S. credibility therefore was a prominent argument for pursuing a war in far-off Vietnam, even if it was costly and victory would be difficult.[5]

Once the United States was in the war, a need to save face may have contributed to its persistence. As the war progressed, U.S. decisionmakers showed a steadily increasing concern for the costs of failure, in both domestic and international political arenas, rather than the costs of fighting. In some sense the prestige of the United States was at stake because of its precarious involvement in the war. Some facts corroborate this view. John McNaughton, assistant secretary of defense for international security affairs, suggested that U.S. aims were "70 percent to avoid a humiliating defeat to our reputation as guarantor." President Johnson was also concerned that withdrawing without having won concessions would "lose us face." No one wanted the enormous U.S. investment in lives, dollars, and political commitment to have been in vain.[6]

Even if the factors just described were not prominent concerns of the leaders themselves, they nevertheless influenced policy because of the value attached to them by *other* domestic political actors. For all of the administrations, political pressures could never be ignored, especially within the divided system of government in Washington. Being seen as soft on communism was a politically punishable offense, with high penalties. Kennedy and Johnson in particular remembered "Republican charges that the Democrats had 'lost' China [to the communists in 1949, as well as the failure to win in Korea] as having harmed their party for a decade." Johnson thought those earlier setbacks would be "chickenshit compared with what might happen if we lost Vietnam." His chief advisors "believed with him that they would take greater punishment from the right by withdrawing than from the left by pursuing the fight."[7]

No leader could withdraw from a confrontation with communist aggression without seriously jeopardizing his subsequent election. As a result, in Tuchman's words, "the alternative of disengagement was always seen to be worse—loss of faith in the American shield abroad and accusations at home of weakness and infirmity against Communism." Domestic public opinion also tended to favor the war up to the later Johnson years. Until 1966 a majority of Americans approved of Johnson's handling of the war.[8] The initial antiwar demonstrations were largely ignored and held to represent troublemakers rather than the opinion of average Americans. Even Nixon was able to make the claim (rightly or wrongly) that a "silent majority" supported him. Last, but by no means least, there was the crucial sentiment that none of the presidents wanted to be the first in American history to lose a war.

None of these explanations need be taken as an overbearing reason for U.S. involvement in Vietnam. U.S. decisionmakers may have perceived horrendous constraints in all options, and simply aimed to eliminate the worst ones. If one of those worst options was the political consequences of withdrawing and the collapse of South Vietnam that was expected to follow, then continuing the war—regardless of cost—may have been perceived as the only acceptable option.[9]

In the following analyses, my aim is not to "explain" the Vietnam war, a task that has already been attempted by plenty of other authors. My aim is to show that, regardless of one's favored theory for the underlying causes of the war, there are still gaps and puzzles as to why the war was pursued the way it was in the face of considerable negative information. The theory of positive illusions may help to fill those gaps.

The Eisenhower Administration (1952–1960)

Information and Reaction

Eisenhower inherited from Truman a heavy commitment to supporting France's war in Indochina. Truman's initial contribution of aircraft and $119 million had steadily increased, by 1952, to $300 million.[10] Eisenhower had the opportunity to reconsider this policy, but he continued the trend, and in 1953 U.S. assistance reached $1 billion. Eisenhower was under no misapprehension about the likely opposition or the dangers of involvement in Vietnam. He was well aware, perhaps better than most given his career, that any military action could be expected to lead to escalation.

Despite the U.S. government's strong desire to prevent the spread of communism, in 1953 the plans division of the army general staff suggested a "reevaluation of the importance of Indochina and Southeast Asia in relation to the possible cost of saving it." Vice Admiral A. C. Davis, the advisor on foreign military affairs to the secretary of defense, declared that "involvement of US forces in the Indochina war should be avoided at all practical costs." A CIA report stated that "even if the United States defeated the Viet-Minh field forces, guerrilla action could be continued indefinitely . . . and [the United States] might have to maintain a military commitment in Indochina for years to come." The army chief of staff, General Matthew B. Ridgway, was opposed to sending ground forces. Having been commander of U.S. forces in the latter part of the Korean War, he knew the complications of fighting a war in Asia, and his advice was not to do it again. Ridgway sent a "large team of specialists, representing every branch of the Army, on an extended visit to Indochina. The result was a comprehensive report stating that success in Indochina would require well over three hundred thousand U.S. troops, high rates of casualties for five to seven years, and an expansionist fiscal policy that would reverse the constraints Eisenhower had placed on the budget and in particular on the military."[11]

The French mountain stronghold of Dien Bien Phu was taken by Vietnamese forces on 7 May 1954, marking the defeat and final withdrawal of the old colonial power. The French experience of 150,000 casualties, in a country they knew well, was not alarming enough to deter American optimism about winning a war in Vietnam. By 1954 evidence that involvement would be a mistake was widespread. The Joint Chiefs were opposed even to sending the small Military Assistance Advisory Group (MAAG) to train the Army of the Republic of Vietnam (ARVN) forces, and they issued a memorandum in August 1954 recommending that the United States "should not participate."[12] Further emissaries were sent to Saigon on information-gathering missions. They returned with the same message: do not get involved.

Senator Mike Mansfield, after his second trip to Vietnam, reported that the situation had if anything worsened, largely because of a "consistent underestimating" of the political and military strength of the Viet Minh. He pressed the point that "unless there is a reasonable expectation of fulfilling our objectives, the continued expenditure of the resources of the citizens of the

United States is unwarranted and inexcusable." General J. Lawton Collins was sent to Paris to consult with the French and evaluate the leadership potential of Ngo Dinh Diem, America's preferred candidate to head the South Vietnamese government. Collins found Diem so unconvincing in his ability either to unite South Vietnam or to compete effectively with Ho Chi Minh that he recommended a "re-evaluation of our plans for assisting Southeast Asia." Although Collins saw withdrawal as an undesirable option, he thought it "may be the only sound solution."[13]

Positive Illusions?

Eisenhower's decisionmaking is considered to have been of high quality in comparison to that of other presidents during the war (although he never had to make the hardest choices), and its quality may have prevented any hasty jump into a direct military commitment. Nevertheless, Eisenhower's administration gradually committed the United States to increasing financial and military assistance, first to the French, then to the South Vietnamese. Eisenhower took risks in providing strong support to Diem and in sending hundreds of American military personnel into Vietnam. His secretary of state, John Foster Dulles, had the task of garnering domestic and international support to hold back the tide of communism in Vietnam. Yet, by the time of the Geneva conference on Indochina's future in May 1953, Dulles had failed to prevent the establishment of a communist regime in the North, had failed to convince Britain or other allies to join the U.S. effort, had failed to keep France in the field, had failed to gain approval from Eisenhower for direct involvement, and had even failed to get France to join the European Defense Community (as a reciprocal move for the massive American aid for France in Indochina). Despite all these indications that the American policy of containing communism was a failure, Dulles "was not prepared to infer from them any reason to re-examine policy."[14]

Given the various pessimistic views on U.S. involvement, why did the United States not only fail to withdraw, but actually escalate? In April 1955 an attempted coup gave reason to believe that the South Vietnamese government under Diem did not meet the standards of performance that Eisenhower himself had specifically made a condition for American aid. It thus offered a perfect chance to exit—but the United States did the reverse and committed itself further. The continued fear of communist expansion appeared to be the overriding factor. Eisenhower even went so far as to support Diem's highly controversial decision to cancel the planned South Vietnam elections (stipulated by the Geneva Accords of 1954) because of a concern that the vote would be "biased" (Ho Chi Minh was expected to win). An independent report by American political scientists suggested that "American aid has built a castle on sand."[15] And yet U.S. financial support soared ever upward. American military personnel had been on the ground since Truman's time (even though the French did not want them), but Eisenhower increased their number from a handful to several hundred. At this stage the war in Indochina was not a major public issue in the United States, but the continued escalation despite considerable counter-evidence implies that U.S. policymakers remained optimistic that they would prevail. The communist National Liberation Front was formed in 1960, and South Vietnam entered into a civil war proper, just in time for Eisenhower to pass on the mess to his successor.

The Kennedy Administration (1961–1963)

Information and Reaction

The new administration took possession of a legacy in Vietnam that its members appeared willing to continue without much change. "As far as the record shows," wrote Barbara Tuchman, "they held no session devoted to re-examination of the engagement they had inherited in Vietnam, nor did they ask themselves to what extent the United States was committed or what was the degree of national interest involved. Nor, so far as it appears in the mountains of memoranda, discussions and options flowing

over the desks, was any long-range look taken at long-range strategy." Even so, Kennedy cannot be accused of ignoring intelligence. Rather, "he dispatched . . . an endless series of upper-
level official missions to assess conditions in Vietnam. Secretary
McNamara was later to go no fewer than five times in 24 months,
and missions at the secondary level went back and forth to Saigon
like bees flying in and out of a hive." Information was also already
flowing back via the MAAG, the U.S. embassy, and the intelligence agencies.[16]

Not all information about progress in Vietnam was negative.
For example, after visiting Vietnam in May 1961, Vice President
Johnson urged, on the broader issue of involvement throughout
Southeast Asia, that "we move forward promptly with a major effort to help these countries defend themselves." William Gibbons
later wrote that in 1961 Kennedy had been "reluctant to move as
fast or as far as some of his advisors recommended." Moreover,
two senators who were later to speak vociferously against involvement, William Fulbright and Mike Mansfield, both argued in
Congress at this time that the president and U.S. foreign policy
should have *more* independent power and trusting support from
Congress, a view that "reflected the general attitude among most
members of Congress at that point."[17]

A new mission was sent in October 1961 following an increase
in Viet Cong infiltration across the border from Laos. It was led
by Maxwell Taylor, military representative of the president (and
soon to become chairman of the Joint Chiefs of Staff), and Walt
Rostow, an ardent hawk of whom Tuchman claims it was a "fore-
gone conclusion" that he "would find reasons for going forward
in Vietnam." Various officials from the state and defense depart-
ments, the Joint Chiefs' offices, and the CIA accompanied them.
The report they produced suggested that, as Tuchman noted,
"the program to 'save South Vietnam' would be made to work
only by the infusion of American armed forces to convince both
sides of [U.S.] seriousness . . . It quite accurately foresaw the
consequences: American prestige, already engaged, would become more so; if the ultimate object was to eliminate insurgency

in the South, 'There is no limit to our possible commitment (unless we attack the source in Hanoi).' Here, in both statement and in parenthesis, the future military problem was formulated."[18]

Since the evidence was to some extent mixed, it was still possible at this point to believe that real American involvement on the ground would swing events against the communists. But even if the information was perceived as simply ambiguous, not negative, committing the United States further was a huge risk to take. William Bundy (deputy assistant secretary of defense) stated in an analysis of the Taylor-Rostow report: "An early and hard-hitting operation has a good chance (70% would be my guess) of *arresting* things and giving Diem a chance to do better and clean up . . . The 30% chance is that we would wind up like the French in 1954; white men can't win this kind of fight." Given, in the best case, ambiguity from this and the various other intelligence sources, Kennedy's decision to extend U.S. involvement was a bold and optimistic move into a foggy unknown. Kennedy increased the number of U.S. personnel tenfold, "a step in some ways comparable to Johnson's escalation in the summer of 1965."[19] He also continued to strongly support Diem's unpopular regime. Meanwhile, negative information kept coming in.

A further report, delivered in December 1962, while generally supportive of U.S. involvement, was explicit in outlining the possible negative consequences, warning that "the war would last longer, cost more in money and lives than anticipated, and that 'the negative side of the ledger is still awesome'." Kennedy was clearly receptive to such reports that he himself commissioned; indeed, "he was aware of the negatives and bothered by them, but he made no adjustment, nor did any of his chief advisors suggest making one."[20]

In fact, as Ernest May notes, "every member of Kennedy's inner circle supported" the military commitment to Vietnam. Originally Dean Rusk was hesitant. Though firmly in favor of preventing the spread of communism, he thought it was a bad idea to make a major commitment of American prestige to what he called a "losing horse." He eventually gave the president his agreement,

but wrote to him that "in doing so, we recognize that the introduction of United States and other SEATO forces may be necessary to achieve this objective." In testimony before the Senate
foreign relations committee, he said: "Can you or should you invest in a regime when you know in your heart that that regime is
not viable?" Caution came from outside Kennedy's inner circle
too. John Kenneth Galbraith, U.S. ambassador to India, warned
Kennedy that his administration's good promise could be "sunk
under the rice fields."[21]

History should also have hinted at significant dangers. Like Eisenhower before him, once in office Kennedy was not apparently
concerned with Vietnam's excellent record of repelling invaders.

> The American failure to find any significance in the defeat of
> the French professional army, including the Foreign Legion, by
> [what were seen as] small, thin-boned, out-of-uniform Asian
> guerrillas is one of the great puzzles of the time. How could
> Dien Bien Phu be so ignored? When David Schoenbrun, corre-
> spondent for CBS, who had covered the French war in Viet-
> nam, tried to persuade the President of the realities of that war
> and of the loss of French officers equivalent each year to a class
> at St. Cyr [the French military academy], Kennedy answered,
> "Well, Mr. Schoenbrun, that was the *French*. They were fight-
> ing for a colony, for an ignoble cause. We're fighting for free-
> dom, to free them from the Communists, from China, for their
> independence."

This is remarkable because Kennedy himself had said of Vietnam
earlier that "if it were ever converted into a white man's war, we
should lose it as the French had lost a decade earlier."[22]

Information from the field should have become alarming. The
failure of the ARVN forces need not have been taken on as a responsibility of the U.S. military. According to William Gibbons's
analysis: "When the South Vietnamese failed to come up and
meet the mark at the advisory level, then we never should have
committed US forces. We should have failed at the advisory ef-

fort and withdrawn." By 1962 the media were also "probing the chinks and finding the short-falls and falsehoods in the compulsive optimism of official briefings." A mission by three senators in late 1962 reported that "a protracted struggle, at best, can be the only realistic forecast." Senator Mansfield, now the majority leader, was asked by Kennedy to visit Vietnam once again in December 1962. He returned to say: "Seven years and $2 billion of United States aid later . . . South Vietnam appears no more stable than it was at the outset." Kennedy said later: "I got angry with Mike for disagreeing so completely, and I got angry with myself because I found myself agreeing with him." If Kennedy himself found at least some of the negative indications convincing, why did he not modify policy?[23]

The enhanced U.S. prestige and public approval of the president resulting from the favorable outcome of the Cuban missile crisis in 1962 offered an opportunity to reevaluate Vietnam policy with much less danger of domestic wrath. A specific exit option arose following the Buddhist revolt in Saigon in 1963 (in which Diem was killed). The revolt demonstrated that the U.S.-supported South Vietnamese government was failing badly. Although Kennedy's assassination soon afterward may have complicated any exit options around this time for Johnson, the revolt did spark serious discussions in Washington in which Robert Kennedy asked "whether a Communist take-over could be successfully resisted with any government. If it could not, now was the time to get out of Vietnam entirely, rather than waiting." Nevertheless, "despite reports to the contrary, policy makers in Saigon and Washington continued to believe that the situation in Vietnam was improving."[24]

Positive Illusions?

It is perhaps notable that Kennedy and the men in his administration were a generation of war winners. "Like the President, many of his associates were combat veterans of World War II . . . Accustomed to success in the war and in their postwar careers, they expected no less in Washington." This may have contributed to an attitude that political problems could be solved by military means. As John Garofano puts it, "Military power and diplomacy were complementary instruments, not alternatives, in Kennedy's approach to crises in Berlin and Cuba as well as in Vietnam and Laos." Revisionists writing about the Cuban missile crisis argue that, in Richard Lebow's words, "Kennedy's successful use of coercive diplomacy led ineluctably to American intervention in Vietnam." That is, his apparent success in repelling communist advances in Cuba may have reinforced a belief that firm U.S. resolve could be successful elsewhere too. David Kaiser also considers the fact that the Kennedy administration represented the so-called GI generation, which he describes as characterized by "relentless optimism" and an "unwillingness to question basic assumptions, or to even admit the possibility of failure . . . the GI generation that led the nation into the war contained almost no doubters about the wisdom or the success of the enterprise."[25]

Even General Maxwell Taylor, who echoed Kennedy's prescient prediction that "only the Vietnamese can defeat the Viet-Cong," was nevertheless confident that the United States could "show them how the job might be done." According to Tuchman, "this was the elemental delusion that underwrote the whole endeavor"—the assumption that the United States would be able to stimulate South Vietnam to win. Robert McNamara, the secretary of defense, was particularly hawkish and "certain of an American victory." He once bragged in a Pentagon briefing, "We have the power to knock any society out of the twentieth century." He had come to government service from a successful commercial and academic background, of which the "training and mental habits had formed in McNamara a man of the implicit belief that, given the necessary material resources and equipment and the correct statistical analysis of relative factors, the job—any job— could be accomplished."[26]

The expectation of victory prevailed despite an acknowledgment that it might not be easy or cheap to attain. A 1961 Vietnam Task Force report stated that "come what may, the U.S. intends to win this battle." Key factions in the U.S. military retained a high level of confidence in victory. General Taylor and General Paul Harkins—who would become the first head of the Military Assistance Command, Vietnam (MACV)—"persisted in transmitting overly optimistic military reports to the President." The Joint Chiefs of Staff had written off the defeat of France as due to "French errors" which "included major political delays and indecisions," so the U.S. military simply had to "make sure we don't repeat their mistakes." The Joint Chiefs noted in parentheses, "The French also tried to build the Panama Canal."[27]

Contrary to the official optimism, sending military advisors to South Vietnam had not had much effect, and "by 1962 the situation had become desperate." While official channels continued to give optimistic assessments, these did not reflect unanimous opinion. "At the ground level, colonels and non-coms and press reporters were more doubtful," and John Kenneth Galbraith, who reported personally from Saigon in 1961 at Kennedy's request, advised against committing U.S. troops because "our soldiers would not deal with the vital weakness." The fragility of Diem's support suggested to him the need to rethink the situation, and he added ominously, "We are now married to failure." Galbraith wrote again to Kennedy in 1962, proposing a political solution that would install a nonaligned government and effect an American withdrawal, and warning that otherwise "we shall replace the French as the colonial force in the area and bleed as the French did." But the Joint Chiefs rejected this proposal and "advocated no change in American policy, but rather that it be 'pursued vigorously to a successful conclusion.' This was the general consensus; Kennedy did not contest it; Galbraith's suggestion died."[28]

The optimism of the military prevailed over the warnings coming from other channels. The key decisionmakers carried on believing, in the face of considerable counter-evidence, that victory would eventually come. The military optimism and can-do attitude may not have been particularly persuasive to Kennedy, who was intensely skeptical of military advice after the Bay of Pigs fiasco and the Cuban missile crisis. He once declared that he "could not believe a word the military was telling him" and "had to read the newspapers to find out what was going on" in Vietnam. Yet, according to John Stoessinger, even Kennedy "became the victim of that particularly American form of hubris that blithely assumed that technology, computerlike efficiency, . . . air power, and, above all, competent American management could overcome any adversary."[29]

The Johnson Administration (1963–1968)

Information and Reaction

Despite certain international and domestic imperatives, Johnson need not have simply picked up where Kennedy left off. As Ernest May points out, "It remained open to him to wash his hands of Vietnam." Fredrik Logevall concurs, on the basis of more recent information, that Johnson indeed had alternative options available to him. Although the option of pulling back was disliked because of both domestic and international concerns given the prestige Kennedy had already invested, it was clear that continued participation "would involve heavy costs, for Johnson's advisers told him almost from the beginning that success might require bombing North Vietnam and ordering substantial American forces into combat in South Vietnam. In effect, Johnson had to decide whether or not to go to war." In fact, the "considerations on one side or other were much like those of [Kennedy in] 1961." And yet by the time Johnson made the decision there were significant new doubts that not only raised the stakes but also lowered the probability of achieving gains: "Recent events in Saigon argued for disengagement, for they made it seem more questionable than ever that South Vietnam deserved to be termed 'free.' Also, they increased significantly the chances of failure. Further, the possibility that the American public might not support a war in Vietnam had become far more apparent . . . And in early 1965, when the President approached decisions for war, significant numbers of Congressmen and editorial writers voiced opposition."[30]

The fear that Southeast Asia would fall to communism was still a major concern, and "compared with 1961, the reasoning remained practically unchanged." Yet, even at the start of Johnson's first full term, Tuchman wrote, "a good look would have revealed that the raison d'être for American intervention had slipped considerably. When the CIA was asked by the President . . . whether, if Laos and South Vietnam fell to Communist control, all Southeast Asia would necessarily follow, the answer was in the negative; that except for Cambodia, 'It is likely that no other nation in the area would quickly succumb to Communism as a result of the fall of Laos and Vietnam'." Thus the whole logic of the original motive was put into question. Johnson asked for this information himself, and then neglected it. He failed to update his policy despite the fact that one of the fundamental reasons for the original U.S. intervention had been identified as invalid. At the same time, the interagency Working Group on Vietnam also warned that the United States could not "guarantee to maintain a non-Communist South Vietnam short of committing ourselves to whatever degree of military action would be required to defeat North Vietnam and probably Communist China militarily." Despite such warnings, "the President, his Secretaries and the Joint Chiefs were sure that American power could force North Vietnam to quit while the United States carefully avoided a clash with China."[31]

Johnson "received a wide variety of advice both informally and formally," and there is "more than adequate evidence to deflate the argument that Johnson heard only the views of a closed 'Tuesday lunch' group. Arguments about groupthink or bureaucratic or organizational roadblocks do not stand up to the archival evidence."[32] Hence other factors must explain the decisions to escalate. One possibility is that early decisions were constrained by a lack of adequate information on enemy strengths, but information was good enough to allow Johnson and his advisors to understand the risks.

By the time Johnson took office, the permanent Military Assistance Command, Vietnam (MACV) was up and running in addition to CICV (Combined Intelligence Center, Vietnam), which the MACV chief of intelligence described as "one of the finest supports of combat intelligence that was ever developed in support of our forces in wartime." One intelligence unit, the Combined Document Exploitation Center, "was dealing with *half a million pages* of captured NLF and NVA material *every month*. About 10 percent was of prime intelligence value." If anything, the difficulty was that there was too much intelligence. As Gelb and Betts put it, "never before have the platters of the political leadership been so filled with the minutiae of war." The Johnson administration also began to reassess the prospects of success:

> The Administration at this stage [in 1965] began to study the chances of "winning." Given a military task, the military had to believe they could accomplish it if they were to believe in themselves and quite naturally demanded more and more men for the purpose. Their statements were positive and the requisitions large. Facing escalation, McNamara asked General Wheeler, Chairman of the Joint Chiefs, what assurance the United States could have "of winning in South Vietnam if we do everything we can." If "winning" meant suppressing all insurgency and eliminating Communists from South Vietnam, Wheeler said, it would take 750,000 to a million men and up to seven years.[33]

Michael Handel argued that a leader's "readiness to discard intelligence that reveals flaws in his policies is particularly strong when his mistakes are otherwise unlikely to be detected in the short run." In Vietnam, "Johnson 'could afford' to ignore intelligence reports on the lack of progress in the Vietnam war," Handel argues, "hoping that the situation was not as bad as it seemed; and since he assumed that the United States could not lose in any event, any final decisions or unfortunate consequences could be passed on to the next administration."[34] Such a theory is not satisfactory, however, because it does not explain those hopes and assumptions, nor the concomitant political imperatives to try to improve the situation, nor the massive escalations.

In 1964 U.S. naval units off the Vietnamese mainland were attacked by gunboats. Both U Thant and Charles de Gaulle took this opportunity to offer Johnson new exit options, either as another Geneva convention or via superpower talks. Neither proposal would have assured a noncommunist South Vietnam, and the Johnson administration ignored them. Johnson and his advisors were of the opinion that talks would signal low U.S. resolve and demoralize the ARVN and the South. Undersecretary of State George Ball was sent to meet with de Gaulle and told him: "The United States 'did not believe in negotiating until our position on the battlefield was so strong that our adversaries might make the requisite concessions.' De Gaulle rejected this position outright. The same illusions, he told Ball, had drawn France into such trouble; Vietnam was a 'hopeless place to fight'; a 'rotten country,' where the United States could not win for all its great resources. Not force but negotiation was the only way."[35]

Ball himself eventually became a strong advocate against ground combat and the bombing campaigns. Standing as the "one convinced and consistent opponent of further military action," he attempted to press the arguments against war.[36] Nevertheless, the policymakers elected to fight and negotiate at the same time, reining themselves in to keep to a limited war while hoping it was enough to force the North to stop fighting. Johnson managed to get a congressional resolution to repel armed attack (the Tonkin Gulf resolution of 7 August 1964). For a third of the Senate 1964 was an election year, and none of them wished to risk appearing not to support American servicemen overseas. The resolution passed and opened the way for deepening military involvement in Vietnam.

General Wallace Greene, commandant of the U.S. Marine Corps, and the army chief of staff, General Harold K. Johnson, estimated that they would need between 500,000 and 750,000 troops and five to seven years to win. By 1965 even Maxwell Taylor, originally a proponent of the ground war, was drafting his own plan for ending U.S. involvement. He wrote that the "white-faced soldier armed, equipped and trained as he is [is] not [a] suitable guerrilla fighter for Asian forests and jungles. [The] French tried to adapt their forces to this mission and failed; I doubt that U.S. forces could do much better."[37]

In Washington, George Ball wrote a number of memoranda urging disengagement. Clark Clifford (who would eventually succeed McNamara as Johnson's secretary of defense) "warned in a private letter [to Johnson] that on the basis of CIA assessments, further build-up of ground forces could become an 'open-end commitment . . . without realistic hope of ultimate victory'." And skepticism was not limited to certain factions in the United States. Although some countries, such as Australia and the Republic of Korea, supported the war, many others increasingly expected U.S. policy in Vietnam to fail. British diplomats from across Southeast Asia, for example, thought the United States could not win.[38]

Johnson presided over a major interagency disagreement on estimates of enemy strengths that has implications for my analysis of whether U.S. expectations exceeded the available evidence. The decisionmakers knew about the dispute, and this should have made them, if anything, more cautious, but instead they deepened U.S. involvement.

In 1967 the CIA estimated the number of Viet Cong to be twice the number predicted by U.S. military intelligence (headed by MACV). At that time the main CIA proponent of the higher estimate, Samuel Adams, campaigned unsuccessfully to get MACV to update their figures, and when that failed, he went directly to the White House. As John Hughes-Wilson highlights, "This was not just some arcane matter of numbers. The answer really would have very real practical military consequences." Both sides stuck steadfastly to their own estimates. After the war, a CBS television show accused General Westmoreland and members of U.S. military intelligence of deliberately deceiving the press, the public, and Washington in order to "lead the people, Congress, the Joint Chiefs and the President to believe we were winning a war, which in fact we were losing." The next day a *New York Times* editorial claimed the show had revealed that Johnson had been "victimized by mendacious intelligence." This was suggested to have "robbed this country of the ability to make critical judgments about its most vital security interests during a time of war."[39]

Westmoreland sued, in a highly publicized case that was eventually settled before any ruling, but only after two and a half years of investigative preparation and five months of trial, which included the examination of 500,000 pages of formerly classified documents. No evidence was found of any such deliberate conspiracy, and this has been corroborated by subsequent analyses. Moreover, "the trial record made it clear that all those who conceivably had a need to know about the 'numbers dispute' for policy-making purposes did know." The hypothesis that Johnson was limited to erroneous information and that this absolved his bellicose policies can therefore be ruled out.[40]

Ambassador Ellsworth Bunker in Saigon sent a message to Walt Rostow at the White House warning of the "devastating impact if it should leak out (as these things often do) that despite all our success in grinding down the VC/NVA here . . . [some statistics showed] . . . that they are really much stronger than ever. Despite all the caveats, this is the inevitable conclusion which most of the press could reach." Hence, though there may have been an intention to keep the dispute from the press, there is no evidence that the object or the result was to deceive the decisionmakers in the conflict, which is the only crucial aspect of this debate for my argument. The higher CIA estimates would have had, if anything, a negative effect on U.S. involvement (justifying not more optimism, but less). Yet what occurred was the opposite—continued escalation—so regardless of which figures were given the most weight, my conclusions remain unchanged. The director of the CIA, Richard Helms, remarked to his crusading colleague Sam Adams that "it would have made no difference to U.S. policy if he had told the White House that there were a million more Viet

Cong." U.S. policymakers were already committed to fighting, and a conviction that they would eventually win was psychologically consistent with that commitment.[41]

Positive Illusions?

In mid-January 1967 General Wheeler told Johnson, "The adverse military tide has been reversed and General Westmoreland has the initiative." The United States, he added, "can win the war if we apply pressure on the enemy relentlessly in the North and South." In April 1967 Westmoreland himself, in a briefing at the White House, said that the enemy numbers within South Vietnam had reached a limit at around 287,000 and that for the first time the "cross-over" point had been reached in the northernmost area, meaning that enemy casualties and defections were more numerous than the replacements who were being recruited. Thus, he claimed, "the US was winning the war of attrition."[42] Johnson may have been reasonable to believe, on the basis of this advice (even if the advice was wrong), that the war was winnable. With regard to the bombing campaign, too, "during the year-long deliberations of 1964–65 . . . even the most pessimistic intelligence estimates conceded some likelihood of success." Thus Johnson did not necessarily plod on with what he should have known was inevitably going to fail. However, this begs the question of why other decisionmakers remained optimistic.

Assessments by other military leaders certainly gave overly optimistic views. David Halberstam notes that, in contrast to the views of many at the front, there was a widespread "false optimism" among high-ranking Americans in Saigon (which struck him "as essentially self-deception"), including a "seemingly unshakable optimism" on the part of U.S. Ambassador Ellsworth Bunker. Bunker apparently believed his generals' assurances that "everything was on schedule and that there was an inevitability to the victory we sought, given the awesome force we had mounted against the North Vietnamese Army and Vietcong." All this was duly reported back to Washington. As for the bombing, evidence in the defense department's own study implied that "the members of the policy-making group were overoptimistic about defeating North Vietnam by means of bombing raids during 1964 and 1965."[43]

Many of Johnson's civilian advisors believed North Vietnam could be coerced by threats against its population and its economy, an illusion that led to the wholly unsuccessful Rolling Thunder air campaign of 1965–1968. The air force chief of staff, General Curtis E. LeMay (and his successor, General John P. McConnell, as well as battlefield commanders), thought that "the military task confronting us is to make it so expensive for the North Vietnamese that they will stop their aggression against South Vietnam and Laos. If we make it too expensive for them, they *will* stop." This confidence was expressed more widely as well: "Within the government and the press, it was frequently argued that North Vietnam was bound to yield when it reached some 'pain level'."[44]

However, a report by the Policy Planning Council concluded that "bombing would not work and predicted, prophetically, that it would imprison the American government . . . This remarkable study was ignored. [Walt] Rostow, who was committed to the bombing, never brought it to the president's attention." George Ball remained a critic, and "every week, in the 'Tuesday lunch group,' Ball would voice his concern with the administration's assumptions about Vietnam. The others would listen politely then proceed to ignore him, all the while feeling good that a critical perspective had been taken into account."[45] Hence Johnson must have heard some, if not all, of the negative reports. But his decisions did not seem to reflect them, as highlighted by Janis:

> There is no evidence to show that President Johnson and his principal advisers personally accepted the invariably pessimistic estimates in the intelligence reports or took seriously the likelihood that further major escalations . . . would actually be needed. The Pentagon Papers indicate that on some important occasions the dire forecasts were simply ignored. In the late fall

of 1964, for example, the high hopes of President Johnson and his principal advisers that Operation Rolling Thunder would break the will of North Vietnam were evidently not diminished by the fact that the entire intelligence community, according to the Department of Defense study, "tended toward a pessimistic view." About a year and a half later, the CIA repeatedly estimated that stepping up the bombing of North Vietnam's oil-storage facilities would not "cripple Communist military operations," and the policy-makers were aware of this prediction. Instead of accepting it, however, they apparently accepted the optimistic estimate from the Pentagon, which asserted that the bombing would "bring the enemy to the conference table or cause the insurgency to wither from lack of support."

Expectations of eventual success held sway in the upper echelons of the administration. As late as 1968 Walt Rostow declared that "history will salute us." The president's press secretary, Bill Moyers, said after resigning that in Johnson's inner circle "there was a confidence, it was never bragged about, it was just there—a residue, perhaps of the confrontation over the missiles in Cuba—that when the chips were really down, the other people would fold."[46]

Chester Cooper noted overoptimism from 1964 right up to the final months of the Johnson administration: "The optimistic predictions that flowered from time to time . . . reflected genuinely held beliefs. While occasional doubts crossed the minds of some, perhaps all, the conviction that the war would end 'soon' and favorably was clutched to the breast like a child's security blanket. Views to the contrary were not favorably received." In the post-war *Westmoreland v. CBS* trial, Rusk testified that "he believed that the war could be won militarily—that is, the US could deny the achievement of Hanoi's goal." Others also remained positive that they could win over what Senator Thomas Dodd, a Democrat from Connecticut, called "a few thousand primitive guerrillas." Johnson himself, though loathing the war that was destroying his plans to develop the "Great Society" at home, nevertheless appears to have expected eventual victory against "that raggedy-ass little fourth-rate country." "Confident of his own power," Tuchman writes, "Johnson believed he could achieve both his aims, domestic and foreign, at once."[47]

But the bombing was not bringing results. At least by the middle of the air campaign it should have been clear that the "guerrilla warfare required little in the way of supplies and next to nothing at all from North Vietnam," and this was made widely known during Senate hearings in August 1967. The CIA/Defense Intelligence Agency report of November 1967 stated: "There have been no indications that difficulties associated with the bombing have been sufficient to force the regime to alter its policy on the war." A report commissioned by the Institute of Defense Analysis similarly noted that "bombing had not created serious difficulties in transportation, the economy or morale."[48] The authors of the report thought that, if anything, the bombing had heightened enemy resolve (a phenomenon that was well known from the experience of strategic bombing in World War II): "The expectation that bombing would erode the determination of Hanoi and its people clearly overestimated the persuasive and disruptive effects of the bombing and, correspondingly, underestimated the tenacity and recuperative capabilities of the North Vietnamese." The Institute of Defense Analysis, after reviewing the report, concluded: "We are unable to devise a bombing campaign in the North to reduce the flow of infiltrating personnel into SVN [South Vietnam]."[49]

While the military apparently remained confident (officially), the pessimism of the other intelligence reports finally succeeded in raising doubts among policymakers. McNamara had received two detailed reports (in August 1966 and May 1967) from the CIA "forecasting that no matter how large a force the US military fielded in South Vietnam, the war there was unwinnable." For McNamara at least, the accumulating information began to dispel any positive illusions that the United States was going to win. In private, according to Tuchman, he began to "show a dawning recognition of futility." Such views had usually quietly left the White

House with those who held them (Roger Hilsman, director of the state department's intelligence bureau, departed in 1964; McGeorge Bundy, Ball, and Moyers in 1966). Congress, at least, still needed convincing, and military leaders were becoming more outspoken about the restraints imposed upon them. At the armed services committee hearings on these issues in August 1967, McNamara rejected a positive assessment of the war:

He cited evidence to show that the bombing program had not significantly reduced the flow of men and supplies, and he disputed the military advice to lift restraints and allow a greater target range. "We have no reason to believe that it would break the will of the North Vietnamese people or sway the purpose of their leaders . . . or provide any confidence that they can be bombed to the negotiating table." Thus, the whole purpose of American strategy was admitted to be futile by the Secretary of Defense.[50]

Then came the Tet offensive of January 1968, which totally undermined the "relentless military optimism" that was being reported back to Washington. Even the optimists' illusions were now being dispelled. McNamara left the government after Tet, and his departure appears to have had a crucial effect on decisionmaking. Johnson ordered the new secretary of defense, Clark Clifford, "to make a complete review of US strategy in Vietnam. To his astonishment, Clifford could not find a single senior officer who believed that the war could be won using the methods the USA was employing." Even though the military's requests were constantly tempered by political pressure to avoid escalating numbers of men and materials sent to Vietnam, the U.S. commitment had already crept up to half a million troops. "In July [1967], Johnson had placed a ceiling on the escalation of ground forces at 525,000, just over the figure General Leclerc, 21 years before, had declared would be required, 'and even then it could not be done'."[51]

Indeed, this was not enough. Following the Tet offensive,

Westmoreland's request for 200,000 more troops was daunting, but "mentally locked in the belief that superior force must prevail, Johnson was not ready to negotiate or disengage on any terms that could be construed as 'losing'." At this point it becomes clear that Johnson had been overoptimistic about the outcome all along. Even Leclerc's pessimistic estimate of the necessary troop numbers had been increased on the basis of new information and experience. In 1965, when he was considering whether to commit ground troops, Johnson had been "warned that attainment of U.S. objectives would require 700,000 to 1,000,000 men and 7 years of warfare in order to force the communists from the field and to pacify the south. Such a level of commitment was beyond what the Johnson administration ever considered." Johnson, it seems, had not updated his thinking over time, and thought the U.S. military could achieve some kind of victory *even without* the forces others told him would be necessary to achieve it. "Because he believed he could not lose, Johnson dropped still more bombs and sent still more men to their death." Even George Ball, the constant critic, announced in 1966, "The one thing we have to do is to win this damned war."[52]

After years of receiving information contradicting his hopes of victory, Johnson began to open up to reality. He lamented in his 1966 State of the Union address: "War is always the same. It is young men dying in the fullness of their promise. It is trying to kill a man that you do not even know well enough to hate. Therefore, to know war is to know that there is still madness in this world." In the polls, a majority expressed dissatisfaction with his handling of the war for the first time in mid-1966, following the air force's admission that its bombs had hit a civilian area of Hanoi, and his approval ratings never recovered. "It was slowly becoming clear to Johnson," Tuchman notes, "that there was no way the Vietnam entanglement could end to his advantage. Military success could not end the war within the eighteen months left of his present term, and with an election ahead, he could not disengage and 'lose' Vietnam . . . and, in Moyers's judgment, 'He knew it. He sensed the war would destroy him politically and wreck his presidency. He was a miserable man.'" Johnson appears to have suffered from poor advice by others with overoptimistic expectations of victory. Nevertheless, it was he who made the decisions to escalate.[53]

The Nixon Administration (1968–1974)

Johnson was not the last president to be made miserable by Vietnam, of course. I will treat Nixon only briefly here, because it was clear by the time he took office that the war was not likely to be won militarily. Nixon had backed U.S. military intervention very early when he was vice president in 1954, recommending that the United States send combat troops if Indochina could not be "saved" in another way. As president, after campaigning as the candidate who would extract the nation from Vietnam, he ended up executing the war with increasing ferocity, just as his predecessors had done. He did withdraw troops, but the air campaign was ratcheted up several notches. Bombing had failed to work before, but the bombings under Nixon were of unprecedented severity and scope, secretly expanding the war into supposed enemy bases in Cambodia. At this time, North Vietnam reduced its guerrilla tactics in favor of large-scale conventional military action. While air power is usually ineffective against civilian or infrastructural targets, it *is* effective against conventional military offensive forces. Thus, although Washington may not have recognized this at the time, the success of Nixon's 1972 bombing campaigns was at least partly due to Hanoi's switch to conventional methods (plus the fact that Nixon imposed lesser demands than Johnson), not to the merits of the new U.S. bombing strategy itself.[54]

Hanoi conceded to U.S. demands on 21 October 1972, but the South stalled over the details of the proposed agreement, triggering the North to back off again. In response, Nixon resumed a devastating assault in the "Christmas bombings" of 18 to 25 December, which rapidly brought the North Vietnamese back to the table. In January 1973 a treaty was finalized and the war, for the United States at least, was finally over.[55]

Nixon had continued to believe in the U.S. capacity to "win."

For him, winning did not mean defeating the North, but preventing the North from defeating the South. He claimed that he had achieved this, and that the failure of Congress and the public to maintain the South Vietnamese government after the U.S. withdrawal was responsible for "losing the peace." His policy paid off, it seems, largely thanks to a coincidental change of military strategy by the North Vietnamese which exposed them to attack from the air. Even so, long after the war, Nixon "still believe[d] that the war was won, while seminars and symposia assemble[d] to inquire why it was lost."[56]

When Saigon finally fell to the communists in 1975, Dean Rusk admitted: "Personally, I made two mistakes. I underestimated the tenacity of the North Vietnamese and overestimated the patience of the American people."[57] Such beliefs characterized a majority of the U.S. decisionmakers throughout the conflict in Vietnam.

Hanoi's Perceptions

Recent work suggests that the North Vietnamese forces and their civilian supporters had no intention of giving up.[58] In guerrilla wars, national movements may never concede so long as a popular will to resist remains. As we saw from the failure of Johnson's bombing campaigns, the insurgency in South Vietnam was sustainable even in total independence from the North. Kennedy's insight that "only the Vietnamese can defeat the Viet-Cong" was an accurate prophecy. In a sense, then, the North Vietnamese were justified in their confidence that they would prevail, even against a vastly superior opponent. They had good evidence to support this, most notably their defeat of the French. As in that earlier conflict, they did not need to defeat the enemy but only to keep fighting longer than the United States was prepared to do. Ho Chi Minh had said as early as 1946: "Kill ten of our men and we will kill one of yours. In the end, it is you who will tire." "Hanoi's intransigence," according to Tuchman, "was indeed tied to a belief that the United States, whether from cost or from rising dissent, would tire first." One U.S. report on the bombing campaign noted: "The regime continues to send thousands of young men and women abroad for higher education and technical training; we consider this evidence of the regime's confidence of the eventual outcome of the war."[59]

There are some indications that the North was overly optimistic in launching the Tet offensive in 1968, in which they were greatly outnumbered (and in the end, suffered a military defeat): "Nothing was said to the attack echelons about replacements or escape routes. The unique form of this plan, coupled with its scale, indicates that the Viet Cong and their North Vietnamese supporters were confident of a victory." Decisionmakers in Hanoi also expected the offensive to spark a popular uprising across the country, but it did not. Part of this apparent overoptimism may have been due to poor information, in which case it does not necessarily implicate positive illusions. The North Vietnamese general Tran Van Tra later wrote: "During Tet of 1968 we did not correctly evaluate the specific balance of forces between ourselves and the enemy, and did not fully realize that the enemy still had considerable capabilities and that our capabilities were limited." Michael Handel also suggests that Tet was based on insufficient information. Nevertheless, in support of the possibility that positive illusions did play some role, General Tran Van Tra added that the objectives "were beyond our actual strength . . . [and based] in part on an illusion of our subjective desires."[60]

But the decision to launch the Tet offensive need not have been based solely on North Vietnamese expectations of victory. General Vo Nguyen Giap, the North's commander in chief and minister of defense, knew that a major offensive at that time might intensify U.S. domestic opinion against the war and also strain the fragile cooperation between the United States and South Vietnam. Both of these outcomes were achieved. Thus even the vastly expensive Tet offensive may have been not overambitious but rather a rational strategy in the pursuit of wider political goals.[61]

At other times, too, captured documents attested to a realistic appreciation by the North Vietnamese of their limitations and their failures in the face of successful U.S. efforts such as Operation Junction City in 1967. The numerous documents were "not the record of a revolutionary force buoyed up by anticipation of final victory." In other words, the VC/NVA forces do not appear to have been overconfident, whether or not their leaders were. Only at the very end of the conflict did those in the North appear to be optimistic about their chances of winning. On 2 May 1972 Henry Kissinger, Nixon's national security advisor, met with North Vietnam's negotiator, Le Duc Tho, who rejected all American proposals because of, according to Kissinger, "Hanoi's conviction that it was so close to victory that it no longer needed even the pretense of negotiations."[62]

Did Positive Illusions Contribute?

Gaps in Other Explanations

Information about the situation in Vietnam was at times faulty, at times misunderstood, not always negative, and sometimes withheld from the White House. Moreover, there were alternative pressures for escalation: the concern for halting communism; U.S. credibility on the international stage; domestic political pressures; public and electoral concerns; the need to keep up pressure to win concessions should it come to negotiated settlement with North Vietnam; the "lesson of history" not to appease aggression; and the mistaken analogies of Korea and the British experience in Malaya (in fact Korea had been a failure, and the British campaign in Malaya had taken twelve years against a much more vulnerable foe).[63]

While these factors provide an understanding of why the war in Vietnam was fought and continued, they do not explain the origin of the belief that the United States could win the war, or the perseverance of that belief in the face of contradictory evidence. It is not enough to argue that leaders chose to fight simply because they felt compelled to, or to appease domestic political pressure. Clearly, such factors did play a role, but it is highly unlikely that they alone, without a concomitant expectation of victory, explain the continued commitment and escalation by a variety of U.S. leaders over twenty-seven years. Indeed, the persistence of controversy about the causes of the war demonstrates that these factors do not provide a satisfactory explanation. Moreover, the widely noted discrepancy between facts and policy has prompted researchers to revert to supplementary psychological and nonrational explanations to fill the gaps in otherwise neat theories (such as Janis's groupthink, Tuchman's folly, or Jervis's range of misperceptions). It is quite clear from individuals' viewpoints as expressed in the Pentagon Papers and other sources, as well as from their actions, that despite the difficulties, key decisionmakers believed the United States would prevail.[64] Four lines of evidence support this argument.

First, key clues about the U.S. involvement in Vietnam come from empirical facts about U.S. actions (rather than statements). The escalations were so large, and so specifically based on requirements from military commanders, that one can rule out the idea that they were mere signals of resolve, intended to pander to political pressure to increase effort. No, they were designed to win the war. Thus the massive U.S. escalations (especially in 1965 and 1967) imply a belief that victory was possible. Robert McNamara told President Johnson that "in my judgment we must go on bending every effort to win," and Johnson himself "wanted do whatever was necessary to win in Vietnam." Each president appears to have maintained an optimism that some kind of victory would eventually come, however painful and costly the war might be along the way. "Every American escalation in the air or on the ground was an expression of the hope that a few more bombs, a few more troops, would bring decisive victory."[65]

Second, alternative explanations hinge on the assumption that once the United States was committed it had few escape options. But this assumption is questionable. Although many external factors affected the different administrations in similar ways, the inauguration of a new president always presented an opportunity to review policy and consider exit options. Indeed, in 1964 Johnson was elected partly on the basis of a relatively dovish manifesto which contrasted with that of his hawkish opponent, Barry Goldwater. Johnson had publicly declared: "We are not going to send American boys nine or ten thousand miles away from home to do what Asian boys ought to be doing for themselves."[66]

Once in office, new presidents suddenly gain access to privileged information that may alter their outlook and decisions. But this should not have affected the Johnson administration, which simply continued in office after Kennedy's assassination. In general, each new administration is expected to make some changes, and at these times some settlement or scaling down from Vietnam was feasible, if still a huge political burden. David Kaiser, Fredrik Logevall, and Barbara Tuchman have argued that it should have been clear to U.S. policymakers—at the time—that withdrawal offered a better option than escalation. This is of course an easy argument to make with the benefit of hindsight. At the time, there was a widespread conviction in both the public and the government that the communist conquest of South Vietnam had to be prevented, and even toward the end of Johnson's term, polls often showed that those who wanted to end the war by winning it outnumbered those who favored ending it by withdrawing. So perhaps escape options were few and undesirable. But if each new president was willing to fight instead, each one must have thought that fighting was the better option. It is difficult to argue that they did so without a belief that they could eventually win—somehow and however long it took.

Third, the hypothesis that the various presidents were pushed into escalation by domestic politics does not hold water. If domestic political pressure was really the reason for U.S. involvement in Vietnam, then one would predict that U.S. leaders would not have wanted to remain involved after Nixon withdrew the American military (when the pressure to win a widely watched war and to stand firm against communism subsided). However, Nixon's successor, Gerald Ford, actually tried to get involved in Vietnam *again*, but this was blocked by Congress: "The Ford administration failed in convincing Congress of the need to reintervene in the war, or even of the need to provide emergency military assistance to South Vietnam."[67] This fits with the hypothesis that positive illusions about American capabilities were partly responsible for U.S. policy in Vietnam: under this hypothesis, one would expect Ford to share his predecessors' belief that the United States could maintain a free South Vietnam.

Fourth, domestic political constraints on Johnson may not have been as great as often assumed. The year of the fateful decision to send combat troops, 1965, was, according to Vice President Humphrey, "the year of minimum political risk for the Johnson administration." David Kaiser notes that the administration "did not decide upon the war out of a fear of a right-wing backlash, or because of a belief that Congress or the American public demanded it." In early 1965, after Johnson's landslide electoral victory and before the critical decision to commit ground troops to the war, "the lack of any real political pressure to go to war had never been more apparent" (especially given Johnson's campaign as the peace candidate against Goldwater).[68] Concerns about political backlash for "losing Vietnam" as the Democrats had "lost" China, or about the McCarthy-inspired dread of communism, did not impose paralyzing constraints on U.S. decisionmakers. Especially following the successful U.S. handling of the Cuban missile crisis and Diem's assassination in Saigon, Johnson's administration had an opportunity and a reason to consider getting out of Vietnam.

In combination, the traditional reasons adduced for the war—containment of communism, U.S. reputation, and domestic politics—do not provide a wholly satisfactory explanation for America's continued involvement in Vietnam. The view that escalation begat escalation, so that the military became mired in something from which it could not extricate itself, has been rejected. U.S. leaders "always had considerable freedom about which way to go in the war," and Kennedy had already set a precedent for prudence by deciding not to intervene militarily in Laos. Logevall and Tuchman have highlighted various opportunities for ending

U.S. participation.[69] Many of these came at times when American prestige need not have suffered too greatly as a result—even given the political pressures to maintain a commitment. To sum up, therefore, these other explanations do not fully account for the U.S. escalation in Vietnam; the additional factor needed to complete the account is an expectation among decisionmakers that they would eventually achieve favorable gains, if not victory.

This is not to say that they blithely expected it. As much as they may have hoped for such a victory, all the U.S. presidents would have loved to get out of the Vietnam war. It was only because they were already fighting it that they had to find a way to win. The problem was that they were not willing to accept defeat as the price of withdrawal. George Ball eventually seemed to admit that such a cost might be worth taking, but his input came too late to affect the decision to send combat troops in 1965. Even those who most strongly opposed escalating the war held out for some "third way," such as a nonaligned government or a negotiated settlement, that would end the conflict without letting the communists triumph. Yet the notion that it was possible to avoid war while ensuring a South Vietnam free of communism was as illusory as the notion that the United States could win the war.[70]

Impact on U.S. Policy

The escalation of the war in spite of ample and systematic evidence from a variety of sources (including, at times, the military, the secretary of defense, the CIA, civilian advisors, and diplomats) that it was unwinnable suggests that decisionmakers maintained positive illusions that the United States would eventually win. Note that for my argument it does not matter whether the Vietnam war was really "winnable" or not. I am only arguing that policymakers perceived that it was. Johnson may have given up on this hope in the final year of his presidency, and Nixon's aims were surely more limited in scope, but each administration nevertheless escalated the war *as if* to achieve a victory that was eventually sure to come. This is consistent with positive illusions in decisionmaking. Jeffrey Race attributed the U.S. government's perseverance, so starkly contrasting with much of the prevailing intelligence, to "an unconscious alteration in the estimate of probabilities." Irving Janis, in his study of biases in group decisionmaking, found that in the case of Vietnam U.S. policymakers were, as Garofano summarized it, "blissfully optimistic about the prospects for success."[71]

I do not mean to imply that expecting a U.S. victory in Vietnam was wholly unjustified at all stages of the war. Indeed, at the beginning of Johnson's second term, Tuchman tells us, "no one doubted" that the United States would be able to "accomplish its aim by superior might."[72] I also do not claim that all intelligence and analysis unambiguously pointed to defeat. In fact American analysts could often identify tangible military gains. The leadership could thus, at times, take logical confidence from military successes (whether genuine or not) that some kind of victory would be possible in the future.

Nevertheless, even John Garofano, who believes the war was caused by "a combination of structural pressures, entrenched mind-sets, and limited information," notes: "A general sense of, if not optimism, then can-do-ism, characterized the preponderance of military advice in the spring and summer of 1965." Hence, even if U.S. involvement in Vietnam is largely explained as the least bad alternative to the costs of inaction, so that decisionmakers were forced to accept the risks of military intervention, positive illusions may help to explain why they were willing to take these risks. Kaiser reports that telephone conversations "show beyond doubt, [that] Johnson, Rusk, McNamara, and Bundy undertook the war and overrode the well-founded doubts of some important subordinates simply because they believed it had to be done and had confidence in the nation's ability to do it." Several officials close to Kennedy and Johnson reported a "sense of omnipotence" among administration members before the Bay of Pigs invasion and again after Johnson's 1964 election, leading them to think that they had a "golden touch."[73]

Positive illusions need not lead to expectations of outright victory. Rather they may lead to expectations of gains, of whatever form, greater than the evidence would predict. Even "the possibility of defeat," Janis noted, "does not preclude a strong element of wishful thinking and even a strong dose of overoptimism about limited hopes such as escaping with their skins intact, successfully postponing defeat indefinitely, and holding out long enough for a lucky break to turn the tide in their favor." Indeed, while there is much evidence that decisionmakers ignored negative omens, "it certainly cannot be said that they maintained grossly overoptimistic illusions about the overall security of the military enterprise in Vietnam. Yet at times there may have been a more limited type of illusion that inclined the policymakers to be willing to take long-shot gambles. Many observations suggest that the group experienced some temporary lapses in realism about the grave material, political and moral risks [and clung to the view that] 'everything will go our way, none of the dangers will seriously affect us.'"[74] Janis attributes this to groupthink, but it is also indicative of more fundamental positive illusions, and both are likely to contribute to an overall explanation. The lapses in realism, the variation in expectations depending on feedback, the gloomier predictions from those closer to the battlefield, and the insensitivity to risk during the implementation stage of the war all conform to antecedent conditions of positive illusions (described in Chapter 2).

In addition to overoptimism about military objectives, there were deeper illusions about the very nature of the conflict. As so many authors have revealed, U.S. policymakers mistakenly treated what was essentially a revolutionary war as a conventional one, and focused on military means to fight it. Kennedy thought the United States could stimulate the South Vietnamese to win because they were fighting for freedom, but according to Tuchman "the assumption that humanity at large shared the democratic Western idea of freedom was an American delusion." The idea is encapsulated in a U.S. army colonel's quip from Stanley Kubrick's film *Full Metal Jacket*: "We are here to help the Vietnamese, because inside every gook there is an American trying to get out." John Lewis Gaddis and Mark Bradley argue that cultural misunderstandings between the United States and Vietnam, particularly Americans' belief in the superiority of Western civilization and its institutions, pervade the entire history of U.S.-Vietnam relations and significantly contributed to the outbreak of the war. General Maxwell Taylor was one person who sometimes did express an awareness of such problematic assumptions; he reported in 1965: "The Vietnamese have the manpower and the basic skills to win this war. What they lack is motivation."[75]

Ernest May believes that the presidents' and their advisors' simplistic historical reasoning had critically misleading influences on their faith in the war. The main analogies they invoked had no substantive relevance to Vietnam, and he suggests that if they had studied the history and culture of Vietnam, they "might have discovered at the outset some truths later painfully learned . . . it might also have led to the recognition that the conflict in Vietnam was in many if not most respects a civil war, the determining forces of which were outgrowths of the Vietnamese past and likely to be affected only marginally by foreigners." It was not that the relevant information was poor, absolving U.S. decisions. The information was plainly available—Taylor's report lamenting a lack of South Vietnamese will to fight formed "one of the longest cables in the history of American diplomacy"—but warnings were not heeded. McNamara would later write: "I didn't think these people had the capacity to fight this way. If I had thought they could take this punishment and fight this well, could enjoy fighting like this, I would have thought differently at the start." He and others believed they were fighting communism, but they were fighting nationalism. People on the ground were aware of this and were reporting it, but U.S. policy failed to reflect it.[76]

Robert Pape, in his analysis of the U.S. bombing campaigns, notes the crucial importance of taking into account the enemy's underlying motivations:

American leaders, both civilian and military, paid insufficient attention to the relationship between American military action and the *enemy's* goals. Proponents of Schelling and Douhet strategies considered means of attacking civilian morale but failed to consider how firm North Vietnamese morale might actually be. Similarly, proponents of interdiction strategies during 1965–1968 planned operations for attacking military targets but failed to consider how much difference destruction of those targets would make to Hanoi's military strategy. Consequently, American leaders failed to realize that no coercive air power strategy could have succeeded during 1965–1968.[77]

In other words, victory was not achievable by military means, whether by ground or by air.[78]

As Garofano put it: "Civilians and military officers alike overestimated the efficacy of airpower . . . and neglected the importance of domestic support for the insurgency." Kaiser concurs: "The loss of the war stemmed not from a failure in civil-military relations but from a failure of either the civilian or the military leadership to understand the nature of the conflict and to define realistic American objectives and strategies." As a result, Stoessinger notes, McNamara's famous statistics were irrelevant: "They overlooked the fact that even if the South Vietnamese forces outnumbered the Vietcong by a ratio of ten to one, it did no good because the one man was willing to fight and die and the ten were not" (as Ho had claimed). T. L. Cubbage, who served in the U.S. intelligence service in Vietnam, corroborates this view:

If the war in Vietnam involved an intelligence failure, it was a general one, namely, the inability to understand the nature of modern guerrilla warfare. The US military continued to think in terms of fighting another conventional Second World War or Korea. The enemy's motivation and strategy were misunderstood, as was the connection between what happened on the battlefield and domestic politics at home . . . the US military and intelligence community . . . failed to understand the overall political implications of fighting a war that cannot be won militarily.[79]

Both Ho Chi Minh and Johnson miscalculated the other's intentions. Neither side thought the other would fight as long and hard as it did. As Gary Hess wrote, "the American command's delusion that the body count could bring victory underestimated North Vietnam's determination and capability . . . intelligence sources correctly predicted that the North Vietnamese would indefinitely replace losses inflicted by the American search-and-destroy strategy." This is not peculiar to the Vietnam war; small nationalist movements often win conflicts even when the odds are heavily against them. Such movements tend to have extremely high resolve that can be sustained indefinitely, and conventional war-fighting strategies are ineffective against a dispersed enemy with a largely invisible support base. This applies to attacks from the air as well; during the Johnson years "North Vietnam was largely immune to conventional coercion." May notes that, "so far as one can discern from available documents and memoirs, no one inquired what precise effects the bombing would achieve towards altering North Vietnamese policy." Decisionmakers simply expected it to work.[80]

If the competing theories I have outlined offered a satisfactory explanation for U.S. involvement in Vietnam, they probably would not have proved so controversial. The debate rages on because some pieces of the puzzle are missing. We can fill in these gaps by recognizing that U.S. decisionmakers were biased to expect victory. But where did that bias come from, and why did it persist in the face of intelligence that contradicted it? I suggest that this systematic bias can be attributed, in part, to the decisionmakers' positive illusions, which led them to overestimate their side's capabilities, underestimate the enemy, neglect intelligence, and inflate the probability of victory. The problem of hindsight is that, had the United States won, their decisions might not have been classified as overly optimistic. But the benefit of hindsight is that we know that, in the end, the U.S. leaders *were* too optimistic in their expectations. Even if they had won the war, the same evidence presented here would demonstrate that they overestimated their capability and underestimated the difficulty, so that the war became far more costly than they expected. Positive illusions are a possible source of this overoptimism.

Ambiguous Information?

I have presented evidence that there was considerable advice against escalation in Vietnam. A critic might argue that, while these negative assessments did exist, the overall information that reached the White House was ambiguous rather than clearly negative. If it was, then perhaps each president simply drew a wrong conclusion from poor data. And in fact intelligence analyses were sometimes hugely ambiguous. For example, an advisor to the Joint Chiefs and a state department official, after heading a mission Kennedy sent to Vietnam, submitted such widely diverging reports that the president asked them, "You two did visit the same country, didn't you?" Later, Johnson would encounter similarly divergent assessments of enemy strengths made by the CIA and MACV, in which "the difference between the estimates was so large it seemed as if each of them had fought a different enemy." With such ambiguity, it is possible that the U.S. presidents simply had to make difficult choices on the basis of unclear information.[81]

However, there is considerable evidence that people selectively interpret ambiguity as confirming beliefs they already hold. In addition, as Robert Jervis points out, they "do not know they are doing so. Instead, . . . they see many events as providing independent confirmation of their beliefs when, in fact, the events would be seen differently by someone who started with different ideas. Thus people see evidence as less ambiguous than it is, think that their views are steadily being confirmed, and so feel justified in holding to them ever more firmly . . . Ambiguous or even discrepant information is ignored, misperceived, or reinterpreted." Thus, if ambiguous information was a problem for U.S. leaders during the Vietnam war, the likelihood is that, rather than weakening positive illusions, it reinforced them in a systematically positive direction.[82]

Suppression of Information?

Intelligence, whether the information it yields is ambiguous or clear, can affect policy only if it reaches the eyes or ears of the policymakers. In the Vietnam conflict, a great deal of information was collected and analyzed and by and large appears to have flowed freely to U.S. leaders. Yet even in Washington there were sometimes significant obstacles, so that openness of debate was impaired. What is more, even the information that was properly reported sometimes came primed with optimism by the messenger. Robert McNamara was a key figure in this closing of debate. According to John Hughes-Wilson:

> By 1968 no real decisions were being delegated down the US military chain of command. Robert McNamara's way of dealing with the military was simple: those who disagreed with him he sacked if he could; and if he couldn't, he sidelined them and choked off their access to the President like some latter-day Renaissance cardinal. Under the Secretary of Defense's baleful influence, LBJ's lack of access to any military subordinate with a point of view that differed from Bob McNamara's would be a major factor in the debacle that was to follow.[83]

McNamara may also have deliberately selected General Westmoreland as a compliant commander of MACV, since according to army colleagues it was an unexpected promotion, as was Westmoreland's subsequent promotion to the chairmanship of the Joint Chiefs of Staff.

And McNamara, as Tuchman reveals, was not the only one who exerted control over information:

> Field officers who had accompanied ARVN units into combat, and learned in bitterness that American training and weapons could not supply the will to fight, did their best to circumvent General Harkins' *suppression of negative reports* and gave their accounts of sorry performance at debriefings in the Pentagon . . .

the battle at Ap Bac in January 1963 . . . bared the failings of ARVN, the inutility of the American program and the hollowness of Headquarters optimism, although no one was allowed to say so. Colonel John Vann, the senior American at Ap Bac, was back at the Pentagon in the summer of 1963 trying to inform the [Army] General Staff. As Maxwell Taylor was the particular patron of General Harkins and held his view, Vann's message could make no headway. A Defense Department spokesman announced that "The corner has definitely been turned towards victory," and CINCPAC foresaw the "inevitable" defeat of the Viet-Cong.[84]

It is not clear how much damage this manipulation may have done to Kennedy's and (in particular) Johnson's ability to make informed decisions, but it is clear that information was not getting through as easily as it should have done. Negative messages were being stalled higher up the decisionmaking chain as well. In Washington the interagency Working Group on Vietnam had exposed a number of problems with U.S. policy. These prompted its chief, Paul Kattenburg of the state department, to predict that the war would require half a million troops and take five or ten years. He also told a meeting (including Rusk, McNamara, Taylor, Bundy, and Vice President Johnson) that Diem's diminishing support implied that the United States should get out. Apparently no one present agreed, and Rusk declared, "We will not pull out of Vietnam until the war is won."[85] Kattenburg was removed from the group and assigned to another post.

Thus, if U.S. leaders did have positive illusions, those illusions seem to have been protected by the closing of debate and violations of democratic process. Kaiser argues that "McNamara and the Pentagon helped hide the true situation from the President, the rest of the government, and the American people, thereby putting off the need to reevaluate American policy."[86] This control subverted the constitutional responsibility of the Joint Chiefs to report to Congress and not just to the military's commander in chief and the secretary of defense. Johnson's decisions may therefore have been influenced by the incremental optimism added to intelligence reports as they moved up from the field, to Saigon, to Washington, to the White House, to the president. Information skewed by the optimism of others may have prevented Johnson from realistically assessing the probability of a U.S. victory. To some extent, then, he may have been a victim of other decision-makers' positive illusions.

If Vietnam was not a quagmire, the literature on it often seems like one. But certain aspects are now clear enough to reveal that accounts of its causes still lack something. For all the reasons just discussed, the idea that bad intelligence about the situation in Vietnam led to ill-informed but at-the-time reasonable decisions can be rejected. Neither Kennedy nor Johnson, according to Ernest May, can "be accused, like Truman in 1950, of overhasty decisionmaking. On the contrary, both presidents permitted months of careful staff work and assigned to it some of the ablest minds around them." Daniel Ellsberg, who leaked the Pentagon Papers to the press, alleged that "a succession of American presidents over the course of 20 years . . . had been supplied with information and nonetheless had chosen to disregard it." The U.S. leaders did not lack information on which to base decisions; the puzzle is that they acted in contradiction to that information. They continued to expect victory in the face of strong evidence that such an expectation was a positive illusion.[87]

Barbara Tuchman's characterization of U.S. action in Vietnam as "folly" (which she defines as behavior contrary to self-interest) does not explain *why* the decisionmakers in this case—or in any of the other fiascos in her book—were subject to such "wooden-headedness." The poor policy decisions regarding Vietnam do appear to contradict the copious available intelligence, as we have seen, but they are more consistent with a deep-seated conviction that victory was possible (or at least that tangible gains were), as predicted by the theory of positive illusions, than with the notion that leaders simply made a series of foolish mistakes.

There is also the hypothesis that the momentum of the war, with all its institutional and social complexities, kept it going despite presidential efforts to bring it to an end. This may help to explain why the different presidents, despite divergent initial intentions, made similar decisions to continue the war. It also suggests why the war might have continued even if the decisionmakers had believed their side was unlikely to win. But each president did not merely continue the war—rather, each one escalated it. And the escalations were far larger than were necessary if the object was simply to demonstrate continued commitment. They represented an intention to win and a belief that winning was possible. Furthermore, the presidents were operating in vastly different contexts. No two of them faced identical problems or identical options. The different presidents act as a dummy variable for diverse political contexts across which a belief in victory remained constant, not as dummies who behaved exactly the same regardless of context. All of them had confidence that the United States would eventually win the war.

Even critics of the view that U.S. decisionmakers really expected victory may find that positive illusions contribute to an understanding of some key instances of optimism. Leslie Gelb and Richard Betts, for example, agree that the U.S. government comprised both "genuine" optimists and pessimists, but they argue that most of the optimism was consciously assumed—to boost the morale of domestic audiences, allies, the military, and the civilian bureaucracy so they would "work and fight hard." Their explanation of why the United States continued the war is that the decisionmakers did hear and reflect on the negative reports and advice, but that policy decisions were shaped by the importance—in the eyes of both hawks and doves—of containing communism and reaching a domestic political compromise. In other words, escalation can be understood (whether or not it was justified) even if the leaders may not have expected to win.[88]

However, as Betts points out, it is important to differentiate between decisionmakers' hopes and their expectations. While U.S. leaders perhaps did not *expect* any outright victory, they did hope for some advantageous outcome. But even if we accept this and judge that there was no expectation of victory, the unwarranted hope still demands an explanation. As Betts put it to me: "The 'positive illusions' argument may help to explain why hope overrode expectation, but presidents rarely expected as much as they hoped for. There were periods of optimism, but fewer than those of pessimism. They hoped they would get lucky, but they were rarely confident."[89] At the least, positive illusions may have contributed to those periods of optimism, which accompanied many of the greatest escalations of U.S. commitment to the war.

Fredrik Logevall recently argued that several U.S. policymakers foresaw disaster in Vietnam, but that the presidents did not take their advice; this view is strongly corroborated by Barbara Tuchman, who holds that decisionmakers should have realized that escalation would bring disaster. Still, as John Garofano points out, this argument "does not explain *why* President Johnson did not take their advice." This suggests a remaining gap in current explanations of U.S. policy on Vietnam, and I believe that the theory of positive illusions offers a compelling way to fill that gap. U.S. leaders may have harbored positive illusions about American capabilities, about their own ability to control events, and about the future. Garofano himself noted that his review of recent literature on Vietnam "points to serious limitations of the rational view of war, which needs to account better for the mindsets that policymakers bring to their tasks." Surely we should not ignore the widespread impact of positive illusions, especially the aspects most relevant to Vietnam, such as the evidence that in the implemental stage of a project positive illusions may "especially blind people to risk."[90]

Like a ticking bomb, the conflict in Vietnam was handled anxiously and indecisively by each of the U.S. presidents between 1946 and 1972, with some voices clamoring to back off and others simultaneously clamoring to defuse it with overwhelming force. Fearing the consequences of both actions, the presidents did neither; they simply dumped the problem onto each successor until it inevitably exploded in someone's face. But it burned everyone's hands along the way, and it badly singed American credibility and prestige. A succession of administrations became obsessed with it, pursuing a war policy without heeding the portents of disaster; as John Stoessinger put it, "Five American presidents based their policies in Indochina not on Asian realities but on their own fears and, ultimately, on their hopes."[91] The result, for the United States, was 59,000 killed, 303,000 injured, and a communist Vietnam. Somehow all the presidents maintained the conviction that the Vietnam war could be won by half-measures (without resorting to total war). But that was—as anticipated by many of their contemporaries, argued by many historians, and then proven by history—an illusion.

Chapter 7

Vanity Dies Hard

Overconfidence in one's own ability is the root of much evil. Vanity, egoism, is the deadliest of all characteristics. This vanity, combined with extreme ignorance of conditions . . . produces more shipwrecks and heartaches than any other part of our mental make-up.

—Alice Foote MacDougall

Hope, it is the quintessential human delusion, simultaneously the source of your greatest strength and your greatest weakness.

—The Architect, *The Matrix Reloaded*

The theory of positive illusions, as we have seen, offers a solution to the puzzle of why states are often so belligerent toward each other that they go to war, at the expense of much blood and treasure, even when the odds are uncertain or against them. In the case studies, I found evidence of positive illusions among leaders on both sides in World War I, and on the U.S. side during the Vietnam war. Chamberlain's overoptimism about Hitler's intentions exacerbated the Munich crisis, as did Khrushchev's overoptimism that the United States would permit Soviet nuclear missiles in Cuba. By the end of the two crises, however, positive illusions were absent. Together, these findings support the prediction that positive illusions are associated with conditions that can change to exacerbate them and cause war, or to reduce them and avert war. It also concurs with Richard Lebow's finding: "Crisis may even prove essential to rapprochement in some instances, in that the shock of acute confrontation or defeat is required to dispel dangerous illusions . . . When initiators recognized and

Table 5. Summary of the results of the case studies (shading indicates evidence of positive illusions).

	Open debate		Closed debate	
	Democratic	Nondemocratic	Democratic	Nondemocratic
	Predicted level of positive illusions			
	Low	Medium	Medium	High
World War I	Triple Entente			Central Powers
Vietnam war			United States	North Vietnam[a]
Munich crisis (before it broke)	Allies[b]			Hitler
Munich crisis (at its end)	Allies			Hitler
Cuban missile crisis (before it broke)	United States[c]			USSR
Cuban missile crisis (at its end)	United States			USSR

a. Some possible positive illusions about the Tet offensive.

b. Some possible positive illusions about adversary's intentions, but not about relative capabilities.

c. Some possible positive illusions about effectiveness of deterrence and efficacy of a military strike.

corrected for initial misjudgments, they usually succeeded in averting war . . . When little or no learning occurred . . . the protagonists remained on a collision course."[1]

Positive illusions were not evident on every side in all cases, but this is not necessarily unexpected. Even if they were present in all cases, in some they may have been outweighed or masked by other factors. As explained in Chapter 2, I deliberately selected tough case studies in which the effects of positive illusions should have been limited, and for which explanations based on alternative theories are plentiful. Finding evidence of positive illusions in such circumstances is a significant success for the theory and indicates that positive illusions do play an important role in provoking war.

The distribution of positive illusions among (and within) the cases suggests that regime type and openness of debate are crucial factors in determining whether positive illusions filter through the decisionmaking process to encourage war. This distribution will be a central focus of my conclusions, as it presents an opportunity to understand why and when positive illusions arise, and how they might be reduced. This comparison is set out in Table 5, which summarizes my findings from the case studies.

Results of the Case Studies

I predicted that positive illusions would be most likely to affect policy in nondemocratic regimes where debate was closed—that is, where leaders' overconfidence would be least opposed. This was borne out in the case of the Central Powers in World War I, but it was unclear in the case of North Vietnam. The prediction of high positive illusions for Hitler in the Munich crisis and for Khrushchev in the Cuban missile crisis is supported by their initially ambitious aims that led to the crises.

In the Vietnam war, the United States was predicted to exhibit a medium level of positive illusions (given that debate was relatively closed, yet within a democracy). Positive illusions were certainly evident, but not overwhelming. They appear to help explain some of the remaining puzzles, but leaders were not blindly optimistic about outright victory.

At the other extreme, I predicted that positive illusions would be least likely to affect policy in democratic regimes with open debate. This was borne out in assessments of capabilities by the Allies in the Munich crisis, and by the United States in the Cuban missile crisis, but it was contradicted by evidence of positive illusions in leaders of the Triple Entente in World War I (though their positive illusions were arguably less strong than those of leaders in the Central Powers). However, the fact that positive illusions were evident even in some of the least expected circumstances suggests that they may play a significant role even where contextual factors should conspire to restrain them.

Covariance with War and Peace?

Type I congruence analysis (described in Chapter 2) reveals that high levels of positive illusions are correlated with high levels of war: while positive illusions were evident in both international crises that did break out into war, they were not evident by the end of the two crises that were resolved peacefully. In addition, the level of positive illusions approximately conformed to that predicted. While these results suggest that there is general support for my theory, certain aspects of the cases deviated from the predictions. These exceptions may shed light on the causal processes.

Although the United States is democratic, positive illusions were evident in its policy toward Vietnam. From the point of view of my theory, this is not unexpected because U.S. decisionmaking concerning the Vietnam war was relatively closed, so if the leaders did harbor positive illusions, a medium amount of those illusions was predicted to survive debate and influence policy. In this particular case, some additional circumstances probably fostered such survival. First, as the Pentagon Papers made clear, the U.S. government to some extent concealed the reality of the situation from the public and the media. Second, to some extent the presidents received unduly favorable military reports from the field, and civilian officials screened out contradictory information. Thus, although good information was being collected, optimism accumulated as the information was passed up the chain of command and was not subject to wide enough scrutiny.

North Vietnamese decisionmaking is difficult to assess because it was conducted in secret and left little documentary evidence. We can say, however, that although nondemocratic and with a closed debate, North Vietnam does not appear to have exhibited overoptimism about winning. Ho Chi Minh was certainly full of faith in his "army," even expecting that ten of his own fighters would die for each one invader killed, but this was a reflection of deep-seated conviction, not overoptimism.[2] The continued willingness to fight reflected a widespread and renewable resolve which is characteristic of nationalist movements. The North's most ambitious military undertaking, the Tet offensive of 1968, perhaps betrayed some elements of overconfidence, but decisionmakers appear to have been aware of the political gains that could be made despite potential failure on the battlefield.

Another case in which positive illusions were predicted to be high because of a nondemocratic regime with closed decisionmaking was Hitler during the Munich crisis. Yet he did not always exhibit behavior consistent with positive illusions. His grandiose aims clearly led to the crisis in the first place, but any positive illusions he may have had about military capabilities were gradually dispelled. At that point, Hitler frequently consulted his generals and advisors, and he updated his assessments on the basis of their advice. Thus it is possible that the German decisionmaking process during the Munich crisis was actually quite open and succeeded in suppressing any overoptimism. (The fact that significantly increased positive illusions coincided with war in 1939 further supports the hypothesis; I will come back to this shortly.)

Khrushchev, though also at the head of a nondemocratic regime with a severely closed decisionmaking process, did not exhibit positive illusions toward the end of the Cuban missile crisis. Although he appears to have been overoptimistic in hoping that the United States would tolerate the Soviet Union's deployment of nuclear missiles in Cuba (thus causing the crisis), and in hoping for more concessions than the Kennedy administration was willing to give (thus prolonging the crisis), the accidents and brinkmanship that intensified the risk of nuclear war quickly destroyed any positive illusions he may have had that the United States would capitulate.

Covariance with Changes in War and Peace?

Type I congruence analysis indicated that positive illusions correlate with instances of war and peace. Type II congruence analysis (see Chapter 2) also reveals a within-case correlation between *changes* in positive illusions and *changes* in war. Holding the overall context constant—that is, focusing on a single conflict over time—reduces the possibility that some unknown third factor is ultimately responsible for the link between positive illusions and war (since that third factor would have to vary in perfect synchrony with both independent and dependent variables).

During the Vietnam war, as shown in Table 6, U.S. escalations appear to be related to the level of positive illusions: the administrations that exhibited most positive illusions were the ones that most escalated the war. The table presents a fairly crude comparison of relative levels of each variable, but it seems to imply that, while many characteristics are held constant over several observations of the same war, escalations did covary with positive illusions. Positive illusions may have been particularly influential in the Vietnam conflict, given the empirical finding that positive illusions may significantly blind people to risk when they are trying to implement a task, and given the experimental correlation between the determination or obligation to implement a project and the illusion of control that people experience.[3]

Although Hitler was neither the leader of a democratic government nor a model of unprejudiced decisionmaking, the debate about German foreign policy was relatively open at the time of the Munich crisis in 1938, but became increasingly closed thereafter. This change covaries with the avoidance of war in 1938 and the eventual expression of Hitler's overconfidence and the outbreak of war in 1939. In the months before Munich, Hitler's insatiable ambitions were temporarily restrained by his advisors, who argued that if Germany initiated a war in 1938 it would lose. Hitler appears to have heeded their advice. By the following year, however, he had begun to trust his own judgment over that of others, and he severely underestimated the allies that would be ranged against him. The gradual unbridling of Hitler's ambitions eventually exploded into one of the greatest examples of overconfidence of all time. In the end, "the downfall of the Third Reich was due in no small measure to Adolf Hitler's inability to realize

Table 6. Variation in positive illusions and relative U.S. escalations in the Vietnam war. The suggestion is that when decisionmaking was less open, positive illusions and attendant overconfidence went unchecked, resulting in an intensification or escalation of the war.

Administration	Positive illusions?	Relative escalation	Decision-making	Potential explanatory factors	
				Expectation	Source of positive illusions
Truman	Not overt	Small	More open	Uncertain	Unquestioned U.S. supremacy
Eisenhower	Not overt	Medium	More open	Uncertain	Unquestioned U.S. supremacy
Kennedy	Some	Large	Less open	Political gains	U.S. supremacy, inner circle
Johnson	Yes	Large	Fairly closed	Political gains, if not victory	Inner circle, military
Nixon	Some	Large (but different)*	Fairly closed	Honorable peace, better bargaining position	Inner circle, himself
Ford	Hint of	Proposed	More open	Political gains	Unclear

*More intensive bombing campaigns.

Note: Relative levels are important because, for example, Kennedy committed only a small number of military personnel, but this represented a major increase in U.S. commitment to the war.

that in strategic terms, the road to everywhere is the road to nowhere."[4]

Importance of Context

Extensive research indicates that a majority of people are subject to positive illusions. But as with all psychological biases, this finding means that people have a *tendency* to experience them, not that they will inevitably appear in every person or at all times. In addition to individual variation, positive illusions are mediated by the context in which a decision is made. Six main antecedent conditions (levels of verifiability, generality, ambiguity, and threat, quality of feedback, and stage of task; see Chapter 2) influence the likelihood of positive illusions, but more important than these for policy outcomes are two aspects of the decisionmaking environment that I considered in my case studies: democratic versus nondemocratic governments and open versus closed debate. They are more important because, regardless of the level of positive illusions held by decisionmakers at the beginning of the policy process, effective decisionmaking should eliminate or reduce them before they are translated into action. I will now consider how these two factors promote or reduce positive illusions.

Regime Type

Positive illusions are hypothesized to influence policy more easily in nondemocratic than in democratic regimes. In the case studies, nondemocracies did appear to be especially prone to the persistence of biased opinions. For example, Hitler's military ambitions were unaffected by the unpopularity of war among the German populace, but public opinion restrained U.S. policy in Vietnam. As the Vietnam case also showed, however, even democracy does not ensure that information is effectively scrutinized or challenged. In fact, the political infighting that is a hallmark of democracy can lead to explicit failures in effective decisionmaking—and, as Barbara Tuchman points out, this may be particularly true of the U.S. government: "The effect of the American Presidency with its power of appointment in the Executive branch is overbearing. Advisers find it hard to say no to the President or to dispute policy because they know that their status, their invitation to the next White House meeting, depends on staying in line. If they are Cabinet officers, they have in the American system no parliamentary seat to return to from which they may retain a voice in government."[5]

Despite imperfections, however, democracy is better at dispelling illusions than nondemocracy. Sumit Ganguly argues that military overoptimism, though evident in the history of both India and Pakistan, was much reduced on the Indian side precisely because India's more democratic institutions served to check unwarranted overconfidence. He further warns that India's current trend away from democratic ideals is likely to permit false optimism to rise dangerously to the surface.[6]

The hypothesis that unfounded positive illusions are more likely to be crushed in democracies may contribute to explaining the so-called democratic peace: the phenomenon that democracies do not fight wars against each other. It may also help to explain another phenomenon suggested by empirical evidence: that when democracies do fight (against states that are not democracies), they tend to win.[7] This is thought to result from their more prudent assessment of situations and their electing to fight only enemies they know they can defeat. Clearly there are historical exceptions such as Vietnam, but, as Victor Hanson observes, democracy can be beneficial overall even when a particular foreign policy fails because of it: "The institutions that can thwart the daily battle progress of Western arms can also ensure the ultimate triumph of its cause. If the Western commitment to self-critique in part caused American defeat in Vietnam, then that institution was also paramount in the explosion of Western global influence in the decades after the war."[8]

Openness of Debate

The case studies revealed that openness of debate also played a significant role in exacerbating or reducing the impact of positive illusions on policy. Hitler's foreign policy decisionmaking, for example, became significantly less open after the Munich crisis, and that change affected the decision for war in 1939. In fact, positive illusions seemed to vary more among styles of debate than they did among regime types. Indeed, positive illusions sometimes correlated with changing levels of openness within the same regime. The U.S. cases are particularly illuminating.

In the Cuban missile crisis, an intensive and expansive search for and debate on U.S. options apparently dispelled or prevented any positive illusions about military solutions. By contrast, decisionmaking about Vietnam became particularly closed in the Johnson administration, and Johnson became less and less exposed to alternative viewpoints. Some scholars have argued that if Kennedy had lived, he would not have escalated the war as Johnson did in 1965, largely because he would have, in John Garofano's words, "heeded advice suggesting that South Vietnam was not willing to save itself." Kennedy had earlier proved able to resist optimistic predictions of a rapid victory regarding a proposed intervention in Laos, and he was suspicious of military advice after the Bay of Pigs fiasco and the Cuban missile crisis. Ultimately, Johnson's more closed decisionmaking environment was a key factor in maintaining optimism. He believed, as James Nathan noted in 1975, that "success in international crises was largely a matter of national guts; that the opponent would yield to superior force; that presidential control of force can be 'suitable,' 'selective,' 'swift,' 'effective,' and 'responsive' to civilian authority; and that crisis management and execution are too dangerous and events move too rapidly for anything but the tightest secrecy."[9]

In Paul Kowert's view, Johnson "suffered a great deal politically from pursuing policies endorsed by ideologically unified top advisors but not subjected to wider scrutiny." He also suffered because others kept information from him, closing the debate before it reached the president. In addition to Robert McNamara's significant suppression of information (described in Chapter 6), during the last year of the Johnson administration Walt Rostow steered negative information and dissenters away from the White House.[10]

Debate about the Vietnam war was somewhat constrained in Congress as well. Opposition to the prevailing policy of continuation and escalation was politically untenable, being interpreted as a lack of support for the soldiers fighting overseas, and as an implicit admission of American failure. In other words, any dissenter in Congress risked being branded as not supporting national security. When new members of Congress convened in 1965, Vice President Hubert Humphrey told them, "If you feel an urge to stand up and make a speech attacking Vietnamese policy, don't make it." He was not asking them to cover up governmental mistakes, but rather offering them professional advice about how to get reelected in the next election.[11]

As the case studies made clear, acquiring good information is only one step toward achieving good decisions. Much more crucial is the openness of debate—the degree to which leaders and institutions encourage diverse and nonpartisan opinions, consider multiple options, exploit intelligence analysis, promote further intelligence gathering, cooperate with intelligence services, and heed advice. If the debate is not open, positive illusions will thrive and persist.

For a striking example, consider the case of Israel before the invasion of Lebanon in 1982. John Garofano notes that Israel's leaders became less and less open to both civilian and military advice, and that Ariel Sharon (then serving as defense minister) and his advisors "over-estimated the time available and under-estimated the cost in lives to achieve their goals." Michael Handel expands on the reasons for this (and quotes the former head of Israeli military intelligence, Shlomo Gazit):

> [Prime Minister Menahem] Begin and Sharon knew what they wanted to do, chose to isolate themselves from their intelligence advisors, and never evinced the slightest doubt that they could achieve their objective . . . The Israeli Defence Forces became bogged down in a Vietnam-style war that could not be won . . . Even more tragic is the fact that "there was nothing at fault with the intelligence analysis and evaluation on Lebanon. The necessary data were all there, the recommendations proved to be sober and realistic." The advice of even the best intelligence organisation in the world is useless when a nation's key decisionmakers are permitted to ignore critical information and indulge wishful thinking unrestrained by legal, political or moral checks and balances.[12]

Implications for Theory

As stressed in Chapter 1, the positive illusions hypothesis adds a novel and illuminating element to key issues in international relations theory. Positive illusions and the overconfidence they spawn are likely to affect not only war but international relations generally. Much of international politics is more about diplomacy, alliances, negotiation, manipulation, and credible threats than it is about war, and positive illusions among leaders may have a significant impact—both good and bad—on these aspects of international relations. In some cases they may enhance commitment and strength, which may increase bargaining power, attract allies, and ultimately serve the national interest. At other times, by raising perceptions and expectations of power and influence, they may undermine advantageous cooperation and agreements. There are also questions about how illusions of moral and ideological supremacy might affect states' attitudes toward the laws of war (and Just War Theory) or toward interstate intervention— whether for selfish or humanitarian goals. Such implications are wide open for future scrutiny; I briefly consider a few others here.

The Gamble of War

One could argue that decisionmakers choose war, not because they are overconfident about their chances of victory, but rather because they are simply willing to take the gamble. War is inherently unpredictable; according to Clausewitz, "No other human activity is so continuously or universally bound up with chance." However, that begs the question: What factors make people willing to take such risks? If anything, going to war aware that the outcome is uncertain is harder to understand than going to war with an erroneous belief in victory. Therefore, even where positive illusions do not promote an unrealistic *expectation* of victory, they may nevertheless contribute to the decision *that it is worth the risk to fight.*

In fact, positive illusions may lead to perceptions that make the gamble of war seem attractive even if victory appears unlikely. For example, they may lead to an underestimation of the costs, an exaggeration of one's capacity to control events if things go badly, an expectation that impressive military performance will force concessions, or an unrealistic optimism that things may turn out well after all. So even where it is evident that a leader did not expect to win, but decided to go down fighting or hoped for a lucky victory, positive illusions may help to explain why. As Clausewitz noted: "When Frederick the Great [of Prussia] perceived in the year 1756 that war was unavoidable and that he was lost unless he could forestall his enemies, it became a necessity for him to initiate hostilities; but at the same time it was an act of boldness, because few men in his position would have dared to act in this way."[13] (Frederick's boldness set off the Seven Years' War, embroiling much of Europe in a costly and protracted conflict that left Prussia devastated and eventually ended with an agreement that essentially restored the prewar status quo.)

In the case of Vietnam I argued that substantial evidence about military, political, and social prospects should have advised against U.S. involvement. But how much of a risk was it to fight? During the war U.S. analysts "consistently foresaw the achievement of military objectives as no more than a fifty-fifty proposition."[14] In such a case, it remains to be understood what led the leaders to believe that this risk was worth taking (if it was really fifty-fifty, they effectively gambled blood and treasure against an equivocal foreign policy objective on the flip of a coin). Positive illusions can help to explain why decisionmakers were willing to accept the risks and the costs.

Many scholars have suggested that prospect theory—which posits, as Robert Jervis puts it, that "actors are prone to accept great risks when they believe they will suffer losses unless they act boldly"—explains many risky decisions made in international conflict (such as the Cuban missile crisis and Japan's decision for war in 1941). However, while prospect theory may indeed fit the way states (or their leaders) behave, it does not explain *why* people become more willing to take risks when they are weighing potential losses. The triggering of positive illusions offers a possible explanation.[15]

Deterrence

Even in the post–Cold War world, deterrence of both conventional and nuclear war remains a significant foreign policy challenge, as does containment of rogue states. Because deterrence theory has traditionally assumed that actors are rational, understanding psychological biases is crucial to developing good deterrence strategies, and positive illusions are likely to be of particular importance. We saw in Chapter 5 that Khrushchev's positive illusions about installing nuclear missiles in Cuba undermined the U.S. deterrence strategy of the time. Similar problems may occur in many other situations: positive illusions on either side may make deterrence much harder than expected. Jervis, writing in the 1980s, warned that biased perceptions might even lead to the kind of failure of deterrence that would be necessary to bring on World War III:

> Given the overwhelming destruction which both sides would expect such a war to bring, it seems hard to see how such a conflict could erupt in the absence of misperception. It would be particularly dangerous if either the United States or the Soviet Union [or China or India and Pakistan today] or both believed that that war was inevitable and that striking first was significantly preferable to allowing the other side to strike first. Since a number of psychological processes could lead people to overestimate these factors, it is particularly important for statesmen to realize the ways in which common perceptual processes can lead to conclusions that are not only incorrect, but also extremely dangerous.[16]

Deterrence is likely to fail if opponents underestimate the threat, overestimate their ability to prevail if war does break out, or believe it is worth risking defeat. (As we shall see in the next chapter, each of these positive illusions may have contributed to Saddam Hussein's behavior in the period before the invasion of Iraq in 2003.)[17]

Realism

The branch of theory known as realism posits that all nations are in a "state of nature," vying with one another to achieve egoistic goals and to maintain their relative power, and that this drives the competitive nature of international relations. However, though egoistic behavior is an essential assumption of realist theory, its origin has not been satisfactorily identified. This "classical" realism, as Bradley Thayer points out, "rest[s] principally on one of two discrete ultimate causes, or intellectual foundations. The first is Reinhold Niebuhr's argument that humans are evil. The second is grounded in the work of Thomas Hobbes and Hans Morgenthau: Humans possess an innate *animus dominandi*, or drive to dominate. Both intellectual foundations are widely considered to be weak, however, because they rely either on a theological force or a metaphysical precept to explain state behavior." As a result of this weakness, most international relations scholars turned away from classical realism to neorealism, which accepts the same observed competitive state behavior but attributes it instead to the pressures of the "anarchic international system," in which all states must arm to ensure their own security given the lack of a higher authority to police them.[18] I argued in Chapter 1 that positive illusions add usefully to the neorealist framework by accounting for war-causing misperceptions.

In recent years there has been a revival of classical realism, and the theory of positive illusions may enhance this framework as well. Vincent Falger has argued that Morgenthau's assumption about a human lust for power may be wrong, but that the resulting theory need not be. In rejecting classical realism, Falger asserts, international relations theorists neglected "the most elementary foundation of human interaction, the biological basis of social behavior and its historical development."[19] I suggest that individual and group positive illusions can rebuild this missing link.

The in-group/out-group bias of social identity theory (SIT) has been advanced as a potential basis for explaining states' egoistic behavior. SIT has an enormous following, is supported by broad and extensive empirical evidence, and appears the most parsimonious theory to account for observed data. Jonathan Mercer suggests that it supplies a plausible driving mechanism for egoistic behavior that was missing from classical realism: "To explain the extreme and ethnocentric nature of [intergroup] competition, SIT posits a universal desire for self-esteem." But this is merely another nebulous assumption, providing no explanation of the *origin* of the posited "universal desire." The adaptive advantages of positive illusions may fill this gap, providing an evolutionary mechanism to explain *why* humans evolved such a fundamental psychological trait.[20]

It is well established that deeply ingrained psychological biases affect human decisionmaking, including decisionmaking in international politics. Positive illusions are not just another bias to add to the list, however. The theory presented in this book builds on a broad and interdisciplinary convergence of research findings on human nature, psychology, and warfare. It also benefits from an explicit explanation of why such biases were adaptive in human evolution, why they vary today, and why they are specifically linked to conflict. This makes it an unusually parsimonious and testable theory.

My task in this book had three components. First, I argued, on the basis of pathbreaking work by Richard Wrangham, Robert Trivers, and Daniel Nettle, that positive illusions were an adaptive trait in our evolutionary past, and that as a result they became an integral aspect of the human psyche. Second, I presented evidence from the work of Shelley Taylor and many other psychologists that positive illusions are widespread among normal people, that they are maintained and compounded by common psychological biases, and that they have specific sources of variation. Third, I argued that positive illusions promote war. To test this hypothesis I examined four international crises of the twentieth century. The results of my case studies concur with a longstanding view, stressed by Geoffrey Blainey in the 1970s and by Stephen Van Evera today, that overoptimism is a primary cause of war—a finding that until now had no satisfactory explanation. The case studies demonstrated that when positive illusions were stamped out in the decisionmaking process, war was averted, but that when positive illusions persisted among policymakers, nations careered into violence. Thus the theory of positive illusions and war may help to solve the War Puzzle.

In the modern world, positive illusions appear to be deleterious because they encourage war. But if they enable their holders to better fight, deter, or defend against enemies, then positive illusions in military and political decisionmakers (as well as in soldiers) may still serve national security interests: even if we live in an anarchic world in which they cause more war, positive illusions may help us survive within it. In modern war, however, they are increasingly likely to wreak havoc. Initiators of war tended to win in the past, but since 1900 have lost about half the time.[21] Today's command, control, and communications operate far from the battlefield, so psychological mechanisms are less likely to be updated by environmental and behavioral cues the way evolution set them up to be. Positive illusions can run riot without the feedback that would normally hold them in check. There are many reasons to believe that positive illusions, like other legacies of our evolution, long ago became embedded in our institutions and our society, and that we often have neither means to detect them nor incentives to correct them.

Positive illusions are as evident today as they were in World War I and Vietnam. In the early years of the twenty-first century they have been exemplified by the Taliban's and Saddam Hussein's fateful defiance of Western coalitions. Leaders of Afghanistan and Iraq surely did not expect to lose as badly or quickly as they did. Western powers, too, continue to suffer from overoptimism in foreign policy. Perhaps this is because, compared with domestic policymaking, foreign policies are less verifiable, are more abstract in design, produce more complex and slower feedback, involve more ambiguous elements, involve implementation of longstanding goals rather than deliberation about goals, and are commonly made in situations perceived as threatening. Under such conditions, positive illusions should reign supreme. As we shall see in the next chapter, such illusions contributed to U.S. policymakers' underestimation of the difficulty of creating a stable democracy in Iraq—in spite of prewar analyses that pointed out the obstacles ahead.

And yet I am optimistic for the future. There are historical beacons of decisionmaking that shine through the fog of illusions, indicating that my optimism may not be *over*optimism. At the time the world came closest to nuclear war, in the Cuban missile crisis of 1962, we also came closest to solving the problem. But vanity dies hard, and we quickly forget the lessons of the past. According to Richard Lebow, a key factor that facilitated a peaceful resolution in 1962 was the "personal relationship" that Kennedy and Khrushchev developed during the crisis. "By its end," Lebow contends, "they had become as much allies as adversaries, struggling against their own hawks and the mounting pressures pushing them toward a military showdown. It is no exaggeration to say that through the mechanism of a public-private deal, they went so far as to conspire with each other against their respective internal opponents."[22] This bizarre alliance was necessary in order to defeat the real enemy, the havoc toward which unbridled overconfidence inexorably drives us: war itself.

Chapter 8

Iraq, 2003

Bush's goals are extraordinarily ambitious, involving remaking not only international politics but recalcitrant societies as well, which is seen as an end in itself and a means to American security. For better or (and?) for worse, the United States has set itself tasks that prudent states would shun.

—Robert Jervis

Some important assumptions turned out to underestimate the problem.

—Paul Wolfowitz, 23 July 2003

The age-old human proclivity to go to war shows no sign of abating. Indeed, there has been a "disquieting constancy in warfare," with more than two million battle deaths in nearly every decade since World War II, and the 1990s was "one of the worst decades in modern history," with thirty-one new outbreaks of war. Recent wars include countries around the globe, from the Congo to Kashmir, from Chechnya to Afghanistan and Iraq. These conflicts are too recent to have been as widely analyzed as the ones in my case studies, and feelings about them are still too strong for any consensus to have developed among historians or international relations scholars. But I believe it is not too soon to investigate whether positive illusions and overconfidence continue to affect international relations, or more specifically, whether they continue to promote war. To do this, I will take a look at the most recent: the war in Iraq that began in March 2003.[1]

By the criteria of the case studies in earlier chapters, the Iraq war should feature few positive illusions. On the Iraqi side, there had been many years of interaction with the United States, options other than war were available (such as cooperating with weapons inspectors), and assessments regarding the likely outcome of war should have been simple, given that Iraq had lost the 1991 Gulf War, and that it was widely known that in the subsequent decade U.S. military strength had grown extensively while Iraq's had declined. On the U.S. side, there was a long period in which to evaluate policy toward Iraq, alternatives to war were available, and U.S. intelligence capabilities (independent of the quality of their interpretation) were at an all-time high.

Nevertheless, there is evidence that both sides exhibited positive illusions. In particular, the Iraqi leader, Saddam Hussein, displayed extraordinary overconfidence in believing he could risk war. Even if he did not expect to win, he clearly underestimated the coalition that opposed him. He apparently thought that the American president, George W. Bush, was bluffing, that pressure from U.S. domestic politics or the international community would prevent war or curtail it before Baghdad was seriously threatened, or, even if that failed, that somehow he would cling to power. Why else would he have so blatantly steered Iraq on a collision course toward war? It is unreasonable to assume that Saddam resigned himself to being defeated, to losing family members and endangering his own life, and to seeing his country occupied by American soldiers. He had demonstrated for decades his desire to stay alive and in power; for him, according to one analysis, "these two goals [were] absolutely paramount."[2] He could have avoided war by providing full access and information about the status of his programs for producing weapons of mass destruction (WMD). His catastrophic risk-taking may be explained by positive illusions—particularly given that erroneous beliefs were unlikely to be corrected in his tyrannical regime, which lacked any semblance of open debate.

On the U.S. side, underlying motives were long in coming and rational in origin (whether they were justified is a separate issue). In the eyes of Bush and his advisors, who had declared a "war on terror" after the destruction of the World Trade Center towers in September 2001, Iraq's refusal to comply with U.N. resolutions demanded action, up to and including war. The U.S. secretary of defense, Donald Rumsfeld, told the Senate armed services committee: "The coalition did not act in Iraq because of dramatic new evidence of Iraq's pursuit of weapons of mass murder. We acted because we saw the existing evidence in a new light, through the prism of our experience on September 11." The U.S. leaders believed that Saddam, who had used chemical weapons in the past, could not be deterred from using WMD or supplying them to terrorists in the future. At a proximate level, U.S. policymakers could consider war a viable policy option because of a well-founded belief in their nation's military superiority. The Americans' technological and organizational supremacy was obvious, and, as we now know, the invasion itself was a crushing military victory.[3]

However, the invasion was always going to be the easiest phase of intervention in Iraq. War made sense only if the subsequent nation building would also be successful. This broader mission, which as I write is far from accomplished, has been plagued with difficulties. While one should be cautious about making judgments with hindsight, it is clear that U.S. policy reflected over-optimistic assumptions and expectations—about the war itself and, most significantly, about the postwar occupation—that conflicted with a number of contemporary assessments.[4]

These optimistic assumptions appear to have directly contributed to the decision that the war should be fought (or at least that the risk of war was worth taking). In addition, mistakes resulting from overconfidence have exacerbated the costs of the undertaking—costs that have accrued in time, dollars, diplomatic relationships, enthusiasm for democracy, and lives. As the journalist Joshua Marshall put it, "the Bush Administration greatly exaggerated the scale and imminence of the danger Saddam posed, while dramatically underestimating the costs and burden of the postwar occupation."[5] How could the democratic United States, with all its checks and balances, be led so astray by its prewar intelligence and then fail to plan for exigencies of occupation that numerous studies predicted?

Accusations of overconfidence may sound like a stereotypical criticism of the Bush administration—but mine is not a political argument. Hawks from the right have as much interest in convincing other states to cooperate without war as do doves from the left. For the effective containment of "rogue states" and the maintenance of a credible deterrent threat, failures are disastrous. When war does come, those at both political extremes want to prosecute it well. Overconfidence in the case of the war in Iraq, if it exists, is bad for the United States as a whole (and the world), not just for President Bush and members of his administration. People who supported the war should be as disappointed by the difficulty and costs of the postwar phase as those who did not—the promises of success and of low economic and military costs were components of its justification. Moreover, if the war was to happen, it presented a rare opportunity to create a democracy in the Middle East. If it were to fail, it would be an opportunity squandered and an experiment not to be repeated for a long time to come.

Iraqi Overconfidence

After Saddam's defeat in 1991, his apparent willingness to bring on a new war in 2003 is surprising. His decision to fight might have been logical if he had intended to stage a large-scale counterattack with weapons of mass destruction—but there is little evidence that he had any such weapons, let alone had them deployed and ready to use (although he may have been led to think so).[6] The decision might also have been logical if he had expected a guerrilla war to drag out the conflict long enough for other actors to demand its termination—but again, resistance strong enough to allow him to remain in power appears to have been a hugely optimistic expectation.[7]

Saddam's past suggests that an overconfident expectation of victory was fairly typical of him. According to Lawrence Freedman of King's College London: "The only wars that Saddam

Hussein has ever won have been against his own people. He miscalculated when he invaded Iran in 1980, and then again in 1990 when he invaded Kuwait." He nevertheless survived each time to reenact such bellicosity. It seems probable, Freedman points out, that in 2003 Saddam was optimistically planning to fight the war in a way that would make it too costly for U.S. domestic politics to bear, as he had hoped to do in 1991: "The idea was to draw the Americans into heavy, and politically intolerable, casualties on the battlefield, but he had no answer to American air power, which pounded his troops into desertion and demoralization, and missed the US Army's ability to maneuver large forces so that the ground attacks came from unexpected directions. Also false was his hope that he could divide the substantial coalition against him, using Scud missiles to frighten the Saudis while goading Israel into a punitive response."[8]

Saddam might have expected such a strategy to work better in 2003 than it had in 1991, given that this time enemy soldiers would have to enter cities like Baghdad, which urban warfare might have turned into modern-day Stalingrads, with enormous casualties. He also seemed to expect to ravage U.S. communication and supply lines, a tactic that worked to some extent, but, as Frederick Kagan of the U.S. Military Academy at West Point later noted, Saddam "underestimated [U.S.] ability to respond even at that sub-tactical level, with troops against troops." The Iraqis, noted the *Washington Post's* Pentagon correspondent Thomas Ricks, were "stunned at the speed of the American advance. They didn't really think it was possible. They'd seen the Americans fight before. They knew the Americans were pretty good. At the same time, I think they were genuinely surprised when the American forces showed up that quickly on the edge of Baghdad." General Raad Al-Hamdani, commander of Saddam's republican guard south of the capital, claimed that his forces were given enough ammunition for six months to a year of fighting, and that he personally expected the conflict to last for two or three months and "turn Iraq into another Vietnam. I thought that

American forces were unable to breach and fight face-to-face, and that we had capabilities to affect the enemy higher than what we actually saw."[9]

Whatever Saddam's strategy, it should be clear that he did not expect to lose so easily, if at all. Why would he have continued to defy U.S. demands if he really expected his regime to be destroyed? In recent years U.N. sanctions had been softened with the oil-for-food program, and they were increasingly likely to be lifted. At the same time, weapons inspections had effectively ended (and indeed, as we now know, Saddam had little, if anything, to hide). Things were going pretty well for Saddam and he could have preserved Iraq's recovery. Kenneth Pollack, a former CIA analyst, wrote: "Only in 2002, when the Bush Administration suddenly focused its attention on Iraq, would Saddam have had any reason to change this view. And then, according to a variety of Iraqi sources, he simply refused to believe that the Americans were serious and would actually invade."[10] So it seems he was overconfident, first, that he would not be attacked, and second, that if he was, he would not fare too badly because of some mix of factors including Iraqi resistance, U.S. domestic politics, uproar in other Arab nations, international discontent, and a fear among Western military planners that he had and would use WMD.

U.S. Overconfidence

On the U.S. side, the key puzzle is not that the decisionmakers were overconfident about defeating Iraq militarily (few doubted that they could do that), but that they were overconfident about the overall goal, which included rebuilding it again afterward. That is the task on which U.S. policy must be judged. A number of detailed analyses (including projects at the state department, the U.S. Army War College, and USAID, and by congressional committees and independent scholars) warned of the political, military, and economic costs of a war with Iraq.[11] Even if some of the analyses were exaggerated in the other direction and some of them wrong, their volume, concordance, and prescience make it hard to argue today that the U.S. administration was not over-confident to some degree. The U.S. government's own reports and war games highlighted the problems and generally advised caution; the administration downplayed these and generally advised action.

Some of the outward confidence that the United States could achieve its objectives was a tactic to bolster support in the Western public and press, and to convince other audiences—not least the Iraqis—that Saddam's regime had no hope of surviving.[12] However, while many public statements may have reflected spin rather than substance, a number of facts demonstrate that U.S. leaders' excessive confidence was also a genuine belief. These facts, outlined below, betray great expectations that cannot be merely the result of media hype or political spin.

The massive movement of coalition troops and equipment to the Middle East before the war began implies that the simultaneous diplomatic wrangling at the United Nations was largely a charade—that the United States intended to invade Iraq with or without U.N. consent. Such a deployment could have been a bluff intended to aid diplomatic efforts, but the sheer scale of the buildup signaled that the war would go ahead, unilaterally if necessary. As Robert Jervis put it: "In the porous American system . . . getting ready to fight entails such extensive military, political, and psychological mobilization that only a leader committed to carrying out the threat is likely to be willing to muster the necessary effort."[13] The predetermined willingness of the United States (and the United Kingdom) to go to war in spite of the disapproval of large factions of public and world opinion meant that their leaders were confident that the war was justified by their own criteria (that destroying Iraq's WMD and Saddam's regime were legitimate reasons for war), and that they would succeed in creating a secure, stable, and democratic Iraq. Going to war without genuinely believing this would have been political suicide.

The assumption that installing a Western-style democracy and a free market economy in Iraq would be worth the enormous cost reflects, as Jervis notes in an article about the wider "Bush doctrine," "the belief, common among powerful states, that its values are universal and their spread will benefit the entire world." According to Jervis, previous experience "calls into question the links between democracy and free markets, each of which can readily undermine the other. But such doubts do not cloud official pronouncements or even off-the-record comments of top officials. The United States now appears to have a faith-based foreign policy." A number of authors have suggested that such a U.S. strategy will ultimately bring its own ruin. The Slovenian philosopher Slavoj Zizek argues that the Bush doctrine comprises fundamentally incompatible goals (spreading democracy, asserting U.S. hegemony, securing oil supplies), whose incompatibility will make success impossible.[14]

The Bush administration also exhibited overconfidence about potential allies, expecting to garner the support of nations in western Europe and elsewhere. The cooperation of Turkey was assumed to be virtually automatic; shortly before the invasion, David Sanger reported in the *New York Times*, members of the administration "expressed no doubt that within days American tanks and troops would be taking up positions along Turkey's long border with Iraq." Ricks remembered "people at the Pentagon telling me, 'Don't worry, Turkey will eventually come on board, just like they did in 1991' . . . I think the U.S. government really did believe that ultimately the Turks would come around."[15] When the Turkish parliament voted against allowing U.S. troops to cross Turkish territory, an entire arm of the invasion had to be eliminated. This clearly unnerved a number of military and civilian planners—and yet the war went ahead. We now know that Turkey's participation was not essential to military victory, but its absence placed a heavier burden on the remaining invasion forces and may have led to problems later. If Turkey had signed on, coalition troops attacking from the north would have passed through the "Sunni Triangle," the insurgent stronghold that was instead left to fester and to become the most violent region after the end of major combat.

Civilian leaders of the United States and the United Kingdom declared that Iraq possessed significant numbers of weapons of mass destruction, and that those weapons posed an *imminent* threat. It is now clear that these claims were hugely exaggerated—though controversy remains over whether the exaggeration was intentional, as a way to gain support for the war, or unintentional, expressing the leaders' genuine beliefs. The mismatch cannot be attributed solely to faulty intelligence. Intelligence was deficient in some respects, but by far the greater problem was a biased and selective reading of it by decisionmakers. Given that the war would plainly expose the existence or nonexistence of WMD in Iraq, the political costs of knowingly exaggerating this threat would be very high (as has since been demonstrated). Hence, as Michael Elliott of *Time* magazine concludes: "There is no doubt many British and U.S. officials really believed that Saddam had at least chemical and biological weapons—the British government certainly would never have taken the risk of waging an unpopular war if it had genuinely thought there was nothing deadly to be found in Iraq." Jervis concurs: "While much remains unclear, it seems that the United States and Britain not only publicly exaggerated, but also privately overestimated, the extent of [Saddam's] weapons of mass destruction." According to Ricks, among the troops at the front, who were constantly suiting up for chemical warfare, "it really was an article of faith that [WMD] would be used," and "officers believed this to their marrow."[16]

Well into the occupation, significant money and effort continued to be expended to locate the missing weapons. Evidently the coalition leaders had been overconfident that they existed. This is the clearest example of leaders neglecting intelligence in favor of prior assumptions, but it is not the *only* example—policy clashed with intelligence in other areas too. Rumsfeld stated in September 2002 that there was "bulletproof" evidence of Iraq's link to al Qaeda. Any such link is now widely regarded as being entirely imaginary—and many intelligence professionals said as much at the time. What did seem bulletproof was the tendency of U.S. leaders to assert that intelligence reports that supported their assumptions were accurate, while contradictory ones were not.[17]

The Bush administration even set up its own ad hoc agency in the Pentagon (the "office of special plans") to conduct its own evaluation of intelligence. Pollack argues that the evaluation involved "selecting reports that supported the Administration's pre-existing position and ignoring all the rest." As a result, intelligence analysts not employed in the office of special plans "spent huge amounts of time fighting bad information and trying to persuade Administration officials not to make policy decisions based on it." The office of special plans sent incriminatory analyses (which sometimes included raw and unverified intelligence) directly to cabinet members. Worse still, this highly unusual information flow sometimes led to public pronouncements of "facts" that intelligence professionals knew to be dubious or wrong. This faulty process applied to information both on WMD and on likely problems of occupation. Pollack concludes: "As best I can tell, these [administration] officials were guilty not of lying but of creative omission. They discussed only those elements of intelligence estimates that served their cause."[18]

An example was the claim that Iraq could have a nuclear weapon within a year. That concern did feature in intelligence analyses as a possibility—but *only* if Iraq could obtain fissile material from abroad, a scenario that was deemed highly unlikely. This idiosyncratic use of information harks back to the psychologist David Dunning's work showing that positive illusions are created, maintained, and reinforced by the selection of criteria and topics that serve one's own interests. Similarly, Kagan points out, "we focused very much on the one thing that we knew we could do, which was destroy the Iraqi military, and didn't think very much about the one thing that was actually going to be very hard to do, which is transition to democracy."[19]

How the War Plan Undermined the Occupation

Overoptimism in the planning of the war—about how many troops were needed and what they were likely to face after a military victory—spawned several failures of the occupation phase. Rumsfeld's doctrine of using small, highly maneuverable forces plus overwhelming aerial bombardment proved successful in achieving quick military victories (both in Afghanistan and in Iraq), but it contained a hidden overoptimism about what these same forces would face the day after victory. In the planning phase, officials played down potential postwar problems partly in order to garner support for launching the war. James Fallows, who investigated the planning process in detail, notes that staff in Rumsfeld's office seem to have held the opinion that "postwar planning was an impediment to war. Because detailed thought about the postwar situation meant facing costs and potential problems . . . it could be seen as an 'antiwar' undertaking." Wishful thinking was therefore almost inevitable—those who were determined to go to war (regardless of what happened at the United Nations) had to assume the war would have positive consequences.[20]

In the critical hours and days after "major combat" ended, according to Kagan, "The problem was simply that we didn't have enough troops, that the troops we had were not trained to transition from war to peacekeeping, and that there was no clear plan in place for how we would do the peacekeeping." Before the war, many in the U.S. military recognized that large numbers of troops would be crucial to ensure law and order after victory. General Eric K. Shinseki, the army chief of staff, expressed this need to a Senate committee in February 2003, arguing that, in line with the War College and other reports, several hundred thousand troops would be needed in the immediate aftermath.[21]

In response, Deputy Secretary of Defense Paul Wolfowitz testified that it was "hard to imagine" that more U.S. forces would be needed for postwar duties than for the invasion itself. Wolfowitz, according to Ricks, "had a pretty optimistic view of Iraq, and postwar Iraq. He really genuinely did think that Shinseki's estimate was off—that it would not take several hundred thousand troops to occupy Iraq . . . because I think Wolfowitz thought that Iraqis generally would welcome us." This was astounding given that, in Fallows's words: "None of the government working groups that had seriously looked into the question had simply 'imagined' that occupying Iraq would be more difficult than defeating it. They had presented years' worth of experience suggesting that this would be the central reality of the undertaking."[22]

After the fall of Baghdad, the relatively small numbers of coalition troops were unable to prevent looting, revenge attacks, dispersal of Iraqi soldiers, and an influx of foreign terrorists—a situation that, as we shall see, had been foreseen by prewar U.S. government analyses but ignored by policymakers. These initial failures would undermine security long afterward. Many critics blamed Rumsfeld for recklessly pushing too small an invasion force, although it should be noted that the smaller force reflected a long-term defense department plan to rely more on technology and less on large numbers of troops. There were also various political motivations for a smaller invasion force in Iraq—to minimize the impact on civilians, to bypass southern cities so as to topple Baghdad and end the war quickly, and to keep the concentration of allied troops funneling through Kuwait to a minimum (in case this proved a target for WMD).[23]

But the key issue remains the military force required for what was to follow. One of the Army War College report's authors, Conrad Crane, points out that "while the rules for achieving military victory with a modernized military against a force as inept as the Iraqis might indeed have been transformed, the rules about maintaining stability and reconstructing regimes have not." This was not guesswork, but a lesson from history: Crane's study showed that successful occupations in the past had deployed vast ground forces and then transferred power quickly.[24]

Defense department sources revealed that Rumsfeld had reduced troop numbers at least six times before the war, "in the face of frequent warnings by his military advisers that such a plan was dangerous and reckless."[25] Fallows reports: "The military's fundamental argument for building up what Rumsfeld considered a wastefully large force is that . . . with too few soldiers, the United States would win the war only to be trapped in an untenable position during the occupation." Marine General Anthony Zinni, a former head of the U.S. Central Command (CENTCOM), told Fallows that Iraq war games in the 1990s had tended to use more forces: "The reason we had those two extra divisions was the security situation. Revenge killings, crime, chaos—this was all foreseeable."[26]

Rumsfeld was a key character in shaping U.S. policy, and he became known, as a reporter for the London *Times* put it, for his "Teflon-like irrepressible confidence . . . In Afghanistan, a war won with air strikes guided by small teams of special forces and ground battles led by militia, Mr. Rumsfeld's vision appeared vindicated. So, too, did his unbridled enthusiasm for a preemptive, aggressive American foreign policy." Secretary of the Army Thomas White, commenting on Rumsfeld and Wolfowitz's rift with the army over troop numbers, noted that neither "is a man that I would say was burdened by a great deal of self-doubt." The military success in Afghanistan convinced them that they would be "absolutely right" in Iraq as well. Had Rumsfeld's preference gone unchecked, there might only have been 75,000 troops in the invasion force, in contrast to the 400,000 demanded by the army. In the end, some 200,000 troops were involved.[27] In this case, the fairly open institutions and civil-military interactions may have had some success in reducing the impact of positive illusions on policy.

Focusing on military requirements for the invasion despite warnings of likely postwar problems left preparations for the occupation underplanned and inadequate. The resulting lack of law and order, humanitarian aid, and civilian services at the outset may have dissuaded other nations from deploying their own peacekeepers into the chaos. Peter Galbraith, a former U.S. ambassador to Croatia, told a congressional committee in June 2003: "When the United States entered Baghdad on April 9, it entered a city largely undamaged by a carefully executed military campaign. However, in the three weeks following the US takeover, unchecked looting effectively gutted every important public institution in the city."[28] The miniature army that won such a decisive victory lacked the size and preparation that many had warned would be necessary to consolidate its success.

There was much talk of "decapitating" the regime, after which Iraq was expected to capitulate instantly. But instead, as one commentator put it, "Iraq became like a chicken running around with its head cut off, in fact in some ways harder to deal with, harder to catch . . . It was an extremely optimistic war plan at its core . . . All I can think is [that the Bush administration] really did believe what they were being told by Iraqi exiles—that this would be a piece of cake after Saddam Hussein was knocked off."[29]

Prewar Assumptions and Postwar Problems

At this writing, long after the invasion, many more American soldiers have been killed in postwar Iraq (after the declared end of "major combat operations" on 1 May 2003) than during the invasion itself, and the total is still rising. Thousands of Iraqi lives have been lost both during the invasion and during the occupation.[30] The continued attacks on the U.S. military, other coalition forces, Iraqi recruits and police, and civilians (including U.N. staff), plus the soaring costs and the controversial progress toward democracy have led many to label U.S. policy in Iraq a failure.[31] Certainly the United States has faced "a more lethal insurgency than it had bargained for." Many of those who opposed the war believe their opinion of U.S. policy has proven correct: win the war the Americans might, but win the peace they would not— or not without too great a cost.[32]

"Winning the peace" was inevitably going to be difficult in a country containing three mutually hostile ethnic groups suddenly set free after decades of tyranny. But it is uncontroversial to say that U.S. policymakers underestimated this difficulty. As Kagan points out: "It's very clear, if you go back and look at our leaders' statements before the war, they thought that it was going to be relatively easy." The unexpected extension of tours of duty for tens of thousands of national guard and reserve troops reveals that the tasks of occupation and reconstruction exceeded what the United States had planned for. As noted at the beginning of this chapter, even Wolfowitz himself admitted in July 2003 that "some important assumptions" had "underestimate[d] the problem."[33]

And this cannot be attributed to a lack of information. Fallows details numerous reports from within the U.S. government that made accurate predictions about what would happen in postwar Iraq. One was the state department's "Future of Iraq" project, which drew on department staff, Iraqi exile organizations, and outside experts. Some of the exiles had a vested interest in promoting the war, but they also had an interest in producing a stable postwar Iraq. The 2,500-page report detailed key tasks to ensure a successful occupation, such as "restoring electricity and water supplies as soon as possible after regime change," as well as ways to disband and reuse the Iraqi army and ways to avert chaos, looting, and fighting in the aftermath of war. It stressed that the United States should approach the reconstruction of Iraq as resembling the rebuilding of Germany and Japan after World War II—that is, requiring years of investment and troop presence.[34]

Another report, from the U.S. Army War College in February 2003, reviewed previous U.S. occupations and identified successful solutions to common problems. It also detailed specific tasks likely to arise in Iraq, noting that prolonged U.S. presence would be resented, so a multinational force should be installed as quickly as possible. The summary of conclusions makes striking reading:

> To be successful, an occupation such as that contemplated after any hostilities in Iraq requires much detailed interagency planning, many forces, multi-year military commitment, and a national commitment to nationbuilding . . . To conduct their share of the essential tasks that must be accomplished to reconstruct an Iraqi state, military forces will be severely taxed in military police, civil affairs, engineer, and transportation units, in addition to possible severe security difficulties . . . An exit strategy

will require the establishment of political stability, which will be difficult to achieve given Iraq's fragmented population, weak political institutions, and propensity for rule by violence.[35]

This report was certainly seen by CENTCOM and the U.S. Office of Reconstruction and Humanitarian Assistance (ORHA).[36] It is unclear why it did not have much impact on policy, but it is clear that the inadequacy of planning for the occupation cannot be blamed on a lack of information. Fallows sums it up this way:

> The [Bush] Administration will be admired in retrospect for how much knowledge it created about the challenge it was taking on. U.S. government predictions about postwar Iraq's problems have proved as accurate as the assessments of prewar Iraq's strategic threat have proved flawed. But the Administration will be condemned for what it did with what was known. The problems the United States has encountered are precisely the ones its own expert agencies warned against . . . And the ongoing financial, diplomatic, and human cost of the Iraq occupation is the more grievous in light of the advance warnings the government had.[37]

The administration was clearly overoptimistic about the level of armed resistance—both during the invasion and after it. Soon after the war began, Pentagon officials "conceded that they had underestimated the resistance they would face in [some] parts of the country," and "had underestimated the vulnerability of the American supply line and the potency of the guerrilla-style resistance led by the 40,000-strong Fedayin militia that is loyal to Saddam." General Wesley Clark (who would later become a Democratic candidate for president) noted early in the war that although the existence of Saddam loyalists had been "well-reported abroad" and CIA analysts had "told policymakers about this threat," it was nevertheless "underestimated" and "somehow it wasn't factored into coalition planning." The military historian John Keegan wrote: "There probably are too few troops, the result of an underestimation of the size of the military problem by people in the Pentagon" exacerbated by "the failure of the Iraqi army to desert in large numbers, as was optimistically expected."[38]

There were similar optimistic expectations about a popular uprising during the invasion. Saddam's regime was brutal and widely despised, but, as an editorial in the *Times* (London) pointed out, past evidence and prewar intelligence gave little reason to expect a rapid revolt against him: "The Shi'ites, who rose up against the regime in the south in 1991 and were slaughtered for their impudence, were going to do nothing so rash this time . . . Western intelligence should have known that."[39]

The insurgency continued long after the declared end of the war. In the summer of 2003 Rumsfeld claimed the attacks were perpetrated by a small number of Ba'athist "dead-enders." By November 2003 a CIA report warned that the guerrilla war was "in danger of escalating out of US control." This report was endorsed by Paul Bremer, head of the U.S. occupation in Iraq, which some speculated was "a possible sign that he was seeking to bypass his superiors in the Pentagon and send a message directly to President George Bush on how bad the situation has become." The fall 2003 acceleration of plans to turn the governance of the country over to Iraqis strongly suggests a realization in the Bush administration that the situation was far worse than expected, and a wish to get out as soon as possible—ideally before the 2004 U.S. elections.[40]

Whether or not there were positive illusions about the security aspects of the occupation, many administration officials "woefully underestimated the cost of reconstructing Iraq."[41] Budget estimates made by those outside the administration were consistently very high (and, with hindsight, accurate). No official estimates were made public until well after the war. (One insider, the White House economic advisor Lawrence Lindsay, had earlier suggested to the *Wall Street Journal* a figure of $100–200 billion, and, Fallows reports, had been forced to resign soon afterward.) Postponing acknowledgment of the war's costs might be seen as an ingenious strategy on the part of the administration: once the

United States was committed in Iraq, Congress was hardly going to refuse to allocate funds needed to avoid national disgrace. But given that Bush had an election to face in 2004, the political risks of underestimates were high enough to lend credence to the notion that members of the administration genuinely believed the costs would be low.

Positive illusions about the financial burden appear to have been buoyed up by two highly optimistic assumptions: that Iraqi infrastructure would be relatively intact after the war; and that Iraqi oil would largely finance the reconstruction. Both were very wrong. The power grid and numerous other crucial elements of Iraq's infrastructure, including oil-production capabilities, were destroyed or badly damaged. Wolfowitz told Congress that Iraq's oil should generate $50–100 billion in revenues over two to three years. The real figures look more like zero in the first year, $12 billion in the second, and $20 billion after that—as long as oil prices stay high. As a report from the Council on Foreign Relations and Rice University put it in December 2002: "There has been a great deal of wishful thinking about Iraqi oil."[42]

In September 2003, at a Senate armed services committee hearing to consider the extra $87 billion requested to finance postwar reconstruction, Democratic Senator Carl Levin admonished Wolfowitz for his positive illusions: "You told Congress in March that, quote, 'We are dealing with a country that can really finance its own reconstruction and relatively soon,' close quote. Talk about rosy scenarios." Republican Senator John McCain stated: "Clearly . . . we underestimated the size of the challenge that we would face." A day earlier, Senator Tom Harkin, a Democrat, had said on the Senate floor: "This may not be Vietnam, but boy, it sure smells like it. And every time I see these bills coming down for the money, it's costing like Vietnam, too."[43]

When confronted with plans for postwar Iraq before the invasion, Bush had been, according to David Sanger, "relentlessly optimistic . . . he talked of an occupation that would resemble the American liberation of Germany and Japan." Yet his administration does not appear to have accepted the implication of those precedents: that the occupation would be lengthy and hugely expensive. A principle of prudent planning is to use conservative (or at least moderate) rather than ideal assumptions. And yet, as a former chairman of the Joint Chiefs of Staff, General John Shalikashvili, put it recently, whatever planning for postwar Iraq the administration did was based on "the most rosy predictions." The War College report forewarned: "The possibility of the United States winning the war and losing the peace in Iraq is real and serious. Rehabilitating Iraq will consequently be an important challenge that threatens to consume huge amounts of resources without guaranteed results."[44]

Did Positive Illusions Contribute?

Before the war, Iraq and the United States had been in a state of mutual hostility for more than a decade. What changed to result in war in 2003? For one thing, the new Bush doctrine involved taking greater risks than ever before to crush perceived threats to U.S. security. Deterring or containing Iraq was no longer seen as a viable option (the perceived failure of deterrence during the 1990s, and the perceived imminence of threat, ruled that out). A contributing factor was that the United States overestimated how easy regime change would be. It is also important to remember that the war was in part caused by the other side: Saddam was overly confident that the Americans would not try to overthrow him, or that if they did, they would find the task too costly and would fail. If Saddam was wrongly led to believe this by yes-men, then positive illusions were maintained by the predicted variables: the constraints of information due to regime type and a closed debate.

Regardless of one's opinion on whether or not the invasion was justified, U.S. policymakers on Iraq betrayed positive illusions concerning all phases of the conflict: the prewar phase (their cause was just; Iraq had WMD; they could achieve their aims unilaterally; costs of reconstruction would be low), the war itself

(U.S. troops would be welcomed as liberators; Iraqis would rise up against Saddam; resistance would fade quickly), and, most significantly, the postwar phase (resistance would be limited; Iraqi troops would provide security and policing; Iraqi infrastructure would be largely intact; oil would pay for reconstruction; Iraq would embrace democracy).

Bad information was part of the problem, but was not solely to blame for administration policy. As Senator Edward Kennedy, a prominent Democrat, cautioned in early 2004: "If we view these events simply as an intelligence failure—rather than a larger failure of decisionmaking and leadership—we will learn the wrong lessons . . . Specific warnings from the intelligence community were consistently ignored as the administration rushed toward war." Pollack, who had seen the war as unfortunate but necessary, wrote: "At the very least we should recognize that the Administration's rush to war was reckless even on the basis of what we thought we knew in March of 2003." Positive illusions, though not expected for the reasons outlined at the beginning of this chapter, contributed significantly to causing the war: Saddam's underestimate of the U.S. threat; the U.S. underestimate of the costs and difficulty of the objective as a whole. As Michael Elliott described them: "A series of flawed assumptions and decisions made before the war started—some based on resolute optimism, some based on naiveté, and some that carried unfortunate unintended consequences . . . bureaucratic infighting, wishful thinking, and . . . an undue influence in Washington exerted by [Iraqi exile] Ahmed Chalabi . . . contributed to a process by which the Bush Administration got Iraq wrong."[45]

Any positive illusions among individuals were likely to have been exacerbated within the fairly isolated Bush clique—whose members needed to unite to defend a bold new national security strategy and Iraq policy against an often hostile civil service, Congress, and public and world opinion. This is a classic groupthink environment. As I suggested in Chapter 1, positive illusions and groupthink biases are likely to reinforce each other dramatically.

According to the political scientist Karen Alter, the Bush team's prewar foreign policy "manifested all the symptoms" of group-think that Irving Janis warned of:

- Illusions of invulnerability leading to excessive optimism and the taking of extreme risks.
- Collective efforts to rationalize leading decisionmakers to discount warnings that might otherwise force them to reconsider.
- Stereotyped views of enemy leaders as too evil to warrant genuine attempts to negotiate and too weak or stupid to counter an attack against them, leading to miscalculations.
- An unquestioned belief in the group's inherent morality, inclining group members to ignore the ethical or moral consequences of their decisions.
- Advocates of the consensus view putting direct pressure on those who express strong arguments against any of the group's stereotypes, illusions, or commitments, making clear that dissent is contrary to what is expected of all loyal members.
- Self-appointed mind guards emerging to protect the group from advice, information, and views that might shatter the shared complacency about the effectiveness or morality of their decisions.
- Self-censorship by people with views deviating from the apparent group consensus, creating an illusion of unanimity within the group.[46]

Robert Jervis argues that there was also widespread "cognitive consistency" in the debate on whether to invade. Those who thought backing down would be disastrous also tended to believe a slew of other interventionist ideas, even though each one is logically independent, such as that Saddam had weapons of mass destruction, that military victory would be swift, and that a secure, stable, and democratic Iraq was achievable. Those who thought war was not necessary tended to believe all the opposite claims.[47]

It is easy to criticize with the benefit of hindsight, of course, and the media undoubtedly hyped divisions in Washington and problems in Iraq. During the war, according to the political scientist and media researcher Robert Entman, Rumsfeld "quite reasonably complained about reporters' seeming demand for instant success." What would members of the Bush administration say in their own defense? The main official line has been to claim that, since everything is uncertain, outcomes cannot be surprising. Of course some things went badly, but others went well. Overall, Iraq and the world are better off without Saddam Hussein. The situation in Iraq will work out in the end.[48] Rumsfeld often focused on uncertainty about the future and on the limits of information. He once mused: "There are known knowns; there are things we know we know. We also know there are known unknowns; that is to say we know there are some things we do not know. But there are also unknown unknowns—the ones we don't know we don't know." But, Slavoj Zizek points out, Rumsfeld forgot the crucial fourth combination: "The unknown knowns, things we don't know that we know—which is precisely the Freudian unconscious . . . In many ways, these unknown knowns, the disavowed beliefs and suppositions we are not even aware of adhering to, may pose an even greater threat. That is indeed the case with the reasons for this war."[49] Zizek's argument is striking when one recalls that positive illusions are predicated on our own self-deception, filtering incoming information to fit what we would like to believe. In the uncertainty about what would happen in Iraq, key decisionmakers do seem to have engaged in such selective reasoning.

With respect to the postwar challenge (the issue of WMD aside), enough *was* known to allow realistic predictions; the U.S. government itself set up projects and commissioned reports to obtain such knowledge. The decisionmakers maintained overly optimistic expectations *in the face of* contradictory evidence. As Fallows asks: "How could the Administration have thought that it was safe to proceed in blithe indifference to the warnings of nearly everyone with operational experience in modern military occupations?"[50]

The theory I have presented in this book helps to explain why positive illusions became a causal factor promoting war in 2003. On both sides, characteristics of two key predictor variables—regime type and openness of debate—contributed to a relaxation of the constraints normally imposed upon assessments of risk. This was obvious for Saddam's Iraq: he presided over a tyranny that killed the bearers of dissenting views, and a bureaucracy that stifled debate and diverse opinion. If he had positive illusions, no one was going to try to knock them out of him. More surprisingly, in the United States, too, the democratic process was undermined in the decision for war, and debate became relatively closed to outside views.

Louis Fisher, of the Congressional Research Service at the Library of Congress, argues that the democratic process failed to exert the normal checks and balances on presidential power (in my terminology, the effective "regime type" operating in Washington shifted away from democracy). Congress approved the Iraq war resolution not by consensus following a rigorous debate, nor even by making a firm decision. In the end, Fisher notes, "the legislation would decide neither for nor against war. That judgment, which the Constitution places in Congress, would now be left in the hands of the President." This predicament arose from a failure to adequately challenge administration policy and war aims, failure to adequately assess the intelligence information, political pressures due to upcoming midterm elections, and, ironically, a belief that giving war powers to the president would signal to Saddam that war was a real possibility, thereby encouraging him to negotiate and *decreasing* the likelihood of war. This last factor was not only a belief among hawks—even President Jacques Chirac of France held this view, and used it to convince the Syrians to vote in favor of the original U.N. resolution.[51]

It appears that this deficiency in the democratic process was perceived by the public. In response to a *New York Times* poll question of 7 October 2002 (three days before Congress passed the war resolution)—"Is Congress asking enough questions about President Bush's policy toward Iraq?"—51 percent of respondents said no, and only 20 percent said yes. Pollack reports that the democratic process was hindered in no small part by those in power: "Only the Administration has access to all the information available to various agencies of the U.S. government—and withholding or downplaying some of that information for its own purposes is a betrayal of that responsibility." Thus Senator Kennedy could claim that "Congress never would have voted to authorize the war if we had known the facts."[52]

In addition, debate over whether war was necessary (largely the WMD issue) and over the occupation became relatively closed. One problem, Pollack notes, was that U.N. weapons inspectors were harassed out of Iraq in December 1998; until then, they had "been a moderating influence on Western intelligence agencies; the information they provided, and the mere fact of their presence in Iraq, helped those agencies stick to reasonable suppositions and keep unsubstantiated fears at bay. After 1998 many analysts increasingly entertained worst-case scenarios—scenarios that gradually became mainstream estimates." And there were more serious problems in Washington. Rumsfeld and his staff willfully prevented full communication between the Pentagon and other organizations planning for postwar Iraq: for example, Fallows reports that Pentagon officials were "forbidden" by Rumsfeld's office to attend CIA exercises on postwar problems, and that senior military personnel were sometimes excluded from high-level meetings.[53]

More generally, the administration stuck to politically and psychologically motivated arguments and intelligence sources. Its official line foreclosed debate and preparations that, though they might have made the prospect of war less attractive, might have resulted in a more effective peace. Kennedy quoted a former director of the state department's bureau of intelligence and research, Greg Thielmann, as having said: "Some of the fault lies with the performance of the intelligence community, but most of it lies with the way senior officials misused the information they were provided . . . They surveyed the data, and picked out what they liked." The administration tended to seek, believe, and propagate intelligence that served its own purposes. Analysts often knew that such intelligence was unreliable, but were unable to maintain a balanced stream of information and instead faced time-consuming challenges to confirm their own challenges. According to Pollack, many in the intelligence community found that "administration officials reacted strongly, negatively, and aggressively when presented with information or analysis that contradicted what they already believed about Iraq."[54]

Both of the failings just discussed—of democratic process and of debate—are reminiscent of the Vietnam years. The Tonkin Gulf resolution of 1964 paralleled the Iraq war resolution: a Congress hoping to avert war by handing over the power to wage it to the president; an increasingly closed debate that prevented intelligence assessments from updating administration policy. In Fisher's words: "The resolutions are virtually identical in transferring to the president the sole decision to go to war and determine its scope and duration. In each case, lawmakers chose to trust in the president, not in themselves. Instead of acting as the people's representatives and preserving the republican form of government, they gave the president unchecked power . . . Placing the power to initiate war in the hands of one person was precisely what the Framers hoped to avoid when they drafted the Constitution."[55]

Conrad Crane noted that "a fair analysis of the war will have to explain why the assumptions about combat operations basically appear to have been correct . . . while those for reconstruction were very wrong."[56] I propose that expected variations in positive illusions may account for this difference. U.S. institutions and individuals had recent experience of war—not only against the same enemy in Iraq itself in 1991, but also against forces in Somalia and Afghanistan. The United States did not, however, have recent experience of occupation and democracy building in Iraq (though it did have some from Bosnia, Kosovo, and Afghanistan). As outlined in Chapter 2, positive illusions decrease as relevant feedback increases. Regarding war, the U.S. armed forces had recent, relevant, and direct feedback. Regarding occupation, they had less. For similar reasons, verifiability was lower and ambiguity higher for postwar tasks than for those involved in the war itself, so we would expect the postwar planning to have involved less specific information that could puncture positive illusions.

It is also possible that whatever levels of positive illusions were present at the two stages, they manifested themselves usefully in war and disastrously in occupation. As we have seen, positive illusions and overconfidence can bring both glory and havoc. In Iraq, the same U.S. optimism and confidence that led to decisive victory may also have led to problems with the occupation. Exaggerated confidence among soldiers and commanders may have contributed to military effectiveness, while the same quality among Pentagon staff may have contributed to poor planning. As an example, Colonel David Perkins, commander of the 3rd Infantry Division's 2nd Brigade, led "a campaign marked by bold maneuvers and risk-taking" that included the two "Thunder Runs" in which high-speed armored convoys blasted their way into the center of Baghdad long before any significant force was ready to move in. The idea was to send a simple message to the Iraqi resistance—that the United States could move as it pleased and seize key locations in the city, so resistance would be useless. A rational goal, but a risky action. Several vehicles were destroyed, ammunition and fuel were getting low, and their headquarters had been hit. Colonel Perkins later noted: "If you laid out a decisionmaking chart, it probably would have said, 'You need to get out now.'" But the daring tactic worked, and the main Iraqi resistance collapsed much sooner than anyone expected.[57]

The small, bold, and maneuverable force that Rumsfeld advocated, and that was epitomized by the "Thunder Runs," may have achieved military glory faster than a larger, slower-moving force could have done. As Bob Woodward put it, "There was a confidence, even an overconfidence, that made [Rumsfeld] the guy you wanted to lead the charge."[58] Yet that same philosophy of small, bold, maneuverable forces is precisely the reason—as many military officers and others argued before the war—that postwar Iraq collapsed instantly into havoc.

Along with warranted confidence that their forces would achieve military victory, U.S. policymakers displayed overconfidence about the wider mission of occupation and regime change. Such overconfidence—and the planning mistakes it fostered—appear to have originated from overly positive initial assumptions (the most important of which appear to be that U.S. troops would be welcomed, that resistance would fade quickly, that former Iraqi soldiers would provide security, and that oil would fund reconstruction). These faulty assumptions allowed the administration to discount reports and recommendations that contradicted them. "The President," Fallows notes, "must have known that however bright the scenarios, the reality of Iraq eighteen months after the war would affect his re-election. The political risk was enormous and obvious. Administration officials must have believed not only that the war was necessary but also that a successful occupation *would not require* any more forethought than they gave it." The tragedy is that the problems the United States has encountered in postwar Iraq "are not only precisely the ones that all the expert bodies of the U.S. government were concerned about, but also they were largely preventable." Fallows suggests that the errors have something to do with "an attitude prevailing in the administration," namely, that "these particular people had grown accustomed to thinking that they were likely to be right, and their critics were likely to be wrong."[59]

I would suggest that positive illusions remain as important today as they were in the Pleistocene (when they helped humans survive), and in 1914, 1965, and 2003 (when they did not). In fact, the more our societies and technology distance us from our evolutionary roots, the more we should expect our evolutionary legacy to lead us into misguided temptation. There may even be aspects of modern war that make assessment of opponents especially vulnerable to error. Antony Beevor argues that in the past there was a greater reliance on "human intelligence," that is, information gathered from people on the ground (a practice as old as language). Nowadays much of this has been replaced with remotely controlled satellite and signals intelligence. Beevor notes the overoptimistic U.S. expectation of a Shi'ite uprising against Saddam as an example of an error that may have occurred largely because of a paucity of human intelligence.[60]

On the larger scale of U.S. grand strategy, the Bush doctrine's precedent for unilateral, preemptive war and to foster an entire state in the Middle East may reflect positive illusions about the ideological supremacy of the United States, its control over world events, and its future security. These three categories closely match forms of positive illusions found by psychologists: self-serving biases, illusions of control, and overoptimistic expectations about the future. As Robert Jervis warned, "the United States may be only the latest in a long line of countries that is unable to place sensible limits on its fears and aspirations."[61]

Appendix

Notes

Acknowledgments

Index

Appendix

1. Alternative Origins of Overconfidence

Positive illusions are not the only source of overconfidence: there are a number of others. These are not mutually exclusive, and two or more may operate simultaneously.

Learning. Overconfidence can arise from a string of past victories. For example, during 1938 and 1939, as Hitler's ever more ambitious demands went effectively unopposed, his confidence increased with each success. Earlier, Napoleon was defeated "not because he was professionally incompetent, but because he became politically over-confident. His successes led him to dysfunctional behaviors like delusions of grandeur, gambling, misperception, distrust of subordinates, and an excessive demand for efficiency that exhausted his troops and officers." All he had gained in his extraordinary career was eventually "negated by his boundless overconfidence."[1] Sequential successes can engender increasing levels of confidence that may be justified up to a point, but confidence can easily become overconfidence.

Religious Conviction. Religious beliefs have inspired people throughout history to believe that their wars are righteous, that they will be victorious, that God will enable them fight better than their opponents, and that they will be rewarded even if they fail. As an extreme example, many Europeans believed that the Children's Crusade of 1212 (thousands of mainly French and German children and poor people) would be able to recapture Palestine from the Saracen armies. Religion has also inspired confidence in the superiority of one's own group over others. Religious teaching, according to Matt Ridley, "has almost always emphasized the difference between the in-group and the out-group: us versus them; Israelite and Philistine; Jew and Gentile; saved and damned; believer and heathen; Arian and Athanasian; Catholic and Orthodox; Protestant and Catholic; Hindu and Muslim; Sunni and Shia. Religion teaches its adherents that they are a chosen race and their nearest rivals are benighted fools or even subhumans. There is nothing especially surprising in this, given the origins of most religions as beleaguered cults in tribally divided, violent societies."[2]

Personality. Certain personality types may tend more toward overconfidence than others. During the war in Vietnam, many authors have claimed, ego and machismo played a role in President Johnson's leadership, and he even "saw the war as a test of his own manliness." Extreme personalities, such as Hitler or Stalin, are often diagnosed as having personality disorders, such as narcissism, psychopathic tendencies, or mania. A number of these disorders are likely to provoke extreme overconfidence.[3]

Neurochemistry. There are numerous chemical triggers that directly alter behavior, and many of these may influence the level of confidence. Alcohol, for example, can reduce inhibitions and promote boisterous behavior, inflated self-assessment, and violence.[4] One of the most important that occurs naturally is testosterone, which has a marked effect on self-confidence, dominance behavior, and confrontational disposition. In dominance hierarchies, high-status individuals tend to have higher testosterone levels than low-status individuals—but if low-status individuals are injected with extra testosterone, they become more aggressive, challenge higher-ranking members of the hierarchy, and are even able to defeat physically superior individuals. As James Dabbs has found, testosterone is most potent in influencing dominance and control "either in combative interpersonal encounters (as among violent criminals or trial lawyers) or on the larger public scene (as among actors or politicians)."[5]

2. Why Overconfidence Beats Accuracy

Where the outcomes of events are uncertain, the evolutionary psychologist Daniel Nettle and his colleagues have shown, *over*estimating the probability of success can outperform perfect rationality. The basic idea is that, although it is possible to be either under- or over-confident, the costs and benefits of these two errors are not symmetrical. Overconfidence can have a greater payoff than both underconfidence and accuracy.[6]

Imagine you are faced with a game leading to success or failure. You can choose to play, for some benefit of success and some cost of failure, or choose not to play, gaining nothing and losing nothing. Opting out will be costly if, *had you played and succeeded*, you would have gained. Ideally, therefore, you should always play when you will win, but you should never play when you will lose. But the outcome is not known—there is only some probability that you will win. So to decide what to do you must weigh up the "expected utility" of each choice (the net gain of each outcome multiplied by the probability that it will occur). If the benefits and costs are equal, then whenever the probability of success is greater than 50 percent, you should play.

However, when the benefits and costs are not equal, the minimum probability of success required to make playing the better option rapidly declines (in a nonlinear fashion) as the ratio of benefits to costs increases, so that it becomes nearly always worth playing even if the probability of success is small. Playing becomes disproportionately more advantageous as the ratio of benefits to costs gets bigger—so you should go for the big benefit even if dicey. At the other extreme, playing becomes disproportionately less advantageous as the costs get bigger relative to benefits—so you should play it safe even if there is a reasonable chance of winning. Figure A illustrates this.

In a perfect world, a rational player would always know the true values of the benefits, the costs, and the probability of success. But knowledge is rarely perfect. Under such uncertainty, all players will have to estimate the probability of success. This, of course, will include some degree of error: even a rational player's estimate will sometimes be a bit too high, at other times a bit too low. Each decision of whether or not to play will be optimal only if the estimated probability is on the "safe" (conservative) side of the curve depicted in Figure A.

Because of this uncertainty, as long as benefits exceed costs, a

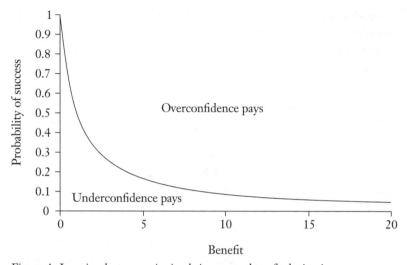

Figure A. In a simple game, winning brings some benefit, losing incurs some cost. The curve describes the minimum probability of winning required to make playing a better choice than not playing. When uncertain of the true probability of winning, a rational player aims to estimate the true value but makes some errors—underestimating in half of them and overestimating in the other half. Wherever benefits exceed costs, an optimistic bias outperforms accurate estimates because even mistakes will tend to fall on the "safe" side above the curve (instead of half above, half below). The curved relationship means that, as the ratio of benefits to costs increases, it becomes nearly always worth playing. In this graph, cost is fixed at 1, so above benefit = 1, benefits always exceed costs. Adapted from D. Nettle, "Adaptive Illusions: Optimism, Control and Human Rationality," in *Emotion, Evolution and Rationality*, ed. D. Evans and P. Cruse (Oxford: Oxford University Press, 2004).

player who overestimates will do better than a rational agent who estimates the true probability. Why? The rational agent aims for the true probability plus some error, so some of his estimates will fall below the true probability, others above it, and on average, half of all his choices will lead to a wrong decision. But if a player systematically overestimates the probability of success, the error component is less likely to knock estimates below the true probability: such estimates will vary precisely as a rational agent's would, but because the bull's-eye is shifted up a bit, even with the error, overestimates are more likely to stay above the curve, resulting in an optimal choice. When benefits exceed costs, therefore, an actor with positive illusions rarely makes a wrong decision. So a rational actor is out-competed by an actor with a baseline positive bias.

Nettle and his colleagues used a computer simulation to test this optimistic advantage. Over hundreds of interactions, they found that an optimistic bias can indeed outperform a rational actor, under the following (intuitive) conditions: when there is a fairly high uncertainty in the assessment of outcome probability, and fairly low uncertainty in the assessment of costs and benefits. When uncertainty in estimating success is very low, there is little error that positive illusions can help to compensate for. But when uncertainty in estimating success is high, it is better to overestimate.[7]

The Nettle team argue that these conditions are highly plausible for human evolution. The costs and benefits accruing from most life events tend to be recurrent and can be learned by experience and observation. Indeed, if they were common enough in human history, their evaluation may have become innate (for example, the obvious benefits of achieving higher social status). By contrast, probability of success is much more difficult to learn, since it depends on contingencies of time and context—and their interactions—such as unpredictable external factors and whether other people decide to compete for the same goal.

Empirically, it has been shown that people tend to give more weight to costs and benefits than to the probability of success, a strategy that may lead to fewer errors. But it seems likely that positive illusions are sensitive to variation in costs and benefits, so that overestimation is somewhat tempered when costs become too high. This also has empirical support: people's positive illusions are moderated by feedback so that they are kept within reasonable bounds.[8] However, because modern life is often unlike our environment of evolutionary adaptation, positive illusions may be less responsive than they should be and may persist even when costs are extremely high, perhaps because they are not triggered by evolutionarily salient stimuli (consider the political or military leader who cables orders across continents to launch thousands of strangers into a war).

Nettle's results strongly suggest that positive illusions are design features, not design flaws. Actors with positive illusions outperform rational actors in plausible conditions. These illusions may have had further advantages in our evolution if they were cognitively faster (able to trump rational calculations in fast-moving life-or-death situations), or cognitively cheaper to develop (able to trump complex rational calculations in the long run because the brain was a costly device for evolution to fashion). As Nettle concludes, "in behavioral decisions where the benefit of success much outweighs the cost of trying and failing, then, under uncertainty, it is adaptive to be optimistic about the chances of success."[9]

It is important to remember that an overconfident bias need not *always* be better than an accurate estimation to pay off in the long run. Evolution—or any other selection process—would favor biases that "historically minimized overall costs or maximized overall benefits." Having one's bluff called every now and then can be better than never bluffing. So a natural overoptimism may "result from *adaptive biases* that exist in the present because they led to survival and reproductive advantages for humans in the past." This realization has led to the development of "error management theory," which proposes that "psychological mechanisms are designed to be predictably biased when the costs of false-positive and false-negative errors were asymmetrical over evolutionary history." In such cases, the brain evolved to exploit the asymmetry.[10]

3. Extremes of Positive Illusions

We know that positive illusions vary among people. Here I outline some key factors responsible for this variation, from depression (where there are hardly any positive illusions) to egotism (where one finds the greatest positive illusions of all).

Depression. Research suggests that positive illusions are an essential element of the mentally healthy mind. By contrast, positive illusions are greatly reduced or absent among people who are depressed. This phenomenon is called "depressive realism." In addition, "depression is one of the few forms of mental illness associated with lower levels of aggression and violence."[11] If positive illusions have an impact on international relations, then we should also expect depression among decisionmakers to have an impact on international relations.

Depression can be triggered by numerous events common to people in their sixties and seventies—typical ages for national leaders. One of the main causes is illness. Herbert Abrams has warned of the consequences: "Depression, so common an effect of illness, is associated with self-doubt and avoidance of decisions or acceptance of responsibility. When depressed individuals can be induced to make decisions, their capabilities are reduced. They have impaired attention, concentration, and memory. Their powers of analysis fail, and they may overemphasize negative information."[12] Depression commonly follows heart attacks, the mere diagnosis of heart disease, strokes, trauma, surgery, cancer, hypertension, and the taking of some prescribed drugs.[13] So depression is likely to have been quite prevalent in twentieth-century U.S. presidents: thirteen of those seventeen presidents suffered one or more of the above while in office (McKinley, Teddy Roosevelt, Taft, Wilson, Harding, Coolidge, FDR, Truman, Eisenhower, Kennedy, Johnson, Nixon, and Reagan).

I offer here one speculative example. Depression may have been important in the two leaders who inherited the U.S. defeat in Vietnam: Johnson and Nixon. Johnson's goal of founding his cherished "Great Society" was undermined by the costs of the war, and he was burdened with the deaths of tens of thousands of U.S. soldiers. (His press secretary wrote: "The dead were coming back in such numbers that LBJ began to grow morose, and sometimes took to bed with the covers pulled above his eyes, as if he could avoid the ghosts of young men marching around in his head.") Did depression contribute to his decision to withdraw from the reelection campaign? Nixon came to office with high hopes of ending the conflict, but encountered all the frustrations and complications of extricating the United States from an increasingly unpopular war. It seems that he became quite seriously depressed, at least following Watergate. Indeed, Henry Kissinger and James Schlesinger took the unusual step of (illegally) demanding that the Joint Chiefs of Staff consult them before carrying out any presidential order. Both Johnson and Nixon were faced with the problem of controlling hugely complex events, and, as Daniel Nettle notes, "the illusion of control disappears amongst the depressed or dysphoric. The [reduced] strength of illusion of control in a person is predictive of their negative mood following task failure, their ease of discouragement in the face of new challenges, and their depressive symptoms in response to life events."[14]

Abrams concluded that when a president is ill, "in both the national and the leader's interest, he should be separated from the burden of decision making in crisis."[15] I agree, but I wonder whether in some respects decisions might benefit from an absence of positive illusions—which might bode well for peace, if not always for the vigor and self-assurance that fortify national security.

Gender. Men tend to have greater positive illusions than women do.[16] This finding fits with what Roy Baumeister describes as the "familiar views of the male ego, male overconfidence, and male tendencies toward escapist patterns (more alcohol and drug abuse, etc.), as well as the greater prevalence of depression, insecurity, and lack of confidence among traditional women." These differences may stem from natural levels of male and female hormones. Men have much higher baseline levels of testosterone than women do, and, as Richard Wrangham notes, "men's testes give them the capacity for a quicker rise in testosterone than women can experience. So women should be less vulnerable to the emotional allure of being drawn into fights based on temporary steroid-induced illusions about their own abilities." Wrangham suggests that this is one reason why there are so many men in politics in the first place: status and power reward them with a regular rush to their evolutionary sensitivities.[17] If positive illusions have an impact on international relations, therefore, we might also predict gender to have an impact.

It is important to point out that the comparatively few female leaders in history have often been as confident and aggressive as many of their male counterparts—think of Boadicea, Margaret Thatcher, Golda Meir. However, there may be a selection process by which only the most aggressive women survive in what is still a male-dominated profession. When Elizabeth Dole decided not to run for the presidency in 2000, Shirley Chisholm (who had run in 1972) commented: "When you make a bid for such a high office, you have to have energy. You have to be very outspoken and assertive, and not be afraid to offend people. She doesn't have the temperament. She's too cautious."[18]

What would women do differently if they obtained power? Eleanor Clift and Tom Brazaitis have made a fascinating study of women "blazing the leadership trail" in U.S. politics. A common opinion about women's aims was articulated by Senator Ted Stevens (a Republican from Alaska), who moaned in 1999 that "women don't support military spending . . . [and] constantly ask him, 'Why do you want to spend more money on the military? Don't they have enough?'" However, there is little systematic evidence for any gender difference in this respect. Congresswoman Jeannette Rankin of Montana voted against U.S. involvement in both World War I (following Germany's declaration of unrestricted submarine warfare against ships in the Atlantic) and World War II (following Pearl Harbor; the only "no" vote in the House). Advocates of women's suffrage tried to induce her to support war to avoid giving the impression that women were hopelessly pacifistic. By contrast, Margaret Chase Smith, the first woman to serve in both the House and the Senate and who once ran for president, "focused on defense issues and had a reputation for being one of the most hawkish members of Congress during the cold war."[19]

In 2001 a record number of women were planning to run for Congress. But after the terrorist attacks of September 11, which drastically altered the salient issues and overshadowed agendas with which women candidates were proving successful, many dropped out or lost support. "Women had to face the hard reality," Clift and Brazaitis note, "that voters may not trust them to lead the country in a time of war." Surveys have shown that women are perceived as "less capable on foreign policy, law-and-order issues, and the economy. And they score significantly lower on the ability to lead during a crisis and the ability to make difficult decisions." As a result, political analysts apparently expect that the first female president will have "the body of a woman with the character traits of a man. More than likely she will come from the moderate-to-conservative segment of the ideological spectrum."[20]

If women are typically more peace-loving than men, then for the time being it appears that atypical women are more likely to reach positions of political power in the United States (and, for similar reasons, in many other countries). This is likely to be driven both by voter preferences ("voters want the American version of Margaret Thatcher, a woman who won't go wobbly in a crisis") and by self-selection effects (women who might go wobbly in a crisis are less likely to want to run for election, as is true among men). If anything, "women frequently go too far in proving their toughness. Seeking credibility, they cater to men's issues—military defense and the economy."[21]

A study by the National Women's Political Caucus showed that women tend to win elections as often as men—when they run for them. There just aren't that many female generals, governors, or oil tycoons for the traditional selection process to draw on (evidence shows that raising campaign money is also more difficult for women), and fewer women choose to run anyway. At the beginning of the twenty-first century, there were 13 women senators (out of 100), and 62 representatives (out of 435). At the current rate of increase, it will be another 250 years before women are equally represented.

The political scientist Rose McDermott has conducted war games between different gender pairs—male-male, male-female, and female-female—in which subjects did not know their opponent's sex. Female-female dyads were far more cooperative, ended up at war much less often than male-male dyads, and obtained higher overall payoffs as a result. In mixed-gender dyads, women were more cooperative initially, but their reactions were similar to men's, often launching war in response to aggression. Significantly, women estimated their chances of winning as lower than did the men.[22]

Gender differences may mean that international relations are especially exposed to the effects of positive illusions—since it is predominantly men in positions of power. Clearly, there are more important factors in international politics than gender, but the reality is that the average man experiences biological influences on behavior—including perhaps testosterone-induced positive illusions—in a way that a woman does not: for better or for worse.

Culture. Positive illusions are a universal human trait, present in all cultures, but the degree to which members of different cultures exhibit positive illusions varies. Asians have been found to be less self-enhancing and more self-deprecating than Westerners. For example, in experiments designed to compare positive illusions, Canadians showed significantly more unrealistic optimism than Japanese. Another study found similar results comparing Asian Americans with Caucasian Americans.[23] The view of self in Eastern cultures appears to include an element of the collective, but when the group is the target of study rather than the individual, Asians still evaluate their groups less positively than North Americans do.[24]

Differences in positive illusions are thought to arise from different pressures in the respective cultural environments: self-enhancement is more acceptable and more advantageous in the West, and many authors have suggested that optimism is particularly fostered in the United States, rooted in the ideological culture of capitalism, materialism, and individualism. Indeed, according to the psychologists David Armor and Shelley Taylor, "Americans are widely regarded as the most optimistic people on earth."[25]

These cultural differences support the idea that positive illusions are not "fixed traits" in human nature that would fail to explain the *variation* in international politics. Instead, they suggest that while positive illusions may constitute an inherent tendency in our psychology, they are malleable and can be socialized to trigger differently. Thus culture is likely to influence the expression of positive illusions.

Ego. Positive illusions also vary with personality type, and can be particularly strong in people with certain personality disorders. Among normal people, they have been shown to be positively correlated with levels of ego, self-esteem, and narcissism. In one study, people with high self-esteem were "especially prone to persist at impossible tasks." In a review of the literature on aggression, Roy Baumeister and Joseph Boden argue that both individual and collective violence can often be attributed to the convergence of two conditions: a high ego, and a threat to that ego.[26]

This is a dangerous state of affairs because "people who overestimate themselves will be constantly at high risk of receiving evaluations that they are not as good as they think (because, in fact, they are not)." A number of studies have shown that those with "inflated self-opinions may be prone to violent or aggressive behavior." Bizarrely, people with high self-esteem often respond to failure by actually raising their predictions about their future performance—a recipe for disaster. Other studies have shown that high self-esteem individuals tend to make excessive and self-defeating commitments. In general, "people who hold high opinions of themselves tend to react irrationally, impulsively and emotionally when someone else presents a serious challenge to those favourable views. Such reactions may often lead to violence and aggression."[27]

This danger is exacerbated among people with psychological disorders, including narcissists (characterized by grandiosity, exhibitionism, and greatly exaggerated opinions of themselves) and psychopaths (who have grossly inflated images of their self-importance). Psychopaths are associated with unusual levels of aggression. People suffering from mania (the highs in the cycles of bipolar disorder), too, have exacerbated positive illusions, which, though sometimes fostering remarkable feats of creativity, can also lead to damaging and dysfunctional behavior.[28]

Ego threats cannot be transplanted easily from the individual level to the workings of governments. Yet state leaders and institutions do seem to display egoistic behavior that often influences national policy. This is no surprise in tyrannies such as those of Stalin or Hitler, but even normal states tend to behave as if their egos are at stake. Egoistic status competition among states plays a key role in international relations theory (and is a fundamental assumption in some branches of it). When there is a perception that a state is slipping down in the hierarchy of status, violence and war are much more likely. Nations whose leaders and public feel that their status is not properly recognized have an increased probability of initiating wars to maintain it (and similar effects have been found in ethnic violence). For example, William Wohlforth argues that threats to Britain's status led to the Crimean and Suez wars of 1854–1856 and 1956, and that the Cold War was principally a game of status between the United States and the USSR.[29] There certainly appear to be strong links between ego, positive illusions, and violence, not only among individuals, but also among groups and nations.

4. Individually Adaptive, Globally Maladaptive

If in the past positive illusions were an adaptive strategy, then they are predicted to be ubiquitous—and apparent on both sides of a conflict. But what is the point of having positive illusions if your opponent also has them? Does this not mean that any advantage would be cancelled out? As the anthropologist Richard Wrangham explains, positive illusions are "'globally maladaptive' (in the sense that self-deception reduces the fitness of the average individual), in the same way as most investment in aggressive anatomy or behavior." But they remain individually advantageous, because an individual cannot afford *not* to have them if others do. Wrangham gives an example:

> The canine teeth of male baboons *Papio anubis* have evolved to be long and sharp, due to an evolutionary arms race among male baboons to possess the most effective weapons. One result is that their canine teeth regularly cause wounds in females and other males. In this sense, the evolution of canine teeth is disadvantageous for the average individual, compared to a hypothetical baboon species in which males have short, blunt canine teeth. In a similar way, I suggest that self-deception has been positively selected in military contests, because without it a player would be less effective (e.g., hesitant or out-bluffed). Nevertheless, the unfortunate result is that conflicts are more frequent and severe than they would be without it. Thus, self-deception in conflicts is disadvantageous for the species as a whole.[30]

Any dangerous adaptation may decrease the mean fitness of a population, but natural selection acts on individual self-interest, not on the population or the species.[31] Reproductively successful individuals will leave more descendants than less successful individuals, so any trait that confers greater success will be selected for without regard to the population as a whole. Evolution is blind, and the genetic mechanism by which it works means that the selfish advantage of initiating or continuing an arms race is overwhelming. Indeed, in a hypothetical world in which no one deceived opponents about strength, the first person who started doing so would have an advantage, and would leave more descendants to inherit the trait, so the behavior would spread. The opportunity to cheat maintains individual selfishness, regardless of increased risk to the population as a whole.[32] Positive illusions are thought to have had a positive effect, on average, over our evolutionary history, but they increase risk-taking behavior and therefore also increase the likelihood of conflict.

This global malady from individual advantage has a parallel in the so-called security dilemma in international relations. States must arm to defend themselves because there is no overarching authority to protect them, but arming scares other states so that they arm too. What is the point in building up armaments to enhance security if your adversary just does the same? The buildup increases fear in the rival, increases the danger of accidents, increases the chance of war, increases the devastation if war does occur, and, ultimately, if the two sides' armaments match, it does not increase security anyway—hence the dilemma. (An exception may be when both sides achieve a second-strike nuclear capability—that is, when each can absorb a nuclear attack and still launch its own nuclear counterattack—in which case each can smash the other's civilization to smithereens regardless of who starts the war. In such a world of "mutually assured destruction," the security dilemma is in some ways averted. Accidents and misperceptions can still cause war, however.)

This is also a simple game-theoretical result. In many types of social dilemma games, rational players end up in a state of mutual defection (noncooperation), even if that outcome is "Pareto-inefficient"—meaning that everyone could have done better. In other words, stupid though it may seem in hindsight, defection occurs despite being costly and self-defeating. Rational actors defect from cooperative outcomes because they cannot be sure that others will behave in good faith, so they defect to avoid being exploited. Even if everyone sees and understands the costs involved, incomplete information regarding the other side's intentions means that both sides fall into the Pareto-inefficient abyss of mutual defection from which it is difficult to escape. If one sees potential threats and fails to respond to them, then one just magnifies the problem because the threat becomes greater. This has an interesting consequence: it may be better to assume that the threat is always real, so as to react appropriately to avoid danger.[33] Hence, in an anarchic international system full of states jostling to protect their own security, it may be better to err on the side of having positive illusions.

Let me quote Wrangham again here, as he sums up both the positive and the negative sides of this arms race:

> In a competitive world, those with positive illusions do well. But like nuclear weapons, which are similarly helpful to the antagonist that possesses them, they are a liability because they intensify the harm of fighting . . . Globally, these traits probably intensify the risk of fighting, and certainly increase the costs. But because the strong survive, they can only be reduced through binding agreements among all players to abandon them.[34]

5. Summary of Hypotheses and Predictions

Table A. Hypotheses and predictions of the positive illusions theory (see Chapter 2).

Hypothesis	Prediction
Main hypotheses	
Positive illusions provoke war (prime hypothesis)	Positive illusions, such as self-aggrandizing, exaggerated control over events, and overoptimism, precede and provoke war
Positive illusions increase overconfidence (explanatory hypothesis A)	Positive illusions lead to overconfidence about relative capabilities, intelligence, and likelihood of success (contingent on 6 antecedent conditions)
Overconfidence provokes war (explanatory hypothesis B)	Overconfidence sways policies toward war (contingent on 2 antecedent conditions)
Intervening phenomena	
Overestimation of own side (and allies)	Decisionmakers overestimate their own capabilities (and those of allies)
Underestimation of enemy (and allies)	Decisionmakers underestimate enemy capabilities (and those of their allies)
Neglect of intelligence	Decisionmakers do not react appropriately to intelligence
Sum of opponents' winning estimates > 1	Decisionmakers are overoptimistic about chances of success

Table B. Predicted levels of positive illusions as a function of six antecedent conditions (see Chapter 2).

Antecedent condition	Expected level of positive illusions		Prediction
	Low	High	
Verifiability	High verifiability	Low verifiability	Positive illusions decline with proximity to verifiable assessments
Generality	Specific level	General/abstract level	Positive illusions decline from more abstract long-term plans to more day-to-day plans on the battlefield
Feedback	End of period	Beginning of period	Positive illusions decline as feedback builds up or approaches
Ambiguity	Clear qualities	Ambiguous qualities	Positive illusions decline from strategic assessment of ambiguous things (enemy intentions, resolve, third-party responses) to tactical assessments of material things (troops, tanks, etc.)
Stage of task	When deliberating	When planning or implementing	Positive illusions increase from deliberating a task to implementing that task
Level of threat	No danger	Danger	Positive illusions increase in threatening circumstances

Table C. Predicted levels of overconfidence as a function of two antecedent conditions: regime type and openness of debate (see Chapter 2).

Hypothesis	Prediction
More democratic regimes are more likely to identify and reduce overconfidence	Overconfidence is reduced in more democratic regimes (high public, media, parliamentary, civil service, and cabinet scrutiny of policy)
More open debate is more likely to identify and reduce overconfidence	Overconfidence is reduced when debate is more inclusive (open and nonpartisan) and expansive (considering many options and viewpoints)

Notes

1. War and Illusions

1. P. Pizarro, *Relation of the Discovery and Conquest of the Kingdoms of Peru* (New York: Cortes Society, 1921); C. R. Markham, *Reports of the Discovery of Peru* (London: Printed for the Hakluyt Society, 1872); J. Diamond, *Guns, Germs and Steel* (London: Vintage, 1998), ch. 3. The Spaniards had only a single cannon, and only twelve guns (even these were early harquebuses, which were difficult to load and fire).

2. S. David, *Military Blunders: The How and Why of Military Failure* (London: Robinson, 1997), 236–251.

3. B. Thomas, *How Israel Was Won: A Concise History of the Arab-Israeli Conflict* (Lanham, Md.: Lexington, 1999), 199. Robert E. Denney, *The Civil War Years: A Day-by-Day Account of the Life of a Nation* (New York: Sterling, 1992); G. Regan, *Someone Had Blundered: A Historical Survey of Military Incompetence* (London: B. T. Batsford, 1987).

4. L. LeShan, *The Psychology of War: Comprehending Its Mystique and Its Madness* (New York: Helios, 2002), 117.

5. G. A. Blainey, *The Causes of War* (New York: Free Press, 1973), 35. R. Jervis, "War and Misperception," *Journal of Interdisciplinary History* 18 (1988): 676. A. Vagts, *Defense and Diplomacy: The Soldier and the Conduct of Foreign Relations* (New York: Kings Crown Press, 1956), 284. S. Van Evera, *Causes of War: Power and the Roots of Conflict* (Ithaca: Cornell University Press, 1999), 16. N. Dixon, *On the Psychology of Military Incompetence* (London: Jonathan Cape, 1976), 45. S. Ganguly, *Conflict Unending: India-Pakistan Tensions since 1947* (New Delhi: Oxford University Press, 2001).

6. R. S. McNamara, *In Retrospect: The Tragedy and Lessons of Vietnam* (New York: Vintage, 1996); L. W. Grau and M. A. Gress, eds., *The Soviet-Afghan War: How a Superpower Fought and Lost*, vol. 3: *The Russian General Staff* (Lawrence: University Press of Kansas, 2002); N. West, *The Secret War for the Falklands: The S.A.S., M.I.6, and the War Whitehall Nearly Lost* (London: Warner, 1997); M. Bowden, *Black Hawk Down* (London: Corgi, 1999); A. Roberts, "NATO's Humanitarian War over Kosovo" *Survival* 41 (1999): 102–123; K. J. Alter, "Is 'Groupthink' Driving Us to War?" *Boston Globe*, 16 Sept. 2002.

7. M. A. Lorell, C. Kelley, and D. R. Hensler, "Casualties, Public Opinion, and Presidential Policy during the Vietnam War," RAND publication R-3060-AF, 1984. R. N. Lebow, *Between Peace and War: The Nature of International Crisis* (Baltimore: Johns Hopkins University Press, 1981), 242. J. G. Stoessinger, *Why Nations Go to War* (New York: St. Martin's, 1998), 211. H. L. Abrams, "Disabled Leaders, Cognition and Crisis Decision Making," *Canadian Papers in Peace Studies* (1990): 136.

8. R. K. Betts, "Must War Find a Way? A Review Essay," *International Security* 24 (1999): 172. D. Lindley, "Is War Rational? The Extent of Miscalculation and Misperception as Causes of War," paper presented at American Political Science Association Conference, 2003. K. Wang and J. L. Ray, "Beginners and

Winners: The Fate of Initiators of Interstate Wars Involving Great Powers since 1495," *International Studies Quarterly* 38 (1994): 139–154. B. B. de Mesquita, *The War Trap* (New Haven: Yale University Press, 1981).

9. Even knowingly weaker sides may choose to fight, for various reasons such as being cornered, defending against attack, and attempting to gain concessions. As Robert Jervis puts it, "a country could rationally go to war even though it was certain it would lose." Jervis, "War and Misperception," 677. Blainey, *Causes of War,* 293. B. L. Slantchev, "The Principle of Convergence in War-time Negotiations," *American Political Science Review* 97 (2003): 621–632.

10. J. D. Fearon, "Rationalist Explanations for War," *International Organization* 49 (1995): 379–414. Betts, "Must War Find a Way," 172.

11. B. Tuchman, *The March of Folly: From Troy to Vietnam* (New York: Knopf, 1984).

12. S. E. Taylor, *Positive Illusions: Creative Self-Deception and the Healthy Mind* (New York: Basic Books, 1989); L. Tiger, *Optimism: The Biology of Hope* (New York: Simon and Schuster, 1979). R. Wrangham, "Is Military Incompetence Adaptive?" *Evolution and Human Behavior* 20 (1999): 3–17.

13. S. E. Miller, S. M. Lynn-Jones, and S. Van Evera, eds., *Military Strategy and the Origins of the First World War* (Princeton: Princeton University Press, 1991), xvi.

14. J. E. Gillham, ed., *The Science of Optimism and Hope: Research Essays in Honor of Martin E. P. Seligman* (Radnor, Pa.: Templeton Foundation, 2000). Tiger, *Optimism.* A. G. Greenwald, "The Totalitarian Ego: Fabrication and Revision of Personal History," *American Psychologist* 35 (1980): 603–618; N. D. Weinstein, "Unrealistic Optimism about Future Life Events," *Journal of Personality and Social Psychology* 39 (1980): 806–820. C. Peterson, "The Future of Optimism," *American Psychologist* 55 (2000): 45.

15. S. E. Taylor and J. D. Brown, "Positive Illusions and Well-Being Revisited: Separating Fact from Fiction," *Psychological Bulletin* 116 (1994): 22, 23. S. E. Taylor and D. A. Armor, "Positive Illusions and Coping with Adversity," *Journal of Personality* 64 (1996): 873–898; S. E. Taylor and J. D. Brown, "Illusion and Well-Being: A Social Psychological Perspective on Mental Health," *Psychological Bulletin* 103 (1988): 193–210.

16. A. Tversky and D. Kahneman, "Judgment under Uncertainty: Heuristics and Biases," *Science* 185 (1974): 1124–31. S. E. Taylor et al., "Maintaining Positive Illusions in the Face of Negative Information: Getting the Facts without Letting Them Get to You," *Journal of Social and Clinical Psychology* 8 (1989): 117; I. L. Janis, *Victims of Groupthink: A Psychological Study of Foreign-Policy Decisions and Fiascoes* (Boston: Houghton Mifflin, 1972). J. Hughes-Wilson, *Military Intelligence Blunders* (New York: Carroll and Graf, 1999), 41; Peterson, "Future of Optimism." Not all cognitive and motivational biases lead to positive illusions at all times. For example, cognitive dissonance or anchoring can lead to overly positive thinking at some times, but overly negative thinking at other times.

17. Tversky and Kahneman, "Judgment under Uncertainty"; H. Simon, "Human Nature in Politics: The Dialogue of Psychology with Political Science," *American Political Science Review* 79 (1985): 293–304; J. H. Barkow, L.

Cosmides, and J. Tooby, eds., *The Adapted Mind: Evolutionary Psychology and the Generation of Culture* (Oxford: Oxford University Press, 1992).

18. J. Henrich et al., "In Search of *Homo Economicus:* Behavioral Experiments in 15 Small-Scale Societies," *American Economic Review* 91 (2001): 73–78. J. A. Rosati, "The Power of Human Cognition in the Study of World Politics," *International Studies Review* 2, no. 3 (2000): 45–75. S. P. Rosen, *War and Human Nature* (Princeton: Princeton University Press, 2004).

19. R. L. Trivers, "The Elements of a Scientific Theory of Self-Deception," *Annals of the New York Academy of Sciences* 907 (2000): 114–131; R. L. Trivers, *Social Evolution* (Menlo Park, Calif.: Benjamin Cummings, 1985). F. B. de Waal, *Good Natured: The Origins of Right and Wrong in Humans and Other Animals* (Cambridge, Mass.: Harvard University Press, 1996); A. P. Møller and J. P. Swaddle, "Social Control of Deception among Status Signaling House Sparrows *Passer Domesticus,*" *Behavioral Ecology and Sociobiology* 20 (1987): 307–311.

20. R. H. Frank, *Passions within Reason: The Strategic Role of the Emotions* (New York: Norton, 1988); G. Gigerenzer and K. Hug, "Domain-Specific Reasoning: Social Contracts, Cheating, and Perspective Change," *Cognition* 43 (1992): 127–171; M. Ridley, *The Origins of Virtue: Human Instincts and the Origins of Cooperation* (London: Penguin, 1996); C. F. Keating and K. R. Heltman, "Dominance and Deception in Children and Adults: Are Leaders the Best Misleaders?" *Personality and Social Psychology Bulletin* 20 (1994): 312–321; C. F. Keating, "Charismatic Faces: Social Status Cues Put Face Appeal in Context," in *Facial Attractiveness: Evolutionary, Cognitive, and Social Perspectives,* ed. G. Rhodes and L. A. Zebrowitz (Westport, Conn.: Ablex, 2002), 153–192.

21. This is an important distinction because humans have been shown to exhibit a number of psychological biases that appear to be simply errors of calculation rather than adaptive heuristics. See Wrangham, "Is Military Incompetence Adaptive?"

22. C. R. Gur and H. A. Sackheim, "Self-Deception: A Concept in Search of a Phenomenon," *Journal of Personality and Social Psychology* 37 (1979): 147–169; R. J. Sternberg and J. Kolligan, eds., *Competence Considered* (New Haven: Yale University Press, 1990). Taylor and Brown, "Illusion and Well-Being," 199.

23. R. F. Baumeister, "The Optimal Margin of Illusion," *Journal of Social and Clinical Psychology* 8 (1989): 184. R. H. Frank, *Choosing the Right Pond: Human Behaviour and the Quest for Status* (Oxford: Oxford University Press, 1985), 31. National Institute of Mental Health, *Basic Behavioral Science for Mental Health,* NIH pub. no. 95–3682 (Washington: Government Printing Office, 1995), 182.

24. Wrangham, "Is Military Incompetence Adaptive?" S. Taylor, personal communication; Taylor and Brown, "Positive Illusions and Well-Being Revisited," 28. L. H. Keeley, *War before Civilization: The Myth of the Peaceful Savage* (Oxford: Oxford University Press, 1996); S. LeBlanc and K. E. Register, *Constant Battles: The Myth of the Peaceful, Noble Savage* (New York: St. Martin's, 2003).

25. R. Wrangham and D. Peterson, *Demonic Males: Apes and the Origins of Human Violence* (London: Bloomsbury, 1996). Keeley, *War before Civilization,* 93, 196–197. Wrangham, "Is Military Incompetence Adaptive," 6.

26. Wrangham, "Is Military Incompetence Adaptive," 4.

27. Peterson, "Future of Optimism," 47. S. E. Taylor and P. M. Gollwitzer, "The Effects of Mindset on Positive Illusions," *Journal of Personality and Social Psychology* 69 (1995): 224; B. S. Lambeth, "Why Submariners Should Talk to Fighter Pilots," RAND Paper RP-864 (2000), 41.

28. Wrangham, "Is Military Incompetence Adaptive," 13, 14. And see D. D. P. Johnson, R. W. Wrangham, and S. P. Rosen, "Is Military Incompetence Adaptive? An Empirical Test with Risk-Taking Behavior in Modern Warfare," *Evolution and Human Behavior* 23 (2002): 245–264. Although the positive illusions hypothesis implies that it is advantageous to bluff an opponent into thinking one is stronger than one actually is, complacency is a potential danger if perceived superiority leads to letting down one's guard; again there is clearly some optimal balance between the two extremes. Sometimes the opposite strategy—duping one's enemy into overconfidence by acting weak—may be useful. But if one is trying to avoid conflict, or trying to force concessions without resorting to violence, it is usually advantageous to bluff strength—this is the basis of deterrence theory. R. Jervis, "Deterrence and Perception," *International Security* 7 (1983).

29. R. Jervis, *Perception and Misperception in International Politics* (Princeton: Princeton University Press, 1976); D. D. P. Johnson and D. R. Tierney, "Essence of Victory: Winning and Losing International Crises," *Security Studies* (in press); T. C. Schelling, *The Strategy of Conflict* (Cambridge, Mass.: Harvard University Press, 1960).

30. A. J. P. Taylor, *The War Lords* (London: Penguin, 1977). K. M. Pollack, "Spies, Lies, and Weapons: What Went Wrong," *Atlantic Monthly* (Jan./Feb. 2004): 79–92.

31. J. M. Dabbs, "Testosterone and the Concept of Dominance," *Behavioral and Brain Sciences* 21 (1998): 370.

32. Wrangham, "Is Military Incompetence Adaptive," 12. C. von Clausewitz, *On War* (1832; Princeton: Princeton University Press, 1976), 190.

33. L. Gelb and R. K. Betts, *The Irony of Vietnam: The System Worked* (Washington: Brookings, 1980), 321.

34. A. J. R. Mack, "Why Big Nations Lose Small Wars: The Politics of Asymmetric Conflict," *World Politics* 27 (1975): 175–200; R. Gabriel, *Military Incompetence: Why the American Military Doesn't Win* (New York: Noonday Press, 1986). A. Arreguín-Toft, "How the Weak Win Wars: A Theory of Asymmetric Conflict," *International Security* 26 (2001): 93–128.

35. G. J. Church, "Lessons from a Lost War," *Time*, 15 Apr. 1985, 40; M. L. Pribbenow, *Victory in Vietnam: The Official History of the People's Army of Vietnam* (Lawrence: Kansas University Press, 2002). J. Garofano, "Deciding on Military Intervention: What Is the Role of Senior Military Leaders?" *Naval War College Review* 53 (2000): 13.

36. Taylor, *Positive Illusions;* Taylor and Armor, "Positive Illusions and Coping with Adversity"; J. E. Starek and C. F. Keating, "Self-Deception and Its Relationship to Success in Competition," *Basic and Applied Social Psychology* 12 (1991): 145–155; S. S. Wright, "Looking at the Self in a Rose-Colored Mirror: Unrealistically Positive Self-Views and Academic Performance," *Journal of Social and Clinical Psychology* 19 (2000): 451–462; T. Mannarelli, "Motiva-

tion, Individuation, and Positive Illusions of Creative Musicians," manuscript; M. K. Surbey and J. J. McNally, "Self-Deception as a Mediator of Cooperation and Defection in Varying Social Contexts Described in the Iterated Prisoner's Dilemma," *Evolution and Human Behavior* 18 (1997): 417–435; S. L. Murray, J. G. Holmes, and D. W. Griffin, "The Benefits of Positive Illusions: Idealization and the Construction of Satisfaction in Close Relationships," *Journal of Personality and Social Psychology* 70 (1996): 79–98; S. L. Murray, J. G. Holmes, and D. W. Griffin, "The Self-Fulfilling Nature of Positive Illusions in Romantic Relationships: Love Is Not Blind, but Prescient," *Journal of Personality and Social Psychology* 71 (1996): 1155–80.

37. Taylor et al., "Maintaining Positive Illusions," 126.

38. R. W. Robins and J. S. Beer, "Positive Illusions about the Self: Short-Term Benefits and Long-Term Costs," *Journal of Personality and Social Psychology* 80 (2001): 341. D. J. Goleman, "What Is Negative about Positive Illusions? When Benefits for the Individual Harm the Collective," *Journal of Social and Clinical Psychology* 8 (1989): 190, 191.

39. Baumeister, "Optimal Margin of Illusion," 177, 181.

40. N. Tinbergen, "On War and Peace in Animals and Man: An Ethologist's Approach to the Biology of Aggression," *Science* 160 (1968): 1411–18.

41. I am grateful to Leif Edward Ottesen Kennair for raising this point.

42. Lebow, *Between Peace and War*, 243.

43. See the studies cited in Taylor, *Positive Illusions*, and in M. H. Bazerman et al., "Negotiation," *Annual Review of Psychology* 51 (2000): 279–314.

44. M. T. Gabriel, J. W. Critelli, and J. S. Ee, "Narcissistic Illusions in Self-Evaluations of Intelligence and Attractiveness," *Journal of Personality* 62 (1994): 143–155; D. M. Messick et al., "Why We Are Fairer Than Others," *Journal of Experimental Social Psychology* 21 (1985): 480–500; O. Svenson, "Are We All Less Risky and More Skillful Than Our Fellow Drivers?" *Acta Psychologica* 47 (1981): 143–148.

45. R. Baumhart, *An Honest Profit* (New York: Prentice-Hall, 1968); L. Larwood, "Swine Flu: A Field Study of Self-Serving Biases," *Journal of Applied Social Psychology* 18 (1978): 283–289; N. D. Weinstein, "Unrealistic Optimism about Susceptibility to Health Problems," *Journal of Behavioral Medicine* 5 (1982): 441–460; L. Larwood and W. Whittaker, "Managerial Myopia: Self-Serving Biases in Organizational Planning," *Journal of Applied Psychology* 62 (1977): 194–198.

46. Weinstein, "Unrealistic Optimism about Future Life Events"; F. W. Irwin, "Stated Expectations as Functions of Probability and Desirability of Outcomes," *Journal of Personality* 21 (1953): 329–335; L. S. Perloff, "Social Comparison and Illusions of Invulnerability to Negative Life Events," in *Coping with Negative Life Events: Clinical and Social Psychological Perspectives*, ed. C. Snyder and C. Ford (New York: Plenum, 1987), 217–242. P. Cross, "Not Can but Will College Teaching Be Improved," *New Directions for Higher Education* 17 (1977): 1–15.

47. C. Snyder, "The 'Illusion' of Uniqueness," *Journal of Humanistic Psychology* 18 (1978): 33–41; L. Robertson, "Car Crashes: Perceived Vulnerability and Willingness to Pay for Crash Protection," *Journal of Community Health* 3 (1977): 136–141; L. S. Perloff and B. Fetzer, "Self-Other Judgments and Perceived

Vulnerability to Victimization," *Journal of Personality and Social Psychology* 50 (1986): 502–510; J. Burger and M. Palmer, "Changes in and Generalization of Unrealistic Optimism Following Experiences with Stressful Events: Reactions to the 1989 California Earthquake," *Personality and Social Psychology Bulletin* 18 (1992): 39–43; N. Kuiper, M. MacDonald, and P. Derry, "Parameters of a Depressive Self-Schema," in *Psychological Perspectives on the Self*, ed. J. Suls and A. Greenwald (Hillsdale, N.J.: Erlbaum, 1983); J. Burger and L. Burns, "The Illusion of Unique Invulnerability and the Use of Effective Contraception," *Personality and Social Psychology Bulletin* 14 (1988): 264–270.

48. Taylor and Brown, "Positive Illusions and Well-Being Revisited," 26.

49. E. J. Langer, "The Illusion of Control," *Journal of Personality and Social Psychology* 32 (1975): 311–328; J. Crocker, "Biased Questions in Judgment of Covariation Studies," *Personality and Social Psychology Bulletin* 8 (1982): 214–220; R. M. Kramer, "The Sinister Attribution Error: Paranoid Cognition and Collective Distrust in Organizations," *Motivation and Emotion* 18 (1994): 199–230; D. T. Miller and M. Ross, "Self-Serving Biases in the Attribution of Causality: Fact or Fiction?" *Psychological Bulletin* 82 (1975): 213–215; M. W. Morris, D. L. H. Sim, and V. Girotto, "Distinguishing Sources of Cooperation in the One-Round Prisoner's Dilemma: Evidence for Cooperative Decisions Based on the Illusion of Control," *Journal of Experimental Social Psychology* 34 (1998): 494–512; E. Shafir and A. Tversky, "Thinking through Uncertainty: Nonconsequential Reasoning and Choice," *Cognitive Psychology* 24 (1992): 449–474.

50. R. M. Kramer, E. Newton, and P. L. Pommerenke, "Self-Enhancement Biases and Negotiator Judgment: Effects of Self-Esteem and Mood," *Organizational Behavior and Human Decision Processing* 56 (1993): 110–133; Bazerman et al., "Negotiation"; R. G. Lim, "Overconfidence in Negotiation Revisited," *International Journal of Conflict Management* 8 (1997): 52–79. Kramer, "Sinister Attribution Error."

51. C. K. W. De Dreu, A. Nauta, and E. van de Vliert, "Self-Serving Evaluations of Conflict Behavior and Escalation of the Dispute," *Journal of Applied Social Psychology* 25 (1995): 2049–66. Jervis, "Deterrence and Perception," 20.

52. Taylor and Brown, "Positive Illusions and Well-Being Revisited," 27. Recent studies have further corroborated the positive illusions perspective by directly testing the theory against two alternatives; see S. E. Taylor et al., "Portrait of the Self-Enhancer: Well Adjusted and Well Liked or Maladjusted and Friendless," *Personality Processes and Individual Differences* 84 (2003): 165–176.

53. Taylor, *Positive Illusions*.

54. College Board survey, 1976–1977, cited in D. Dunning, J. A. Meyerowitz, and A. D. Holzberg, "Ambiguity and Self-Evaluation: The Role of Idiosyncratic Trait Definitions in Self-Serving Assessments of Ability," *Journal of Personality and Social Psychology* 57 (1989): 1082–90.

55. Y. Klar and E. E. Giladi, "No One in My Group Can Be Below the Group's Average: A Robust Positivity Bias in Favor of Anonymous Peers," *Journal of Personality and Social Psychology* 73 (1997): 885–901; J. D. Brown, "Evaluations of Self and Others: Self-Enhancement Biases in Social Judgments," *Social Cognition* 4 (1986): 353–376; D. W. Griffin, D. Dunning, and L. Ross, "The Role

of Construal Processes in Overconfident Predictions about the Self and Others," *Journal of Personality and Social Psychology* 59 (1990): 1128–39; Langer, "Illusion of Control." Wrangham, "Is Military Incompetence Adaptive"; D. L. Hamilton and T. K. Trolier, "Stereotypes and Stereotyping: An Overview of the Cognitive Approach," in *Prejudice, Discrimination, and Racism*, ed. J. R. Dovidio and S. L. Gaertner (Orlando, Fla.: Academic Press, 1986), 127–163; D. Druckman, "Nationalism, Patriotism and Group Loyalty: A Social Psychological Perspective," *Mershon International Studies Review* (Apr. 1994): 43–68. Y. Klar, "Way beyond Compare: Nonselective Superiority and Inferiority Biases in Judging Randomly Assigned Group Members Relative to Their Peers," *Journal of Experimental Social Psychology* 38 (2002): 331–351; Goleman, "What Is Negative about Positive Illusions," 194.

56. H. Tajfel, "Social Identity and Intergroup Behavior," *Social Science Information* 13 (1974): 65–93; J. C. Turner, "A Self-Categorization Theory," in *Rediscovering the Social Group*, ed. Turner et al. (Oxford: Basil Blackwell, 1987). M. Cinnirella, "A Social Identity Perspective on European Integration," in *Changing European Identities*, ed. G. M. Breakwell and E. Lyons (Oxford: Butterworth Heinemann, 1996), 253–254.

57. R. J. Robinson and D. Keltner, "Defending the Status Quo: Power and Bias in Social Conflict," *Personality and Social Psychology Bulletin* 23 (1997): 1066–77.

58. R. F. Baumeister and J. M. Boden, "Aggression and the Self: High Self-Esteem, Low Self-Control, and Ego Threat," in *Human Aggression*, ed. R. G. Geen and E. Donnerstein (San Diego: Academic Press, 1998), 115, 116. D. Chirot, *Modern Tyrants: The Power and Prevalence of Evil in Our Age* (New York: Free Press, 1994). J. M. Rabbie, "Group Processes as Stimulants of Aggression," in *Aggression and War*, ed. J. Groebel and R. A. Hinde (Cambridge: Cambridge University Press, 1989), 141–155.

59. Janis, *Victims of Groupthink*; Alter, "Is 'Groupthink' Driving Us to War?"; Goleman, "What Is Negative about Positive Illusions," 194. Paul t'Hart notes that while groupthink can indeed spawn overoptimism when a decision is seen as a potential opportunity, if the decision is already seen as very risky, groupthink may result in collective avoidance. So it may not have a systematic influence on war. t'Hart, *Groupthink in Government: A Study of Small Groups and Policy Failure* (Amsterdam: Swets and Zeitlinger, 1990). Stereotyping an enemy as evil seems very prevalent. This was, for example, Dean Acheson's view in negotiating with the Soviets during the Cuban missile crisis. See G. Allison and P. Zelikow, *Essence of Decision: Explaining the Cuban Missile Crisis* (New York: Longman, 1999). One is also inclined to think of Reagan's "Evil Empire" and G. W. Bush's "Axis of Evil," though these were apparently designed largely for propaganda purposes.

60. V. D. Volkan, "The Need to Have Enemies and Allies: A Developmental Approach," *Political Psychology* 6 (1985): 219. N. C. Meier, *Military Psychology* (New York: Harper, 1943), 9.

61. Wrangham, "Is Military Incompetence Adaptive"; S. Van Evera, "Hypotheses on Nationalism and War," *International Security* 18 (1998): 27; Dixon, *Psychology of Military Incompetence*.

62. LeShan, *Psychology of War*, 110, 111. L. Van Boven, D. Dunning, and G.

Loewenstein, "Egocentric Empathy Gaps between Owners and Buyers: Misperceptions of the Endowment Effect," *Journal of Personality and Social Psychology* 79 (2000): 66–76.

63. R. Shenkman, *Presidential Ambition: Gaining Power at Any Cost* (New York: HarperCollins, 1999), 122, xii, 338.

64. A. Ehrenhalt, *The United States of Ambition: Politicians, Power and the Pursuit of Office* (New York: Times Books, 1992), xviii, xx, 254.

65. Clausewitz, *On War*, 192. Taylor, *Positive Illusions*; A. M. Ludwig, *King of the Mountain: The Nature of Political Leadership* (Lexington: University of Kentucky Press, 2002).

66. Tuchman, *March of Folly*, 286. Baumeister, "Optimal Margin of Illusion," 186.

67. See, e.g., P. E. Tetlock, "Social Psychology and World Politics," in *Handbook of Social Psychology*, ed. D. Gilbert, S. Fiske, and G. Lindzey (New York: McGraw Hill, 1998), 868–912; J. S. Levy, "Loss Aversion, Framing Effects and International Conflict," in *Handbook of War Studies 2*, ed. M. I. Midlarsky (Ann Arbor: University of Michigan Press, 2000), 193–221.

68. Fearon, "Rationalist Explanations for War," 380.

69. Ibid., 395. His two other conditions for war within the rationalist framework are "commitment problems," in which a state cannot convince another of how it will behave in the future, and "indivisible issues," in which the object of contention cannot be divided between rival factions. See also R. A. Hinde, "Aggression and War: Individuals, Groups and States," in *Behavior, Society and International Conflict*, ed. P. E. Tetlock, J. L. Husbands, and R. Jervis (Oxford: Oxford University Press, 1993).

70. The rational choice approach has some drawbacks. Even rational actors may not arrive at the same conclusions from the same information. To illustrate this point, Jonathan Kirshner notes that over three years of American football games, six neutral experts disagreed on who would win 74 percent of the time. As Kirshner points out, such disagreement is much *more* likely in predicting something as complex as the outcomes of war. John Garofano similarly argues that "symmetry or asymmetry in available information may be irrelevant for leaderships who understand that strategy, mobilization, organizational effectiveness, the introduction of new technologies, and other factors may decisively affect the outcome of certain kinds of war. The greater the unknowns in war, and the more adaptable the governments, the less meaningful is hard information." J. D. Kirshner, "Rationalist Explanations for War?" *Security Studies* 10 (2000): 143–150. J. Garofano, "Tragedy or Choice in Vietnam? Learning to Think Outside the Archival Box," *International Security* 26 (2002): 166.

71. D. Kahneman, P. Slovic, and A. Tversky, *Judgment under Uncertainty: Heuristics and Biases* (Cambridge: Cambridge University Press, 1982); Simon, "Human Nature in Politics"; J. H. Kagel and A. E. Roth, eds., *The Handbook of Experimental Economics* (Princeton: Princeton University Press, 1995).

72. Frank, *Passions within Reason*; A. R. Damasio, *Descartes' Error: Emotion, Reason and the Human Brain* (New York: Avon, 1994); T. Burnham and J. Phelan, *Mean Genes: From Sex to Money to Food, Taming Our Primal Instincts* (New York: Penguin, 2001). Barkow et al., *Adapted Mind*.

73. Allison and Zelikow, *Essence of Decision*; LeShan, *Psychology of War*; Rose

McDermott, *Political Psychology in International Relations* (Ann Arbor: University of Michigan Press, 2004); Rosen, *War and Human Nature.*

74. K. N. Waltz, *Theory of International Politics* (New York: McGraw-Hill, 1979); J. J. Mearsheimer, *The Tragedy of Great Power Politics* (New York: Norton, 2001). Mearsheimer argues that states worry only about others' capabilities, not their intentions. Since the latter are unknowable, states always have to assume the worst.

75. These four aspects may be perceived as exaggerated for all competitors, as well as for oneself. Perceived easy conquest, for example, may generate an undue fear of attack, as well as undue expectation of an easy victory. However, even if a state exaggerates the ease of conquest for everyone, if it chooses war to escape vulnerability it must be especially optimistic, since the war will be even more difficult against an enemy that can exploit the same advantages. This is supported by history: modern great powers have been defeated only twice by unprovoked aggressors, but six times by provoked aggressors. Five of the six losers initiated war on the basis of "fantasy-driven defensive bellicosity." Van Evera, *Causes of War,* 192.

76. Ibid., 19.

77. Lebow, *Between Peace and War,* 242.

78. Ibid., 244–246. G. Martel, *The Origins of the First World War* (Harlow: Longman, 1987), 58–59. Fearon, "Rationalist Explanations for War," 399.

79. Ganguly, *Conflict Unending,* 7.

80. M. Hastings, *The Korean War* (London: M. Joseph, 1987). Lebow, *Between Peace and War,* 246. Garofano, "Deciding on Military Intervention," 9.

81. Lebow, *Between Peace and War,* 246. David, *Military Blunders,* 272, 278.

82. Hughes-Wilson, *Military Intelligence Blunders,* 257. T. N. Dupuy, *Numbers, Prediction, and War: Using History to Evaluate Combat Factors and Predict the Outcome of Battles* (New York: Bobbs-Merrill, 1985). Thomas, *How Israel Was Won,* 199.

83. Dupuy, *Numbers, Prediction, and War,* 37, 138. R. Patai, *The Arab Mind* (New York: Scribner, 1973), quoted by Dupuy, 138. Thomas, *How Israel Was Won,* 198.

2. Looking for Illusions

1. See, e.g., K. N. Waltz, *Man, the State and War: A Theoretical Analysis* (New York: Columbia University Press, 1959); H. Morgenthau, *Politics among Nations* (New York: Knopf, 1956).

2. V. S. E. Falger, "Human Nature in Modern International Relations, Part I: Theoretical Backgrounds," *Research in Biopolitics* 5 (1997): 155–175.

3. D. A. Welch, *Justice and the Genesis of War* (Cambridge: Cambridge University Press, 1993), 3. C. Peterson, "The Future of Optimism," *American Psychologist* 55 (2000): 51.

4. R. W. Robins and J. S. Beer, "Positive Illusions about the Self: Short-Term Benefits and Long-Term Costs," *Journal of Personality and Social Psychology* 80 (2001): 349.

5. Peterson, "Future of Optimism," 46. L. Tiger, *Optimism: The Biology of Hope* (New York: Simon and Schuster, 1979), 162.

6. S. E. Taylor et al., "Portrait of the Self-Enhancer: Well Adjusted and Well

Liked or Maladjusted and Friendless," *Personality Processes and Individual Differences* 84 (2003): 166, 174.

7. S. E. Taylor et al., "Maintaining Positive Illusions in the Face of Negative Information: Getting the Facts without Letting Them Get to You," *Journal of Social and Clinical Psychology* 8 (1989).

8. E. A. Cohen and J. Gooch, *Military Misfortunes: The Anatomy of Failure in War* (New York: Vintage, 1991); R. Jervis, *System Effects: Complexity in Political and Social Life* (Princeton: Princeton University Press, 1997).

9. J. Burger and M. Palmer, "Changes in and Generalization of Unrealistic Optimism Following Experiences with Stressful Events: Reactions to the 1989 California Earthquake," *Personality and Social Psychology Bulletin* 18 (1992): 39–43. People lower their optimistic estimates when exposed to the resources and strengths of others: see N. D. Weinstein and E. Lachendro, "Egocentrism as a Source of Unrealistic Optimism," *Personality and Social Psychology Bulletin* 8 (1982): 195–200.

10. Taylor et al., "Maintaining Positive Illusions," 124. J. A. Shepperd, J. A. Ouellette, and J. K. Fernandez, "Abandoning Unrealistic Optimism: Performance Estimates and the Temporal Proximity of Self-Relevant Feedback," *Journal of Personality and Social Psychology* 70 (1996): 845.

11. P. E. Tetlock, "The Impact of Accountability on Judgment and Choice: Toward a Social Contingency Model," in *Advances in Experimental Psychology*, ed. M. P. Zanna (New York: Academic Press, 1992), 331–376.

12. R. F. Baumeister and J. M. Boden, "Aggression and the Self: High Self-Esteem, Low Self-Control, and Ego Threat," in *Human Aggression*, ed. R. G. Geen and E. Donnerstein (San Diego: Academic Press, 1998), 111–137.

13. This may be either a cognitive bias due to differential availability of information, or a motivational bias. N. D. Weinstein, "Unrealistic Optimism about Future Life Events," *Journal of Personality and Social Psychology* 39 (1980): 806–820; Weinstein and Lachendro, "Egocentrism as a Source of Unrealistic Optimism."

14. D. Dunning, J. A. Meyerowitz, and A. D. Holzberg, "Ambiguity and Self-Evaluation: The Role of Idiosyncratic Trait Definitions in Self-Serving Assessments of Ability," *Journal of Personality and Social Psychology* 57 (1989): 1089.

15. For a review of this research see D. Dunning, "A Newer Look: Motivated Social Cognition and the Schematic Representation of Social Concepts," *Psychological Inquiry* 10 (1999): 1–11.

16. J. D. Kirshner, "Rationalist Explanations for War?" *Security Studies* 10 (2000): 143–150.

17. M. I. Handel, ed., *Leaders and Intelligence* (London: Frank Cass, 1989), 13.

18. S. E. Taylor and P. M. Gollwitzer, "The Effects of Mindset on Positive Illusions," *Journal of Personality and Social Psychology* 69 (1995): 223.

19. Ibid., 220.

20. Ibid., 220–221, 224. D. A. Armor and S. E. Taylor, "The Effects of Mindset on Behavior: Self-Regulation in Deliberative and Implemental Frames of Mind," *Personality and Social Psychology Bulletin* 29 (2003): 93.

21. D. J. Goleman, "What Is Negative about Positive Illusions? When Benefits for the Individual Harm the Collective," *Journal of Social and Clinical Psychology*

8 (1989): 195. R. Wrangham, "Is Military Incompetence Adaptive?" *Evolution and Human Behavior* 20 (1999): 3–17; Baumeister and Boden, "Aggression and the Self"; L. LeShan, *The Psychology of War: Comprehending Its Mystique and Its Madness* (New York: Helios, 2002).

22. Taylor et al., "Maintaining Positive Illusions," 127.

23. Overconfidence has several possible origins (see the Appendix), but positive illusions can be distinguished from other sources of overconfidence (learning, cognitive dissonance, and so on) in three ways. First, positive illusions manifest specific traits (overestimation of oneself compared to others, illusions of control over events, and overoptimistic expectations of the future). Second, the six antecedent conditions of positive illusions (described above) together form a suite of factors that other sources of overconfidence do not match. Third, positive illusions predict a *systematically positive* bias, whereas other types of misperceptions may sometimes lead to a positive bias but at other times lead to a negative bias. These features suggest that positive illusions are uniquely identifiable and may be particularly associated with war and conflict.

24. N. C. Meier, *Military Psychology* (New York: Harper, 1943).

25. See S. Kernell, *Going Public: New Strategies for Presidential Leadership* (Washington: CQ Press, 1998).

26. Handel, *Leaders and Intelligence*. P. A. Kowert, *Groupthink or Deadlock: When Do Leaders Learn from Their Advisors?* (Albany: SUNY Press, 2002), 8.

27. E. R. May, "Cabinet, Tsar, Kaiser: Three Approaches to Assessment," in *Knowing One's Enemies: Intelligence Assessment before the Two World Wars*, ed. May (Princeton: Princeton University Press, 1984), 36.

28. Crises may be biased in the same way (states normally do not get into either wars or crises). However, the theory predicts that positive illusions play a *greater* role in crises that did develop into war than in those that did not. A logical next step would be to look for an absence of positive illusions in "nonevent" data (i.e. times of peace where nothing happened). While an interesting possibility for future studies, this has methodological problems. For instance, against whom does one not have positive illusions? What time period does one study that is representative? See C. Achen and D. Snidal, "Rational Deterrence Theory and Comparative Case Studies," *World Politics* 41 (1989): 143–169.

29. For an example of this approach see D. A. Welch, *Justice and the Genesis of War* (Cambridge: Cambridge University Press, 1993). His study of wars among former great powers found, despite no expected effect, significant evidence that state behavior is influenced by the pursuit of justice by state leaders.

30. R. S. McNamara, *In Retrospect: The Tragedy and Lessons of Vietnam* (New York: Vintage, 1996), xxi.

31. Taylor and Gollwitzer, "Effects of Mindset on Positive Illusions," 213. Information is extremely difficult to evaluate. The quality and amount of information are likely to have varied among the cases, and it would be interesting to examine this directly as an additional antecedent condition influencing positive illusions (because positive illusions should be corrected faster where there is good intelligence and constant feedback than in situations where there is bad intelligence and poor information flow). However, it is difficult to come up with credible measurements of information availability, or even to generate

valid rankings among cases. It is the *perceived* rather than the *actual* information that is crucial, but this is even harder to measure. Moreover, how would one deal with changing intelligence capabilities over time? One might argue that by the time of the Cuban missile crisis and Vietnam intelligence was much better resourced than and technologically superior to that during the Munich crisis or at the outbreak of World War I. However, such factors need not change the *relative* quality of the information among cases. It was unclear to decisionmakers at Munich, for instance, exactly which states the opposing coalitions would eventually comprise in the event of war. No improvement of intelligence technology is likely to create a sea change in such fundamental uncertainties.

32. Shepperd, Ouellette, and Fernandez, "Abandoning Unrealistic Optimism," 845.

33. I. N. Gallhofer and W. E. Saris, *Foreign Policy Decision-Making: A Qualitative and Quantitative Analysis of Political Argumentation* (Westport, Conn.: Praeger, 1996); G. Allison and P. Zelikow, *Essence of Decision* (New York: Longman, 1999).

3. World War I

1. A. Mombauer, *The Origins of the First World War: Controversies and Consensus* (London: Longman, 2002).

2. G. Martel, *The Origins of the First World War* (Harlow: Longman, 1987), 85.

3. Ibid., 81. S. Van Evera, *Causes of War* (Ithaca: Cornell University Press, 1999), 19–20.

4. See Mombauer, *Origins of the First World War*, 154.

5. Martel, *Origins of the First World War*, 5.

6. S. M. Lynn-Jones, "Detente and Deterrence: Anglo-German Relations, 1911–1914," in *Military Strategy and the Origins of the First World War*, ed. S. E. Miller, S. M. Lynn-Jones, and S. Van Evera (Princeton: Princeton University Press, 1991), 165–194. Mombauer, *Origins of the First World War*, 223.

7. J. Snyder, "Civil-Military Relations and the Cult of the Offensive, 1914 and 1984," in *Military Strategy and the First World War*, ed. Miller, Lynn-Jones, and Van Evera, 20–58. Martel, *First World War*, 84.

8. Snyder, "Civil-Military Relations," 21.

9. J. Garofano, "Deciding on Military Intervention: What Is the Role of Senior Military Leaders?" *Naval War College Review* 53 (2000): 1–19. M. Howard, "Men against Fire: Expectations of War in 1914," in *Military Strategy and the First World War*, ed. Miller, Lynn-Jones, and Van Evera, 3–19.

10. Snyder, "Civil-Military Relations"; Van Evera, *Causes of War*.

11. Van Evera, *Causes of War*, 195.

12. S. Van Evera, "Offense, Defense, and the Causes of War," *International Security* 22 (1998): 5–43.

13. Van Evera, *Causes of War*, 239.

14. Mombauer, *Origins of the First World War*, 3.

15. G. A. Blainey, *The Causes of War* (New York: Free Press, 1973), 36. Van Evera, *Causes of War*, 19.

16. A. Vagts, *Defense and Diplomacy: The Soldier and the Conduct of Foreign Relations* (New York: Kings Crown Press, 1956), 307. J. Merriman, *Modern Europe:*

From the Renaissance to the Present (London: Norton, 1996), 1039. Martel, *Origins of the First World War*, 6.

17. J. K. Tanenbaum, "French Estimates of Germany's Operational War Plans," in *Knowing One's Enemies: Intelligence Assessment before the Two World Wars*, ed. E. R. May (Princeton: Princeton University Press, 1984), 169. Van Evera, *Causes of War*, 206. For more examples of overoptimism see the books by Blainey and Van Evera.

18. Blainey, *Causes of War*, 38. Tanenbaum, "French Estimates of Germany's Plans," 171. Merriman, *Modern Europe*, 1041.

19. E. A. Cohen and J. Gooch, *Military Misfortunes: The Anatomy of Failure in War* (New York: Vintage, 1991), 14. Van Evera, *Causes of War*, 197, 33–34.

20. Van Evera, *Causes of War*, 25.

21. Blainey, *Causes of War*, 39. Van Evera, *Causes of War*, 196.

22. Blainey, *Causes of War*, 37–38. Martel, *Origins of the First World War*, 90, 5. P. M. Kennedy, "Great Britain before 1914," in *Knowing One's Enemies*, ed. May, 191–192. Van Evera, *Causes of War*, 33.

23. Kennedy, "Great Britain before 1914," 194, 192. Van Evera, *Causes of War*, 197.

24. Kennedy, "Great Britain before 1914," 175.

25. Ibid., 185, 186, 188.

26. Ibid., 188, 196, 202.

27. Merriman, *Modern Europe*, 1039–45. Kennedy, "Great Britain before 1914," 204.

28. J. G. Stoessinger, *Why Nations Go to War* (New York: St. Martin's, 1998), 211. Van Evera, *Causes of War*, 19, 204.

29. Van Evera, *Causes of War*, 204.

30. Ibid., 19, 143, 222.

31. Merriman, *Modern Europe*, 1040. Martel, *Origins of the First World War*, 81, 85.

32. Blainey, *Causes of War*, 36.

33. Ibid., 37. Merriman, *Modern Europe*, 1045.

34. Blainey, *Causes of War*, 37.

35. Kennedy, "Great Britain before 1914," 199.

36. Ibid., 198, 199. Van Evera, *Causes of War*, 25.

37. S. Weintraub, *Silent Night: The Remarkable Christmas Truce of 1914* (London: Simon and Schuster, 2001), 6.

38. Van Evera, *Causes of War*, 33–34.

39. Mombauer, *Origins of the First World War*, 208–209. Mombauer notes that considerable confidence has been assigned to the theories themselves: "During the 1950s it was felt that historians moved 'on safe ground' regarding the First World War, as Walther Hubatsch asserted, just as in the 1930s George P. Gooch had been similarly confident that the riddle of the origins of the war had been solved" (224). Do historians exhibit positive illusions about their theories, in the way that 94 percent of college professors rate their work as above average? (See Chapter 1.)

40. Blainey, *Causes of War*, 41, 40.

41. Van Evera, *Causes of War*.

42. Cohen and Gooch, *Military Misfortunes*, 12, 134.

43. Ibid., 136.
44. Snyder, "Civil-Military Relations," 22. Van Evera, *Causes of War*, 196.
45. Snyder, "Civil-Military Relations," 20–21.
46. Other explanations that have been offered for the complacency in 1914 do not seem to be enough. The "short war" expectation, for example, could have arisen from the experience of recent European history in which most wars had indeed been decided very quickly. However, as Blainey argues, expectations of a short war do not explain why each side also expected to be victorious: "From the expectations which preceded more than a score of wars since 1700, a curious parallel emerges. Nations confident of victory in a forthcoming war were usually confident that victory would come quickly. Nations which entered a war reluctantly, hoping to avoid defeat rather than snatch victory, were more inclined to believe that they were embarking on a long struggle. The kinds of arguments and intuitions which encouraged leaders to expect a victorious war strongly influenced their belief that the war would also be swift. The belief in a short war was mainly the overflow from the reservoir of conscious superiority." Blainey, *Causes of War*, 41.
47. Martel, *Origins of the First World War*, 86.
48. Ibid., 87, 83. S. D. Sagan, "1914 Revisited: Allies, Offense, and Instability," in *Military Strategy and the First World War*, ed. Miller, Lynn-Jones, and Van Evera, 109–133.
49. Martel, *Origins of the First World War*, 86. Mombauer, *Origins of the First World War*, 15. Richard K. Betts, "Suicide from Fear of Death?" *Foreign Affairs*, Jan./Feb. 2003.
50. Van Evera, *Causes of War*, 137, 141.
51. E. R. May, "Cabinet, Tsar, Kaiser: Three Approaches to Assessment," in *Knowing One's Enemies*, 11–36. Martel, *Origins of the First World War*, 82. Van Evera, *Causes of War*, 138.
52. May, "Cabinet, Tsar, Kaiser," 32.
53. Cohen and Gooch, *Military Misfortunes*, 13.
54. Blainey, *Causes of War*, 39. Van Evera, *Causes of War*, 228.
55. Kennedy, "Great Britain before 1914," 203.
56. Y. Klar, D. Zakay, and K. Sharvit, "'If I Don't Get Blown Up . . .': Realism in Face of Terrorism in an Israeli Nationwide Sample," *Risk, Decision and Policy* 7 (2002): 203–219. These authors also note that "optimism is mainly found when people believe that avoiding the negative consequences of the risk is within their powers" (18).
57. Stoessinger, *Why Nations Go to War*, xii. A. G. Greenwald, "The Totalitarian Ego: Fabrication and Revision of Personal History," *American Psychologist* 35 (1980): 603–618. Merriman, *Modern Europe*, 1045.

4. The Munich Crisis

1. M. Brecher, J. Wilkenfield, and S. Moser, *Crises in the Twentieth Century* (Oxford: Pergamon, 1988), 165–167.
2. C. Andrew, "Churchill and Intelligence," in *Leaders and Intelligence*, ed. M. I. Handel (London: Frank Cass, 1989), 190. A. J. P. Taylor, *The War Lords* (London: Penguin, 1977), 45.

3. R. Jervis, "War and Misperception," *Journal of Interdisciplinary History* 18 (1988): 685–686.

4. Andrew, "Churchill and Intelligence," 185; P. Neville, *Winston Churchill: Statesman or Opportunist?* (London: Hodder and Stoughton, 1996). G. H. Snyder and P. Diesing, *Conflict among Nations: Bargaining, Decision-Making, and System Structures in International Crises* (Princeton: Princeton University Press, 1977), 551. J. L. Richardson, *Crisis Diplomacy: The Great Powers since the Mid-Nineteenth Century* (Cambridge: Cambridge University Press, 1994), 137.

5. Richardson, *Crisis Diplomacy*, 153.

6. D. Dutton, *Neville Chamberlain* (London: Arnold, 2001), 22.

7. Neville, *Churchill*, 12. Chamberlain died a month after leaving office in 1940, so we do not have a detailed record of his perceptions of what happened, nor did he have a chance to defend his actions for history. As Churchill once said, history is kind to those who write it.

8. Keynes, letter to W. W. Stewart, 14 Nov. 1937, in D. Moggridge, ed., *The Collected Writings of John Maynard Keynes*, vol. 21: *Activities 1931–1939* (Cambridge: Cambridge University Press, 1982), 428.

9. Neville, *Churchill*, 85. Richardson, *Crisis Diplomacy*, 153, 149.

10. R. Jervis, "Deterrence and Perception," *International Security* 7 (1983): 14, 15. Richardson, *Crisis Diplomacy*, 153.

11. Jervis, "Deterrence and Perception," 17.

12. Snyder and Diesing, *Conflict among Nations*, 552. Dutton, *Neville Chamberlain*, 23.

13. Richardson, *Crisis Diplomacy*, 136, 153.

14. J. J. Mearsheimer, *The Tragedy of Great Power Politics* (New York: Norton, 2001), 165. S. G. Walker and M. Schafer, "The Contributions of Operational Code Analysis to Foreign Policy Theory: Beliefs as Causal Mechanisms," in *Advances in Foreign Policy Analysis*, ed. A. Mintz (New York: Palgrave, in press). Neville, *Churchill*, 84. If stalling for time was an objective, it was a misguided one, according to Mearsheimer, because "the balance shifted against the Allies after Munich: they probably would have been better off going to war against Germany in 1938 over Czechoslovakia rather than over Poland in 1939."

15. D. Jablonsky, "The Paradox of Duality: Adolf Hitler and the Concept of Military Surprise," in *Leaders and Intelligence*, ed. Handel, 73; H. C. Deutsch, "Commanding Generals and the Uses of Intelligence," ibid., 194–260; Z. Shore, *What Hitler Knew: The Battle for Information in Nazi Foreign Policy* (Oxford: Oxford University Press, 2002).

16. Brecher, Wilkenfield, and Moser, *Crises in the Twentieth Century*, 164.

17. I. N. Gallhofer and W. E. Saris, *Foreign Policy Decision-Making: A Qualitative and Quantitative Analysis of Political Argumentation* (Westport, Conn.: Praeger, 1996), 74, 75.

18. W. S. Churchill, *The Second World War*, vol. 1: *The Gathering Storm* (London: Cassell, 1948), 302. Mussolini "was deluded and led himself astray by the shows he put on. As he looked at these masses of marching troops shown to him on the screen, he really believed that Italy had an army of five million. The actual figure was not much more than a million when it came to the point. The five million was a phrase he had once used; he used it so often, it

got into his own head. In exactly the same way, he came to believe that Italy had the most powerful navy in the Mediterranean." Taylor, *War Lords*, 21.

19. Jablonsky, "Paradox of Duality," 100, 101. Hitler's tactic of deception was the reverse of certain views held in Britain, where some leaders thought it would be better to *avoid* building up armaments in order to mask the number they potentially *could* have, leaving the opponent to guess what formidable armies might be raised against them should they choose to attack. See Jervis, "Deterrence and Perception," 6.

20. A. J. P. Taylor, *The Origins of the Second World War* (London: Penguin, 1964), 97.

21. Keynes, interview with the *New Statesman*, 28 Jan. 1939, in *Collected Writings*, vol. 21, 498, 499.

22. Richardson, *Crisis Diplomacy*, 153. Walker and Schafer, "Contributions of Operational Code Analysis."

23. J. Merriman, *Modern Europe: From the Renaissance to the Present* (London: Norton, 1996), 1236. Walker and Schafer, "Contributions of Operational Code Analysis," manuscript, 18. E. Fröhlich, ed., *Die Tagebücher Von Joseph Goebbels, Teil I. Aufzeichnungen 1923–1941. Band 7, Juli 1939–März 1940* (Munich: K. G. Saur, 1998), 87.

24. Dutton, *Neville Chamberlain*, 12.

25. Richardson, *Crisis Diplomacy*, 152.

26. D. A. Welch, *Justice and the Genesis of War* (Cambridge: Cambridge University Press, 1993), 130. Richardson, *Crisis Diplomacy*, 154.

27. Richardson, *Crisis Diplomacy*, 135.

28. Ibid., 267–271. Those three were the Crimean War crisis (1853–1854), the Russo-Japanese crisis (1903–1904), and, not least, the crisis of 1938.

29. Jablonsky, "Paradox of Duality," 57. Originally from General Franz Halder's diaries, I, 14 Aug. 1939, 6, 8.

30. E. R. May, *Strange Victory: Hitler's Conquest of France* (New York: Hill and Wang, 2000); M. L. B. Bloch, *Strange Defeat: A Statement of Evidence Written in 1940* (New York: Oxford University Press, 1949). Churchill, *Second World War*, vol. 1, 300.

31. Churchill, *Second World War*, vol. 1, 320; the description is from 3 Sept. 1939. Jablonsky, "Paradox of Duality," 67.

32. Handel, *Leaders and Intelligence*, 22. Jablonsky, "Paradox of Duality," 75, 73; Shore, *What Hitler Knew*.

33. Jablonsky, "Paradox of Duality," 75. Taylor, *War Lords*.

34. Jablonsky, "Paradox of Duality," 72, 77.

35. Ibid., 74. Handel, *Leaders and Intelligence*, 21–22.

36. Welch, *Justice and the Genesis of War*, 130.

37. Jablonsky, "Paradox of Duality," 61. Jervis, "Deterrence and Perception," 7. Taylor, *War Lords*, 46, 49. Gallhofer and Saris, *Foreign Policy Decision-Making*, 77.

38. Jablonsky, "Paradox of Duality," 61, 77.

39. Ibid., 101.

40. Ibid., 94, 92–95.

41. D. Rooney, *Military Mavericks: Extraordinary Men of Battle* (London: Cassell 1999), 124. Jablonsky, "Paradox of Duality," 66.

42. R. Hingley, *Russia: A Concise History* (London: Thames and Hudson, 1991). Jablonsky, "Paradox of Duality," 111, n161. J. G. Stoessinger, *Why Nations Go to War* (New York: St. Martin's, 1998), xii. Taylor, *War Lords*, 53, 54.

43. Stoessinger, *Why Nations Go to War*, 210; A. Beevor, *Stalingrad* (London: Penguin, 1998); see also Jablonsky, "Paradox of Duality," 95. Taylor, *War Lords*, 53.

44. Jablonsky, "Paradox of Duality," 78.

5. The Cuban Missile Crisis

1. G. Allison and P. Zelikow, *Essence of Decision: Explaining the Cuban Missile Crisis* (New York: Longman, 1999), 79.

2. L. Freedman, *Kennedy's Wars: Berlin, Cuba, Laos, Vietnam* (Oxford: Oxford University Press, 2000), 216; P. Nash, *The Other Missiles of October: Eisenhower, Kennedy and the Jupiters, 1957–1963* (Chapel Hill: University of North Carolina Press, 1997).

3. R. N. Lebow, "Domestic Politics and the Cuban Missile Crisis," *Diplomatic History* 14 (1990): 482, 481. D. C. Copeland, *The Origins of Major War* (Ithaca: Cornell University Press, 2000), 190.

4. Lebow, "Domestic Politics." S. M. Stern, *Averting the Final Failure: John F. Kennedy and the Secret Cuban Missile Crisis Meetings* (Stanford: Stanford University Press, 2003), 24.

5. Lebow, "Domestic Politics"; Allison and Zelikow, *Essence of Decision*. The bargaining-chip thesis can be defended by invoking the fact that the Soviets did, in the end, gain a U.S. non-invasion pledge toward Cuba (and the removal of missiles in Turkey). But this had not been expected. Extending the crisis to try and extract these concessions massively increased the risk of a U.S. invasion of Cuba, rather than ensuring the opposite. Even if using the missiles as a bargaining chip was an aim of Khrushchev's, therefore, it was not the principal aim, so achieving permanent missile bases was a crucial condition of the project's utility.

6. Lebow, "Domestic Politics," 487.

7. Ibid., 481, 490, 480. E. R. May and P. D. Zelikow, *The Kennedy Tapes: Inside the White House during the Cuban Missile Crisis* (Cambridge, Mass.: Harvard University Press, 1996), 668; see also A. Fursenko and T. Naftali, *One Hell of a Gamble: Khrushchev, Castro, and Kennedy, 1958–1964* (New York: Norton, 1997).

8. S. Van Evera, *Causes of War* (Ithaca: Cornell University Press, 1999), 135. B. Greiner, "The Cuban Missile Crisis Reconsidered: The Soviet View: An Interview with Sergo Mikoyan," *Diplomatic History* 14 (1990): 213. Mikoyan worked as a foreign ministry official and political secretary to his father, Anastas Mikoyan, who was first deputy prime minister and second only to Khrushchev.

9. J. Hughes-Wilson, *Military Intelligence Blunders* (New York: Carroll and Graf, 1999). D. B. Bobrow, "Stories Remembered and Forgotten," *Journal of Conflict Resolution* 33 (1989): 197–198.

10. Greiner, "Interview with Sergo Mikoyan." Allison and Zelikow, *Essence of Decision*.

11. A number of disadvantages were put forward by different members of

ExComm. I. N. Gallhofer and W. E. Saris, *Foreign Policy Decision-Making: A Qualitative and Quantitative Analysis of Political Argumentation* (Westport, Conn.: Praeger, 1996); May and Zelikow, *Kennedy Tapes.*

12. Bobrow, "Stories Remembered and Forgotten," 197–198. Allison and Zelikow, *Essence of Decision,* 353–354. The authority to fire SAMs had been delegated to Soviet field commanders; see ibid.; Greiner, "Interview with Sergo Mikoyan."

13. Gallhofer and Saris, *Foreign Policy Decision-Making,* 96. S. J. Thorson and D. A. Sylvan, "Counterfactuals and the Cuban Missile Crisis," *International Studies Quarterly* 26 (1982): 540.

14. Lebow, "Domestic Politics," 477. J. G. Blight, J. S. Nye, and D. A. Welch, "The Cuban Missile Crisis Revisited," *Foreign Affairs* (1987): 177.

15. Copeland, *Origins of Major War,* 189. Gallhofer and Saris, *Foreign Policy Decision-Making,* 82. Blight, Nye, and Welch, "Cuban Missile Crisis Revisited," 175.

16. Allison and Zelikow, *Essence of Decision,* 227. May and Zelikow, *Kennedy Tapes,* 133.

17. G. Allison, A. Carnesale, and J. S. Nye, eds., *Hawks, Doves and Owls: An Agenda for Avoiding Nuclear War* (New York: Norton, 1986). Gallhofer and Saris, *Foreign Policy Decision-Making,* 86.

18. Thorson and Sylvan, "Counterfactuals and the Cuban Missile Crisis," 539.

19. P. M. Gollwitzer and R. Kinney, "Effects of Deliberative and Implemental Mind-Sets on the Illusion of Control," *Journal of Personality and Social Psychology* 56 (1989): 531–542. R. N. Lebow, *Between Peace and War: The Nature of International Crisis* (Baltimore: Johns Hopkins University Press, 1981). G. A. Blainey, *The Causes of War* (New York: Free Press, 1973), 39.

20. When the U-2 entered Soviet airspace on 27 October, Soviet fighters were scrambled. U.S. fighters were also scrambled to escort the U-2 home. As a standard procedure under the by-then-high level of security alert, the U.S. jets were armed with nuclear-tipped air-to-air missiles. It was later that same day that Soviet antiaircraft missile crews in Cuba shot down a U-2, nearly triggering an automatic retaliatory strike by the U.S. air force. Allison and Zelikow, *Essence of Decision.*

21. Lebow, *Between Peace and War,* 302–303.

22. Bobrow, "Stories Remembered and Forgotten." T. C. Sorensen, *Kennedy* (New York: Harper and Row, 1965). Although it may be possible to reduce positive illusions in initial deliberations, they may naturally resurface *during* war on account of their psychological function to increase and aid performance in times of stress and threat.

23. May and Zelikow, *Kennedy Tapes.*

24. I. L. Janis, *Victims of Groupthink: A Psychological Study of Foreign-Policy Decisions and Fiascoes* (Boston: Houghton Mifflin, 1972). D. D. P. Johnson and D. R. Tierney, "Essence of Victory: Winning and Losing International Crises," *Security Studies* (in press). R. Kennedy, *Thirteen Days* (New York: Norton, 1969), 128.

25. W. Poundstone, *Prisoner's Dilemma: John Von Neumann, Game Theory and the Puzzle of the Bomb* (Oxford: Oxford University Press, 1992), 209. Khrushchev

may not have known that the United States was planning to scrap those missiles anyway, but the idea that they might represent a tolerable U.S. concession was not new and had been widely discussed.

26. Other possible originators of the suggestion include the Soviet defense minister, Rodion Y. Malinovsky, and Bertrand Russell. Ibid., ch. 10.

27. P. Zelikow, "American Policy and Cuba, 1961–63," *Diplomatic History* 24 (2000): 333.

28. C. Schmidt, "Preference, Beliefs, Knowledge and Crisis in the International Decision-Making Process: A Theoretical Approach through Qualitative Games," in *Game Theory and International Relations: Preferences, Information and Empirical Evidence*, ed. P. Allan and C. Schmidt (Aldershot, UK: Edward Elgar, 1994), 97–122.

29. Freedman, *Kennedy's Wars*, 197.

30. Bobrow, "Stories Remembered and Forgotten," 194; Lebow, "Domestic Politics," 482–483.

31. May and Zelikow, *Kennedy Tapes*, 107. R. Jervis, "Deterrence and Perception," *International Security* 7 (1983): 28.

32. B. J. Bernstein, "The Week We Almost Went to War," *Bulletin of Atomic Scientists* 32 (1976): 20. Bobrow, "Stories Remembered and Forgotten," 194. This was originally argued by Lebow in "Domestic Politics."

33. Address to the United Nations, 25 Sept. 1961.

6. Vietnam

1. D. Ellsberg, "The Quagmire Myth and the Stalemate Machine," *Public Policy* (Spring 1971): 217–274. E. R. May, *Lessons of the Past: The Use and Misuse of History in American Foreign Policy* (Oxford: Oxford University Press, 1973), ch. 4.

2. D. Kaiser, *American Tragedy: Kennedy, Johnson, and the Origins of the Vietnam War* (Cambridge, Mass.: Harvard University Press, 2000); F. Logevall, *Choosing War: The Lost Chance for Peace and the Escalation of War in Vietnam* (Berkeley: University of California Press, 1999). B. Tuchman, *The March of Folly: From Troy to Vietnam* (New York: Knopf, 1984), 274, 283.

3. Ellsberg quoted in I. L. Janis, *Victims of Groupthink: A Psychological Study of Foreign-Policy Decisions and Fiascoes* (Boston: Houghton Mifflin, 1972), 107–109. L. Gelb and R. K. Betts, *The Irony of Vietnam: The System Worked* (Washington: Brookings, 1980), 2–3, 299; my italics.

4. U.S. Department of Defense, *The Pentagon Papers: The Defense Department History of United States Decisionmaking on Vietnam* (Boston: Beacon Press, 1971), Senator Gravel ed., vol. 2, 664. May, *Lessons of the Past*.

5. May, *Lessons of the Past*, 101, 103–104. Gelb and Betts, *Irony of Vietnam*, 70.

6. *Pentagon Papers*, vol. 3, 695. R. S. McNamara, *In Retrospect: The Tragedy and Lessons of Vietnam* (New York: Vintage, 1996), 191.

7. May, *Lessons of the Past*, 99. J. Garofano, "Tragedy or Choice in Vietnam? Learning to Think outside the Archival Box," *International Security* 26 (2002): 165. Tuchman, *March of Folly*, 318–319

8. Garofano, "Tragedy or Choice," 165. Tuchman, *March of Folly*, 297. Gallup Polls.

9. Garofano, "Tragedy or Choice," 143–168.

10. J. G. Stoessinger, *Why Nations Go to War* (New York: St. Martin's, 1998).
11. *Pentagon Papers*, vol. 1, 89. J. Garofano, "Deciding on Military Intervention: What Is the Role of Senior Military Leaders?" *Naval War College Review* 53 (2000): 14.
12. *Pentagon Papers*, vol. 1, 215. They added, however, that if "political considerations are overriding" they would "agree to the assignment."
13. Tuchman, *March of Folly*, 274. *Pentagon Papers*, vol. 1, 226.
14. P. A. Kowert, *Groupthink or Deadlock: When Do Leaders Learn from Their Advisors?* (Albany: SUNY Press, 2002); J. P. Burke and F. I. Greenstein, "Presidential Personality and National Security Leadership: A Comparative Analysis of Vietnam Decisionmaking," *International Political Science Review* 10 (1989): 73–92. Tuchman, *March of Folly*, 268.
15. Tuchman, *March of Folly*, 280. The study was conducted by Michigan State University between 1955 and 1962 and directed by Wesley Fishel.
16. Ibid., 283, 294.
17. W. C. Gibbons, *The United States Government and the Vietnam War: Executive and Legislative Roles and Relationships* (Princeton: Princeton University Press, 1986), vol. 2, 45, 58, 127.
18. Tuchman, *March of Folly*, 295, citing *Pentagon Papers*, vol. 2, 90.
19. *Pentagon Papers*, vol. 2, 79. Garofano, "Tragedy or Choice," 156.
20. Tuchman, *March of Folly*, 302, 303.
21. May, *Lessons of the Past*, 94, 95. *Pentagon Papers*, vol. 2, 105, 113. Tuchman, *March of Folly*, 296–297.
22. Tuchman, *March of Folly*, 287.
23. Gibbons, *The U.S. Government and the Vietnam War*, vol. 3, 173; vol. 2, 134. Tuchman, *March of Folly*, 301, 302. K. O'Donnell, D. F. Powers, and J. McCarthy, *Johnny We Hardly Knew Ye: Memories of John Fitzgerald Kennedy* (New York: Pocket Books, 1973), 15.
24. *Pentagon Papers*, vol. 2, 243. Gibbons, *The U.S. Government and the Vietnam War*, vol. 2, 58.
25. Tuchman, *March of Folly*, 286. Garofano, "Tragedy or Choice," 161. R. N. Lebow, "Domestic Politics and the Cuban Missile Crisis," *Diplomatic History* 14 (1990): 488. Kaiser, *American Tragedy*, 8.
26. Tuchman, *March of Folly*, 296, 285, 297. Stoessinger, *Why Nations Go to War*, 93.
27. Gibbons, *The U.S. Government and the Vietnam War*, vol. 2, 38, report to National Security Council, 11 May 1961. Stoessinger, *Why Nations Go to War*, 93. *Pentagon Papers*, vol. 3, 625.
28. Stoessinger, *Why Nations Go to War*, 93. Tuchman, *March of Folly*, 300, 301. Galbraith's advice had not always been consistent; he had argued at one point in 1961 that they should even consider replacing Diem with a military government, after which the war could be won relatively quickly and easily. See Gelb and Betts, *Irony of Vietnam*, 87.
29. D. Halberstam, *The Best and the Brightest* (New York: Penguin, 1972), 345. Stoessinger, *Why Nations Go to War*, 94.
30. Quotations from May, *Lessons of the Past*, 102. Logevall, *Choosing War*.
31. May, *Lessons of the Past*, 103. Tuchman, *March of Folly*, 319, 321. *Pentagon Papers*, vol. 3, 217.

32. Garofano, "Tragedy or Choice," 157. See also D. M. Barret, *Uncertain Warriors: Lyndon Johnson and His Vietnam Advisers* (Lawrence: University Press of Kansas, 1993); D. C. Humphrey, "Tuesday Lunch at the Johnson White House: A Preliminary Assessment," *Diplomatic History* 8 (1984): 81–101.

33. T. L. Cubbage, "Westmoreland vs. CBS: Was Intelligence Corrupted by Policy Demands?" in *Leaders and Intelligence*, ed. M. I. Handel (London: Frank Cass, 1989), 123. J. Hughes-Wilson, *Military Intelligence Blunders* (New York: Carroll and Graf, 1999), 187. Gelb and Betts, *Irony of Vietnam*, 299. Tuchman, *March of Folly*, 330. Though "if 'winning' meant demonstrating to the Viet-Cong that they could not win, a lesser force would be enough." *Pentagon Papers*, vol. 4, 290–292.

34. Handel, *Leaders and Intelligence*, 9, 19. Note that, in contrast, "when a military commander misuses intelligence, he sees the results immediately: troops may be defeated or he may suffer visible losses in terms of soldiers' lives, lost equipment or terrain" (19).

35. Tuchman, *March of Folly*, 317. De Gaulle's proposal is in *Pentagon Papers*, vol. 2, 193.

36. May, *Lessons of the Past*, 104.

37. Garofano, "Deciding on Military Intervention," 11. *Pentagon Papers*, vol. 3, 419.

38. Tuchman, *March of Folly*, 329. Logevall, *Choosing War.*

39. Hughes-Wilson, *Military Intelligence Blunders*, 191. Cubbage, "Westmoreland vs. CBS," 142. The final quotation is from the CBS television program proposal, ibid., 138.

40. R. Adler, *Reckless Disregard: Westmoreland v. CBS et al., Sharon v. Time* (New York: Knopf, 1986); Cubbage, "Westmoreland vs. CBS," 147. As Cubbage documents, there were indeed some indications of political pressure to cap enemy force estimates; see "Westmoreland vs. CBS," 118–180. However, Cubbage also reports that Johnson's national security advisor, Walt Rostow, told an interviewer that "he, and through him President Johnson, had been aware of the debate between MACV and the CIA concerning whether the numbers . . . had been underestimated by MACV. He said that neither he nor Johnson was aware of any MACV effort to put a ceiling on the enemy strength or to deceive the White House about the enemy." Rostow confirmed this in a letter to the *New York Times* on 7 Feb. 1982: "Johnson was fully aware of the Viet Cong Order of Battle Debate." Ibid., 139, 143. Maxwell Taylor wrote in the *Washington Post* that he had been aware as well. In any case, intelligence estimates were not limited to these channels; for example, the NSA also provided independent information.

41. Cubbage, "Westmoreland vs. CBS," 131, 135.

42. Ibid., 147, 124.

43. Halberstam, *Best and Brightest*, viii. Janis, *Victims of Groupthink*, 121.

44. R. A. Pape, *Bombing to Win: Air Power and Coercion in War* (Ithaca: Cornell University Press, 1996), 180. May, *Lessons of the Past*, 126.

45. Stoessinger, *Why Nations Go to War*, 95. Kowert, *Groupthink or Deadlock*, 160.

46. Janis, *Victims of Groupthink*, 106–107, 120.

47. C. L. Cooper, *The Lost Crusade: America in Vietnam* (New York: Dodd, Mead,

1970), 424. Cubbage, "Westmoreland vs. CBS," 148. Tuchman, *March of Folly*, 313, 321, 319.

48. Pape, *Bombing to Win*, 192. Original hearings: U.S. Congress, Senate Committee on Armed Services, Preparedness Investigating Subcommittee, *Air War against North Vietnam*, 90th Cong., 1st sess., pt. 2 (16 Aug. 1967), 194. Tuchman, *March of Folly*, 337. *Pentagon Papers*, vol. 4, Final Report, 3 Jan. 1968.

49. *Pentagon Papers*, vol. 4, 224–225.

50. Cubbage, "Westmoreland vs. CBS," 147. Tuchman, *March of Folly*, 338, 345.

51. Halberstam, *Best and Brightest*, ix. Hughes-Wilson, *Military Intelligence Blunders*, 216. Tuchman, *March of Folly*, 347.

52. Tuchman, *March of Folly*, 349. G. H. Hess, *Vietnam and the United States: Origins and Legacy of War* (Boston: Twayne, 1990), 177. Stoessinger, *Why Nations Go to War*, 100. H. F. Graff, *The Tuesday Cabinet: Deliberation and Decision on Peace and War under Lyndon B. Johnson* (Englewood Cliffs, N.J.: Prentice-Hall, 1970), 73.

53. State of the Union address, 12 Jan. 1966. Tuchman, *March of Folly*, 339, 334.

54. Stoessinger, *Why Nations Go to War*, 86. Pape, *Bombing to Win*; A. Arreguín-Toft, "How the Weak Win Wars: A Theory of Asymmetric Conflict," *International Security* 26 (2001): 93–128.

55. Pape, *Bombing to Win*, 174.

56. R. Nixon, *No More Vietnams* (New York: Arbor House, 1985), York, 104. D. Fromkin and J. Chase, "What *Are* the Lessons of Vietnam?" *Foreign Affairs* 63 (1985): 725.

57. Rusk, interview on ABC TV, 3 Apr. 1975, cited in Stoessinger, *Why Nations Go to War*, 106.

58. M. L. Pribbenow, *Victory in Vietnam: The Official History of the People's Army of Vietnam* (Lawrence: Kansas University Press, 2002).

59. G. J. Church, "Lessons from a Lost War," *Time*, 15 Apr. 1985, 40. Tuchman, *March of Folly*, 343. *Pentagon Papers*, vol. 4, 224.

60. Cubbage, "Westmoreland vs. CBS," 119. S. Karnow, *Vietnam: A History* (New York: Penguin, 1984), 544. Handel, *Leaders and Intelligence*, 27.

61. Hughes-Wilson, *Military Intelligence Blunders*, 177.

62. Ibid., 172–173. H. A. Kissinger, *White House Years* (Boston: Little, Brown, 1979), 1175.

63. May, *Lessons of the Past*, ch. 4.

64. One might counter this claim with the argument that U.S. decisionmakers were fighting and escalating to attain better bargaining chips in a negotiated solution. But even if this is accurate, at the very least they must have believed that increased military action would improve the situation in their favor—otherwise they would not have expected to gain bargaining chips.

65. *Pentagon Papers*, vol. 2, 193. Garofano, "Tragedy or Choice," 156. Stoessinger, *Why Nations Go to War*, 211.

66. Tuchman, *March of Folly*, 314.

67. Z. Maoz, *Paradoxes of War: On the Art of National Self-Entrapment* (London: Unwin Hyman, 1990), 289; Stoessinger, *Why Nations Go to War*, 106. Ford tried to get $300 million in emergency military aid. See T. C. Jespersen, "The Bitter End and the Lost Chance in Vietnam: Congress, the Ford Administra-

tion, and the Battle over Vietnam, 1975–1976," *Diplomatic History* 24 (2000): 269.

68. Logevall, *Choosing War,* 347. Kaiser, *American Tragedy,* 5, 391.

69. Gelb and Betts, *Irony of Vietnam.* Logevall, *Choosing War,* xvii; Kaiser, *American Tragedy.* Tuchman, *March of Folly.*

70. Richard Betts, personal communication.

71. C. D. Walton, *The Myth of Inevitable U.S. Defeat in Vietnam* (London: Frank Cass, 2002); L. Sorley, *A Better War: The Unexamined Victories and Final Tragedy of America's Last Years in Vietnam* (New York: Harcourt, 1999). J. Race, "Vietnam Intervention: Systematic Distortion in Policy Making," *Armed Forces and Society* (1976): 377–396. Garofano, "Tragedy or Choice," 148.

72. Tuchman, *March of Folly,* 319.

73. Garofano, "Tragedy or Choice," 146. Garofano, "Deciding on Military Intervention," 12. Kaiser, *American Tragedy,* 6. Janis, *Victims of Groupthink,* 105. Janis thought this meant that "they shared a staunch faith that somehow everything would come out right, despite all the gloomy predictions in the intelligence reports prepared by their underlings."

74. Janis, *Victims of Groupthink,* 106, 121.

75. Tuchman, *March of Folly,* 256. J. L. Gaddis and M. Bradley, *Imagining Vietnam and America: The Making of Postcolonial Vietnam, 1919–1950* (Chapel Hill: University of North Carolina Press, 2000). Gibbons, *The U.S. Government and the Vietnam War,* vol. 2, 388, Report of 6 Jan. 1965.

76. May, *Lessons of the Past,* 120. Kaiser, *American Tragedy,* 386. McNamara quoted in Halberstam, *Best and Brightest,* 55.

77. Pape, *Bombing to Win,* 210. The Schelling strategy is to gradually increase the punishment inflicted on infrastructure targets, aiming to coerce the enemy to negotiate; the Douhet strategy is to bomb the civilian population to induce an antigovernment revolt or concessions.

78. Some—notably military—sources claim that the United States could have succeeded in Vietnam. They argue that U.S. victory was prevented by political restrictions on the military—that unrestricted bombing, invasion of the North, and a blockade of Haiphong harbor would have won the war. It has even been suggested that the blatant signals that the U.S. would *not* take these steps were a major mistake, which let the North Vietnamese know they could continue fighting in the South while being largely untouchable in the North (apart from the bombing). See Hess, *Vietnam and the United States,* 174; Sorley, *A Better War.*

79. Garofano, "Deciding on Military Intervention," 12. Kaiser, *American Tragedy,* 6. Stoessinger, *Why Nations Go to War,* 99. Cubbage, "Westmoreland vs. CBS," 27.

80. Garofano, "Tragedy or Choice," 165. Hess, *Vietnam and the United States,* 174. A. J. R. Mack, "Why Big Nations Lose Small Wars: The Politics of Asymmetric Conflict," *World Politics* 27 (1975): 175–200; Arreguín-Toft, "How the Weak Win Wars." Pape, *Bombing to Win,* 195. May, *Lessons of the Past,* 127.

81. *Pentagon Papers,* vol. 3, 23. Handel, *Leaders and Intelligence,* 25.

82. R. Jervis, "Deterrence and Perception," *International Security* 7 (1983): 21, 24.

83. Handel, *Leaders and Intelligence.* Hughes-Wilson, *Military Intelligence Blunders,* 194, 186.

84. Tuchman, *March of Folly*, 308, my italics.

85. *Pentagon Papers*, vol. 2, 241.

86. Kaiser, *American Tragedy*, 4.

87. May, *Lessons of the Past*, 115. Ellsberg quoted in Fromkin and Chase, "What *Are* the Lessons of Vietnam," 725.

88. Gelb and Betts, *Irony of Vietnam*, 321, 3.

89. Richard Betts, personal communication.

90. Logevall, *Choosing War;* Tuchman, *March of Folly;* see also Kaiser, *American Tragedy.* Garofano, "Tragedy or Choice," 153, 146. S. E. Taylor and P. M. Gollwitzer, "The Effects of Mindset on Positive Illusions," *Journal of Personality and Social Psychology* 69 (1995): 220.

91. Stoessinger, *Why Nations Go to War,* xii.

7. Vanity Dies Hard

1. R. N. Lebow, *Between Peace and War: The Nature of International Crisis* (Baltimore: Johns Hopkins University Press, 1981), 332.

2. M. L. Pribbenow, *Victory in Vietnam: The Official History of the People's Army of Vietnam* (Lawrence: Kansas University Press, 2002).

3. S. E. Taylor and P. M. Gollwitzer, "The Effects of Mindset on Positive Illusions," *Journal of Personality and Social Psychology* 69 (1995): 213–226; P. M. Gollwitzer and R. Kinney, "Effects of Deliberative and Implemental Mind-Sets on the Illusion of Control," *Journal of Personality and Social Psychology* 56 (1989): 531–542.

4. T. Taylor, *The Breaking Wave* (New York: Simon and Schuster, 1967), 298.

5. B. Tuchman, *The March of Folly: From Troy to Vietnam* (New York: Knopf, 1984), 338–339.

6. S. Ganguly, *Conflict Unending: India-Pakistan Tensions since 1947* (New Delhi: Oxford University Press, 2001).

7. D. Reiter and A. C. Stam, *Democracies at War* (Princeton: Princeton University Press, 2002); W. Reed and D. H. Clark, "War Initiators and War Winners: The Consequences of Linking Theories of Democratic War Success," *Journal of Conflict Resolution* 44 (2000): 378–395.

8. R. Gabriel, *Military Incompetence: Why the American Military Doesn't Win* (New York: Noonday Press, 1986); A. Arreguín-Toft, "How the Weak Win Wars: A Theory of Asymmetric Conflict," *International Security* 26 (2001): 93–128. V. D. Hanson, *Carnage and Culture: Landmark Battles in the Rise of Western Power* (New York: Anchor, 2001), 439.

9. J. Garofano, "Tragedy or Choice in Vietnam? Learning to Think outside the Archival Box," *International Security* 26 (2002): 143–168. David Kaiser, *American Tragedy: Kennedy, Johnson, and the Origins of the Vietnam War* (Cambridge, Mass.: Harvard University Press, 2000). J. A. Nathan, "The Missile Crisis: His Finest Hour Now," *World Politics* 27 (1975): 280–281.

10. P. A. Kowert, *Groupthink or Deadlock: When Do Leaders Learn from Their Advisors?* (Albany: SUNY Press, 2002), 164. T. Hoopes, *The Limits of Intervention* (New York: McKay, 1969). In 1986 the U.S. Congress passed the Goldwater-Nichols Department of Defense Reorganization Act, intended "to remove the reputed civilian filter represented by the secretary of defense and to prevent

the suppression of dissenting opinions." While this may have helped, it is not thought to have solved the problem entirely—the selection and education of the military service chiefs and Joint Chiefs of Staff chairman remains politically motivated. J. Garofano, "Deciding on Military Intervention: What Is the Role of Senior Military Leaders?" *Naval War College Review* 53 (2000): 8, 16.

11. Tuchman, *March of Folly*, 334. Defense contractors also had an important influence (there were three hundred lobbyists funded by the Pentagon on Capitol Hill), and the military wooed legislators' support with a series of VIP events. Moreover, as Tuchman notes, at that time 25 percent of members of Congress were reserve army officers.

12. Garofano, "Tragedy or Choice," 168. M. I. Handel, ed., *Leaders and Intelligence* (London: Frank Cass, 1989), 32–33.

13. C. von Clausewitz, *On War* (1832; Princeton: Princeton University Press, 1976), 85, 191.

14. G. H. Hess, *Vietnam and the United States: Origins and Legacy of War* (Boston: Twayne, 1990), 177.

15. D. Kahneman and A. Tversky, "Prospect Theory: An Analysis of Decisions under Risk," *Econometrica* 47 (1979): 263–291; M. L. Haas, "Prospect Theory and the Cuban Missile Crisis," *International Studies Quarterly* (2001): 241–270; J. S. Levy, "Loss Aversion, Framing Effects and International Conflict," in *Handbook of War Studies* 2, ed. M. I. Midlarsky (Ann Arbor: University of Michigan Press, 2000), 193–221; A. S. Levi and G. Whyte, "A Cross-Cultural Exploration of the Reference Dependence of Crucial Group Decisions under Risk," *Journal of Conflict Resolution* 41 (1997): 792–813. R. Jervis, "Understanding the Bush Doctrine," *Political Science Quarterly* 118, no. 3 (2003): 383. Rose McDermott, *Risk-Taking in International Politics: Prospect Theory in American Foreign Policy* (Ann Arbor: University of Michigan Press, 1998).

16. R. Jervis, "War and Misperception," *Journal of Interdisciplinary History* 18 (1988): 700.

17. See R. Jervis, "The Confrontation between Iraq and the U.S.: Implications for the Theory and Practice of Deterrence," *European Journal of International Relations* 9, no. 2 (2003): 315–337. J. J. Mearsheimer and S. M. Walt, "An Unnecessary War," in *The Iraq War Reader: History, Documents, Opinions*, ed. M. L. Sifry and C. Cerf (New York: Touchstone, 2003), 414–424.

18. H. Morgenthau, *Politics among Nations* (New York: Knopf, 1956). B. A. Thayer, "Bringing in Darwin: Evolutionary Theory, Realism, and International Politics," *International Security* 25 (2000): 125. K. N. Waltz, *Theory of International Politics* (New York: McGraw-Hill, 1979).

19. V. S. E. Falger, "Human Nature in Modern International Relations, Part I: Theoretical Backgrounds," *Research in Biopolitics* 5 (1997): 171.

20. J. Mercer, "Anarchy and Identity," *International Organization* 49 (1995): 242. See S. E. Taylor, *Positive Illusions: Creative Self-Deception and the Healthy Mind* (New York: Basic Books, 1989).

21. D. Lindley, "Is War Rational? The Extent of Miscalculation and Misperception as Causes of War," paper presented at American Political Science Association Conference, 2003.

22. R. N. Lebow, "Domestic Politics and the Cuban Missile Crisis," *Diplomatic History* 14 (1990): 491–492.

8. Iraq, 2003

1. M. R. Sarkees, F. W. Wayman, and J. D. Singer, "Inter-State, Intra-State, and Extra-State Wars: A Comprehensive Look at Their Distribution over Time, 1816–1997" *International Studies Quarterly* 47 (2003): 49.

2. J. J. Mearsheimer and S. M. Walt, "An Unnecessary War," in *The Iraq War Reader: History, Documents, Opinions*, ed. M. L. Sifry and C. Cerf (New York: Touchstone, 2003), 423.

3. D. H. Rumsfeld, "Testimony on Iraq (Transcript): Testimony as Delivered by Secretary of Defense Donald H. Rumsfeld," Senate Armed Services Committee, Washington, 9 July 2003. Mearsheimer and Walt, "An Unnecessary War."

4. R. M. Entman, *Projections of Power: Framing News, Public Opinion, and U.S. Foreign Policy* (Chicago: University of Chicago Press, 2004); J. Fallows, "Blind into Baghdad," *Atlantic* (Jan./Feb. 2004): 74.

5. J. M. Marshall, "Remaking the World: Bush and the Conservatives," *Foreign Affairs* (Nov./Dec. 2003): 142.

6. N. Gibbs and M. Ware, "Chasing a Mirage," *Time*, 6 Oct. 2003.

7. The Taliban leaders' ruinous defiance of Western coalitions in the 2002 Afghanistan war suggests a similar overconfidence that, somehow, American-led forces would fail to oust them.

8. L. Freedman, "The Dictator's Strategy: Delay to Survive," *Times* (London), 30 Mar. 2003.

9. Frederick W. Kagan, Interview, PBS, 29 Jan. 2004. Thomas E. Ricks, Interview, PBS, 28 Jan. 2004. Lt.-General Raad Al-Hamdani, Interview, PBS, Undated, 2004.

10. K. M. Pollack, "Spies, Lies, and Weapons: What Went Wrong," *Atlantic Monthly* (Jan./Feb. 2004): 85.

11. See examples in Fallows, "Blind into Baghdad"; *The Iraq War Reader*, ed. Sifry and Cerf; and W. D. Nordhaus, S. E. Miller, C. Kaysen, et al., "War with Iraq: Costs, Consequences, and Alternatives," *American Academy of Arts and Sciences Committee on International Security Studies (CISS)*, 2002.

12. C. Krauthammer, "Plan B for Baghdad," *Washington Post*, 4 Apr. 2003.

13. R. Jervis, "The Confrontation between Iraq and the U.S.: Implications for the Theory and Practice of Deterrence," *European Journal of International Relations* 9 (2003): 326.

14. R. Jervis, "Understanding the Bush Doctrine," *Political Science Quarterly* 118, no. 3 (2003): 366, 367. S. Zizek, "Iraq's False Promises," *Foreign Policy* 140 (Jan./Feb. 2004): 42–49.

15. D. E. Sanger, "A Stalwart of Certainty: Bush Undeterred on Iraq," *New York Times*, 3 Mar. 2003. Ricks, Interview, 28 Jan. 2004.

16. Pollack, "Spies, Lies, and Weapons"; L. Fisher, "Deciding on War against Iraq: Institutional Failures," *Political Science Quarterly* 118 (2003): 389–410. M. Elliott, "So, What Went Wrong?" *Time*, 6 Oct. 2003, 33. Jervis, "Understanding the Bush Doctrine," 371. Ricks, Interview, 28 Jan. 2004.

17. E. Schmitt, "Rumsfeld Says U.S. Has 'Bulletproof' Evidence of Iraq's Links to Al Qaeda," *New York Times,* 28 Sept. 2002.

18. Pollack, "Spies, Lies, and Weapons," 88, 90.

19. D. Dunning, J. A. Meyerowitz, and A. D. Holzberg, "Ambiguity and Self-Evaluation: The Role of Idiosyncratic Trait Definitions in Self-Serving Assessments of Ability," *Journal of Personality and Social Psychology* 57 (1989): 1082–90. Kagan, Interview, 29 Jan. 2004.

20. Fallows, "Blind into Baghdad," 58.

21. Kagan, Interview, 29 Jan. 2004. Senate Armed Services Committee, 25 Feb. 2003, "On the Posture of the United States Army."

22. Ricks, Interview, 28 Jan. 2004. Fallows, "Blind into Baghdad," 73. In Afghanistan, as in Iraq, the policy of deploying smaller forces had been successful in achieving a military victory but may have had negative repercussions in the long term. First, the United States had relied on local warlords to bear the brunt of the fighting, and these factions gained power from the war. Second, the Taliban were not entirely eradicated and still posed a significant danger to the new state. Third, security in general remained poor. Fourth, and perhaps most significant given the motive for that war, the use of smaller U.S. forces "may also have contributed to Osama bin Laden's escape by leaving the early searching to poorly equipped Afghan militias and Pakistani border forces with no strong motivation to succeed." Editorial, "High Risks in Afghanistan," *New York Times,* 17 Nov. 2003.

23. C. C. Crane and W. A. Terrill, *Reconstructing Iraq: Insights, Challenges, and Missions for Military Forces in a Post-Conflict Scenario* (Carlisle, Pa.: U.S. Army War College, 2003). L. F. Kaplan, "Rumsfeld's Bad Options: Strategic Attack," *New Republic,* 14 Apr. 2003.

24. Conrad Crane, U.S. Army War College, personal communication.

25. T. Reid, "Washington Hawks Face Unfriendly Fire for 'Cheap War,'" *Times* (London), 31 Mar. 2003.

26. Fallows, "Blind into Baghdad," 64, 65.

27. T. Reid, "Rumsfeld Shows Strain as He Comes in the Line of Fire," *Times* (London), 29 Mar. 2003. Thomas White, Interview, PBS, 31 Jan. 2004. Fallows, "Blind into Baghdad."

28. P. W. Galbraith, Testimony before the Senate Foreign Relations Committee, 12 June 2003, "U.S. Postwar Policies in Iraq," 3.

29. Ricks, Interview, 28 Jan. 2004.

30. See *http://iraqbodycount.net/* and Human Rights Watch, "Off Target: The Conduct of the War and Civilian Casualties in Iraq," *http://hrw.org/reports/2003/usa1203.*

31. There are similar but less well reported problems in postwar Afghanistan (not enough money spent on reconstruction, failure to muster a solid international peacekeeping force), a situation that, according to a *New York Times* editorial of November 2003, cannot simply be attributed to bad luck, but rather "flows from a succession of bad American policy decisions." Editorial, "High Risks in Afghanistan."

32. Unattributed, "Iraq: Failure Begins to Look Possible," *Economist,* 1 Nov. 2003. M. John, "'Old Europe' Feels Vindicated on Iraq," Reuters, 13 Nov. 2003.

The Bush administration would not agree, of course. On the one-year anniversary of the invasion the White House website reports that "substantial progress is being made on all fronts" and that "for the first time in the lives of most Iraqis," democracy, human rights, and freedom are within reach. "Nearly three dozen" countries have made financial contributions, nineteen have supplied personnel for Operation Iraqi Freedom; the food distribution system is "functioning"; all universities are open. The website also lists "signs of" better security, better infrastructure and services, "cultural rebirth," economic renewal, and steps taken to "improve the lives" of Iraqi women. All laudable achievements. At the same time, the fact that the White House needs to list such things as "ten examples of international support" or "ten signs of democracy" suggests a certain defensiveness, an awareness that U.S. achievements in Iraq are, at the least, not obvious. See *www.whitehouse.gov/infocus/iraq/*.

33. Kagan, Interview, 29 Jan. 2004. Paul Wolfowitz, Pentagon press briefing, 23 July 2003.

34. Fallows, "Blind into Baghdad," 70.

35. Crane and Terrill, *Reconstructing Iraq*, 1.

36. Conrad Crane, personal communication.

37. Fallows, "Blind into Baghdad," 54.

38. R. Watson and M. Evans, "US Calls Up 30,000 New Troops," *Times* (London), 27 Mar. 2003. J. Keegan, "This Is Not Vietnam: The Allies Are Well on the Way to Victory," *Daily Telegraph*, 1 Apr. 2003.

39. Editorial, "Tell It Straight," *Times* (London), 30 Mar. 2003.

40. U. Kher, "3 Flawed Assumptions about Postwar Iraq," *Time*, 22 Sept. 2003. J. Borger and R. McCarthy, "We Could Lose This Situation," *Guardian*, 13 Nov. 2003.

41. Elliott, "So, What Went Wrong?" 35.

42. Kher, "3 Flawed Assumptions about Postwar Iraq." Elliott, "So, What Went Wrong?" 36. Rice University, James A. Baker III Institute for Public Policy and Council on Foreign Relations, *Guiding Principles for U.S. Post-Conflict Policy in Iraq* (Dec. 2002), 10

43. A. Stone, "Senators Grill Defense Official about Iraq Price Tag," *USA Today*, 10 Sept. 2003. Paul Wolfowitz, Testimony to Senate Armed Services Committee, "Helping Win the War on Terror," 9 Sept. 2003.

44. Sanger, "A Stalwart of Certainty." General John M. Shalikashvili, "Iraq and Afghanistan: A Military View," talk at Stanford University, 3 Mar. 2004. Crane and Terrill, *Reconstructing Iraq*, 42.

45. Senator Edward M. Kennedy, Speech to the Council on Foreign Relations, 5 Feb. 2004. Pollack, "Spies, Lies, and Weapons," 90. Elliott, "So, What Went Wrong?" 32–33.

46. K. J. Alter, "Is 'Groupthink' Driving Us to War?" *Boston Globe*, 21 Sept. 2002.

47. Jervis, "Confrontation between Iraq and the U.S.," 318.

48. Entman, *Projections of Power*, 119. And see *www.whitehouse.gov/infocus/iraq/* and *www.cpa-iraq.org/*

49. Zizek, "Iraq's False Promises," 47.

50. Fallows, "Blind into Baghdad," 74.

51. Fisher, "Deciding on War against Iraq," 404. Jervis, "Confrontation between Iraq and the U.S." "Joint Resolution to Authorize the Use of United States Armed Forces against Iraq," 107th Congress, 2nd sess., Resolution 114, 10 Oct. 2002.

52. Fisher, "Deciding on War against Iraq," 403. Pollack, "Spies, Lies, and Weapons," 90. Kennedy, Speech to the Council on Foreign Relations, 5 Feb. 2004.

53. Fisher, "Deciding on War against Iraq." Pollack, "Spies, Lies, and Weapons," 86, 92. Fallows, "Blind into Baghdad."

54. Thielmann quoted in Senator Edward M. Kennedy, Speech to the Council on Foreign Relations, 5 Feb. 2004. Pollack, "Spies, Lies, and Weapons," 88.

55. Fisher, "Deciding on War against Iraq," 405, 410.

56. Conrad Crane, personal communication.

57. Colonel David Perkins, Interview, PBS, Undated, 2004.

58. Bob Woodward, *Plan of Attack* (New York: Simon and Schuster, 2004), 264.

59. Fallows, "Blind into Baghdad," 74. Fallows, Interview, 28 Jan. 2004.

60. A. Beevor, "Warfare May Have Changed but Its Outcome Is Always Unknown," *Times* (London), 29 Mar. 2003.

61. Jervis, "Understanding the Bush Doctrine," 366.

Appendix

1. D. Jablonsky, "The Paradox of Duality: Adolf Hitler and the Concept of Military Surprise," in *Leaders and Intelligence*, ed. M. I. Handel (London: Frank Cass, 1989), 55–117. A. Perlmutter, "Military Incompetence and Failure: A Historical Comparative and Analytical Evaluation," *Journal of Strategic Studies* 1 (1978): 123.

2. M. Ridley, *The Origins of Virtue: Human Instincts and the Origins of Cooperation* (London: Penguin, 1996), 191.

3. F. I. Greenstein, *The Presidential Difference: Leadership Style from F.D.R. to Bill Clinton* (New York: Free Press, 2000); J. P. Burke and F. I. Greenstein, "Presidential Personality and National Security Leadership: A Comparative Analysis of Vietnam Decision-Making," *International Political Science Review* 10 (1989): 73–92. F. Logevall, *Choosing War: The Lost Chance for Peace and the Escalation of War in Vietnam* (Berkeley: University of California Press, 1999), 393. A. Bullock, *Hitler and Stalin: Parallel Lives* (London: HarperCollins, 1991).

4. R. F. Baumeister and J. M. Boden, "Aggression and the Self: High Self-Esteem, Low Self-Control, and Ego Threat," in *Human Aggression*, ed. R. G. Geen and E. Donnerstein (San Diego: Academic Press, 1998), 111–137.

5. A. Mazur and A. Booth, "Testosterone and Dominance in Men," *Behavioral and Brain Sciences* 21 (1998): 353–397; J. M. Dabbs, "Hormonal Influences in Nonviolent Dominance," National Science Foundation Final Report SBR-9511600, 1999, available at *www.gsu.edu/~psyjmd/NSF96–99.html*. J. M. Dabbs, "Testosterone Measurements in Clinical and Social Psychology," *Journal of Social and Clinical Psychology* 11 (1992): 302.

6. D. Nettle, "Adaptive Illusions: Optimism, Control and Human Rationality," in *Emotion, Evolution and Rationality*, ed. D. Evans and P. Cruse (Oxford: Oxford University Press, 2004). M. G. Hasleton and D. M. Buss, "Error Management Theory: A New Perspective on Biases in Cross-Sex Mind Reading," *Journal of Personality and Social Psychology* 78 (2000): 81–91.

7. D. Evans, A. Heuvelink, and D. Nettle, "Are Motivational Biases Adaptive? An Agent-Based Model of Human Judgment under Uncertainty," available at *www.dylan.org.uk/bias.pdf.*

8. S. E. Taylor et al., "Maintaining Positive Illusions in the Face of Negative Information: Getting the Facts without Letting Them Get to You," *Journal of Social and Clinical Psychology* 8 (1989): 114–129.

9. Nettle, "Adaptive Illusions," 13.

10. Hasleton and Buss, "Error Management Theory," 90, 81.

11. L. B. Alloy and L. Y. Abramson, "Judgment of Contingency in Depressed and Non-Depressed Subjects: Sadder but Wiser?" *Journal of Experimental Psychology* 108 (1979): 443–479. If anything, depressed people become *negatively* biased in their evaluations. Baumeister and Boden, "Aggression and the Self," 115.

12. H. L. Abrams, "Disabled Leaders, Cognition and Crisis Decision Making," *Canadian Papers in Peace Studies* (1990): 140.

13. Ibid. Other drugs have the opposite effect; anesthetics, for example, can "induce inhibitions, or encourage overconfidence" (140).

14. Bill Moyers, "On the Costs of War," PBS interview, 18 Oct. 2002, *www.pbs.org/now/commentary/moyers14.html.* Nettle, "Adaptive Illusions."

15. Abrams, "Disabled Leaders," 142.

16. See, e.g., S. E. Taylor and P. M. Gollwitzer, "The Effects of Mindset on Positive Illusions," *Journal of Personality and Social Psychology* 69 (1995).

17. R. F. Baumeister, "The Optimal Margin of Illusion," *Journal of Social and Clinical Psychology* 8 (1989): 186; see also S. Baron-Cohen, *The Essential Difference: The Truth about the Male and Female Brain* (Boulder: Perseus, 2003). R. W. Wrangham, *The Cooking Ape* (Boston: Houghton Mifflin, in press).

18. E. Clift and T. Brazaitis, *Madam President: Women Blazing the Leadership Trail* (New York: Routledge, 2003), xxiii.

19. Ibid., xi, xxii.

20. Ibid., ix, xvii, xi.

21. Ibid., xiv, xii.

22. R. McDermott and J. Cowden, "Sex Differences in a Crisis Simulation Game," paper presented at the American Political Science Association meeting, 27 Aug. 2003; R. McDermott and J. Cowden, "The Effects of Uncertainty and Sex in a Crisis Simulation Game," *International Relations* 27 (2001): 353–380.

23. C. Sedikides, L. Gaertner, and Y. Toguchi, "Pancultural Self-Enhancement," *Journal of Personality and Social Psychology* 84 (2003): 60–79. C. Peterson, "The Future of Optimism," *American Psychologist* 55 (2000): 52. S. Kitayama et al., "Individual and Collective Processes in the Construction of the Self: Self-Enhancement in the United States and Self-Criticism in Japan," *Journal of Personality and Social Psychology* 72 (1997): 1245–67.

24. S. J. Heine and D. R. Lehman, "Cultural Variation in Unrealistic Optimism: Does the West Feel More Invulnerable Than the East?" *Journal of Personality and Social Psychology* 68 (1995): 595–607. E. C. Chang, "Evidence for the Cultural Specificity of Pessimism in Asians vs. Caucasians: A Test of a General Negativity Hypothesis," *Personality and Individual Differences* 21 (1996): 819–822. S. J. Heine and D. R. Lehman, "The Cultural Construction of Self-En-

hancement: An Examination of Group-Serving Biases," *Journal of Personality and Social Psychology* 72 (1997): 1268–83.

25. See Peterson, "Future of Optimism." D. A. Armor and S. E. Taylor, "Situated Optimism: Specific Outcome Expectancies and Self-Regulation," *Advances in Experimental Social Psychology* 30 (1998): 361.

26. R. W. Robins and J. S. Beer, "Positive Illusions about the Self: Short-Term Benefits and Long-Term Costs," *Journal of Personality and Social Psychology* 80 (2001): 340–352. Baumeister, "Optimal Margin of Illusion," 177. Baumeister and Boden, "Aggression and the Self," 123.

27. Baumeister and Boden, "Aggression and the Self," 119, 115.

28. Ibid. S. E. Taylor, *Positive Illusions: Creative Self-Deception and the Healthy Mind* (New York: Basic Books, 1989).

29. M. I. Midlarsky, *On War: Political Violence in the International System* (New York: Free Press, 1975); R. D. Petersen, *Understanding Ethnic Violence: Fear, Hatred, and Resentment in Twentieth-Century Eastern Europe* (Cambridge: Cambridge University Press, 2002). W. C. Wohlforth, "The Stability of a Unipolar World," *International Security* 24 (1999): 5–41.

30. R. Wrangham, "Is Military Incompetence Adaptive?" *Evolution and Human Behavior* 20 (1999): 11.

31. See S. Pinker, *The Blank Slate: The Modern Denial of Human Nature* (London: Allen Lane, 2002).

32. R. J. Herrnstein, "Darwinism and Behaviorism: Parallels and Intersections," in *Evolution and Its Influence*, ed. A. Grafen (Oxford: Clarendon Press, 1989), 35–61.

33. See R. Jervis, "Deterrence and Perception," *International Security* 7 (1983): 19.

34. Wrangham, *The Cooking Ape.*

Acknowledgments

I am indebted to numerous people who were instrumental in the development of this book, particularly those who saw value in striking out across disciplinary lines. Special thanks are due to the Kennedy Memorial Trust, which supported my initial research at Harvard University, and to Richard Wrangham, whose ideas and enthusiasm inspired me to start this project. I also thank the Swiss Government, which generously supported my work in Geneva, where I received excellent advice and help from Pierre Allan, Hanspeter Kriesi, Alexis Keller, Philippe Braillard, Elise Lebreque, Nicholas Travaglione, Jean-Marie Kagabo, and Chris Boyd.

I am grateful to the Olin Institute for Strategic Studies for a wonderful year putting the book together at Harvard University, and especially for the interest and guidance of Stephen Peter Rosen. While at Harvard I benefited immensely from the help of Samuel Huntington, Monica Duffy Toft, Ann Townes, Deborah Lee, Cdr. Kenneth Barrett, Alexander Downes, Kelly Greenhill, Lt. Col. Robert Hopkins, Kimberly and Fred Kagan, Greg Koblenz, Erez Manela, Elizabeth Stanley-Mitchell, Michael Reynolds, Paul Schulte, and especially Colin Dueck. Lino and Anna Pertile have my gratitude for welcoming me into the community and life of Eliot House.

Many thanks are due to the Center for International Security and Cooperation at Stanford University, where Dean Wilkening, Michael May, Chris Chyba, Scott Sagan, Lynn Eden, Barbara Platt, and the California coast were sources of great encouragement and inspiration while I finished the book.

A number of others have significantly contributed to my evolving thoughts and ideas, most among them Dominic Tierney, who has read and salvaged more of my writing than I would wish to inflict upon anyone, but also Richard Betts, Terry Burnham, Conrad Crane, Gabriella de la Rosa, John Garofano, Scott Gartner, Brian Hare, Jack Hirschleifer, Robert Jervis, Roger and Jenny Johnson, Gordon Martel, Rose McDermott, Greg Mitrovich, Daniel Nettle, Azeem Sutterwalla, Shelley Taylor, Robert Trivers, Stephen Walker, Mike Wilson, Richard Wrangham, and Luis Zaballa.

Michael Fisher at Harvard University Press is due my great appreciation for his encouragement, advice, ideas, and support. Among the many others at the Press to whom I owe thanks, I must single out Camille Smith for her skill and perceptiveness in transforming the manuscript well beyond my expectations.

Finally, I thank a remarkable collection of family and friends whose encouragement and inspiration were invaluable during the writing of this book: Dennis and Kiyomi Briscoe, Nick Brown, Roger, Jenny and Becci Johnson, Gavin King, Duncan and Elizabeth McCombie, Mark Molesky, Juliette Talbot, Dominic Tierney, Andrew Tuddenham and, especially, for her patience, many sacrifices, and love, Gabriella de la Rosa.

Index

Abrams, Herbert, 3–4, 227–228
Accuracy: of assessment, 6, 11, 13; versus overconfidence, 222–226
Acheson, Dean, 117, 245n59
Adams, Samuel, 145–147
Adaptive overconfidence, 5–18
Adaptive positive illusions, 15–16
Afghanistan, 3, 14–15, 189, 191, 201, 203, 215–216, 264n7, 265nn22,31
Air power, 92, 101, 148–150, 153, 105, 261n78
Alexander the Great, 37
Alliances, 60–62, 87, 90, 190
Alter, Karen, 21–22, 211
Alternative origins of overconfidence, 221–222, 249n23
Alternative proximate factors, elimination of, 51–52, 58–59
Ambiguous attributes, 43–44, 166
Anarchy, 29–30, 187
Antecedent conditions: for positive illusions, 39–47; for overconfidence, 47–49
Appeasement, 89–90, 92–94, 98, 129
Arab-Israeli War, 18
Armor, David, 25, 231
Arms race, 6, 61, 108–124, 234
Army War College, 196, 201–202, 205–206, 209
Assessment: accuracy of, 6, 11, 13; insufficient time for, 51; World War I, 58–59, 63, 66–76; Munich crisis, 85–89, 92, 94–95, 100, 102; Cuban missile crisis, 108–118, 120; Vietnam War, 125–127, 131–156; invasion of Iraq, 192–200, 206, 213. *See also* Feedback
Attributes: general versus specific, 41; ambiguous versus clear, 43–44
Austria, 91, 99, 102
Austria-Hungary, in World War I, 58–84

Bachmann, Admiral, 74
Baghdad, 195, 202–203, 216

Balkans crises, 60–61, 81
Ball, George, 144–145, 148, 151–152, 160
Battle of Britain, 92, 101
Baumeister, Roy, 9–10, 16, 21, 26, 42–43, 47, 228, 231
Bay of Pigs invasion, 3, 111, 121, 140–141, 161, 182
Beer, Jennifer, 16
Beevor, Anthony, 217–218
Begin, Menachem, 183
Belgium, 61, 67–69, 71, 74–75, 79, 81
Benes, Edvard, 90
Bethmann-Hollweg, Theobald von, 73
Betts, Richard, 4, 14, 128, 143, 170–171
Biases: optimistic, 7, 21, 24–26, 45; cognitive, 8; motivational, 8; offensive, 13
Bin Laden, Osama, 265n22
Bismarck, Otto von, 80
Blainey, Geoffrey, 2–3, 29, 35, 58, 65–67, 73, 76–77, 82, 189, 252n46
Block, Ivan, 78
Bluffing, 6, 9, 11–13, 17, 27, 88–89, 95, 110, 192, 226, 242n28
Bobrow, Davis, 124
Boden, Joseph, 231
Bradley, Mark, 163
Brazaitis, Tom, 229
Bremer, Paul, 207
Brinkmanship, 3–4, 80, 90, 177
Britain, 3, 12, 23, 37, 133, 145, 156, 232; in World War I, 58–84; during Munich crisis, 85–100, 173–175, 254n19; in World War II, 100–101, 103–104; and invasion of Iraq, 197–199
Brown, Jonathon, 7, 9
Bundy, McGeorge, 151, 161, 168
Bundy, William, 136
Bunker, Ellsworth, 146–147
Bush, George W., 21, 191–194, 196, 198, 200, 204, 206–212, 214, 217–218, 266n32

Cambodia, 142, 153
Case studies, 50–51, 175–179
Castelnau, Noël-Marie-Joseph-Édouard de, 66
Castro, Fidel, 117
Central Intelligence Agency, 114, 117, 132, 135, 142, 145–146, 149–150, 160, 166, 206–207, 214, 259n40
Central Powers, 58–84, 173–175
Chalabi, Ahmed, 210
Chamberlain, Neville, 85–86, 88–94, 96–99, 173, 253n7
Chicken, game of, 122–123
China, 32–33, 64, 127, 129–130, 137, 142, 159, 186
Chirac, Jacques, 213
Chisholm, Shirley, 228–229
Churchill, Winston, 1, 77, 89–90, 101, 253n7
Cinnirella, Marco, 21
Clark, Wesley, 206
Clausewitz, Carl von, 13–14, 25, 184–185
Clifford, Clark, 145, 151
Clift, Eleanor, 229
Closed debate, 48–49, 174–179, 181–183, 192
Coalitions, 195, 206
Cognitive dissonance, 240n16
Cohen, Eliot, 77–78, 82
Cold War, 46, 129, 232
Collins, J. Lawton, 133
Communism, 46, 128–131, 133–134, 136–139, 142–143, 149, 156, 158–160, 163, 170
Complacency, 23, 74, 101
Confidence, 1, 3, 14, 17, 25, 27
Congress, U.S., 127, 137, 137, 142, 144–145, 150–151, 154, 158–159, 168, 182–183, 193, 196, 203, 208, 210, 213–215, 229, 262n10
Congruence analysis, 55, 176–179
Conscious strategies, 12, 17, 28
Constitution, U.S., 213, 215
Containment, 129, 133, 170, 194, 209
Context, importance of, 179–183
Cooper, Chester, 149
Coordination game, 122–123
Crane, Conrad, 202, 215

Crete, 104
Crimean War, 232, 254n28
Cuban missile crisis, 26, 50, 108–124, 138–139, 141, 149, 159, 173–175, 177, 181–182, 185–186, 190, 245n59, 249n31, 255n5, 256n20; background, 109–110; Soviet Union, 110–113; United States, 113–118; positive illusions in, 118–124
Cubbage, T. L., 164
Cult of the offensive, 62–64
Custer, George A., 2
Czechoslovakia, 87, 90–91, 93, 95–96, 98–99, 102, 253n14

Dabbs, James, 222
Daladier, Édouard, 87, 90, 96
David, Saul, 33
Davis, A. C., 131–132
Debate, openness of, 48–49, 174–179, 181–183, 192
Defense Department, U.S., 148–149, 168, 202, 262n10; Reorganization Act, 262n10
Defense Intelligence Agency, 150
De Gaulle, Charles, 144
Democracy, 25, 47–48, 168, 174–175, 180–181, 193–194, 197–198, 204, 213–214
Depression, 226–228
Deterrence, 13, 27, 92, 111, 118, 124, 186–187, 194, 209, 242n28
Diem, Ngo Dinh, 133–134, 136, 138, 140, 159, 168, 258n28
Diesing, Paul, 85
Dillon, Douglas, 117
Diplomacy, 81, 86–87, 90, 93, 96–97, 99, 139, 193, 197. See also Negotiations
Dixon, Norman, 3
Dobrynin, Anatoly, 110
Dodd, Thomas, 149
Dole, Elizabeth, 228–229
Domino theory, 129
Douhet strategy, 164, 261n77
Dulles, John Foster, 129, 133
Dunning, David, 43–44, 200
Dupuy, T. H., 33

Eden, Anthony, 89
Ego, 231–233
Ehrenhalt, Alan, 25
Eisenhower, Dwight D., 46, 126, 129, 131–134, 137, 179
Elazar, David, 2
Elliott, Michael, 199, 210
Ellsberg, Daniel, 128, 169
Entman, Robert, 212
Error management theory, 226
Escalation, 157–160, 178–179, 182
Esher, Viscount (Reginald Brett), 68–70
European Defense Community, 133
Evolutionary basis to overconfidence, 5, 8–11, 15–17, 30, 226
Executive committee (Cuban missile crisis), 108–110, 114–121, 123

Falger, Vincent, 187–188
Fallows, James, 201–203, 205–207, 212–214, 217
False optimism, 4, 29–30, 64, 147
Fearon, James, 28, 31
Feedback, 216; of specific situations, 39–41; beginning versus end period, 41–43. *See also* Assessment
Ferdinand, Archduke, 60
Fighting ability, 10
First-mover advantage, 30
Fischer, Fritz, 60–61
Fisher, Louis, 213, 215
Foch, Ferdinand, 67
Ford, Gerald, 158–159, 179
France, 131–134, 136–137, 140, 144–145, 154, 213; in World War I, 58–84; during Munich crisis, 85–91, 93–97, 99, 173–175; in World War II, 100–101, 103–106
François-Poncet, André, 89
Franco-Prussian War, 66
Frank, Robert, 10
Freedman, Lawrence, 194–195
Fulbright, William, 135

Gaddis, John Lewis, 163
Galbraith, John Kenneth, 137, 140, 258n28

Galbraith, Peter, 203
Gallhofer, Irmtraud, 116
Gallipoli, Turkey, 77–78
Gamble of war, 184–186
Ganguly, Sumit, 3, 29, 31–32, 180–181
Garofano, John, 32, 139, 161, 164, 171, 182–183, 246n70
Gazit, Shlomo, 183
Gelb, Leslie, 14, 128, 143, 170
Gender, 228–230
Germany, 6, 8, 50, 55, 205, 208; in World War I, 58–84; during Munich crisis, 85–100, 173–175, 177–178, 180–181; in World War II, 100–107, 178, 253n14
Gibbons, William, 135, 137–138
Goals, deliberating/implementing, 44–46
Goebbels, Joseph, 98
Goering, Hermann, 104
Goldwater, Barry, 158–159
Goleman, David, 16, 20–21, 46
Gollwitzer, Peter, 11, 44
Gooch, George P., 251n39
Gooch, John, 77–78, 82
Great Society, 149, 227
Greene, Wallace, 144
Grey, Edward, 81
Gromyko, Andrei, 111
Group positive illusions, 20–23
Groupthink, 21–22, 121, 142, 157, 162, 210–211, 245n59
Gulf War, 14, 191–192, 194–195, 215

Haeseler, Count, 72
Haig, Douglas, 82
Halberstam, David, 147
Halder, Franz, 103, 105
Halifax, Earl of (Edward F. L. Wood), 89, 93
Hamdani, Raad Al-, 194
Handel, Michael, 44, 143, 155, 183
Hanson, Victor, 181
Harkin, Tom, 208
Harkins, Paul, 140, 167–168
Hastings, Max, 32
Helms, Richard, 146–147

Hess, Gary, 165
Hilsman, Roger, 151
Hitler, Adolf, 26, 39, 85–90, 92–100, 102–107, 173–175, 177–178, 180–181, 221–222, 232, 254n19
Hobbes, Thomas, 187
Hochberg, Count, 72
Ho Chi Minh, 14, 133–134, 154, 164–165, 176
Howard, Michael, 63
Hubatsch, Walther, 251n39
Hughes-Wilson, John, 33, 145, 167
Human nature, traits of, 37–38
Humphrey, Hubert H., 159, 183
Hunter-gatherer societies, 10–11, 15, 17, 217

Inclusive decisionmaking, 49
India, 3, 32, 181, 186
In-group positive illusions, 22–23
Inskip, Thomas, 85
Institute of Defense Analysis, 150
Intercontinental ballistic missiles, 108–124
Iraq, invasion of, 3, 13–14, 22, 51, 124, 187, 189–190, 191–218, 266n32; Iraqi overconfidence, 194–196; U.S. overconfidence, 196–200; occupation undermined by war plan, 200–204; prewar assumptions/postwar problems, 204–209; positive illusions in, 209–213
Israel, 2, 18, 33, 83, 183, 195
Italy, 12, 74; during Munich crisis, 87, 89–90, 95–96, 253n18

Jablonsky, David, 102
Jagow, Gottlieb von, 73
Janis, Irving, 21, 121, 128, 148–149, 157, 161–162, 211, 261n73
Japan, 23, 31, 68, 83, 100, 185, 205, 208
Jervis, Robert, 3, 88, 157, 166, 185–186, 191, 197–199, 211–212, 218, 240n9
Joffre, Joseph, 66–67
Johnson, Harold K., 14, 144
Johnson, Lyndon B., 46, 51, 126–128,

130, 135–136, 138, 141–154, 157–161, 165–169, 171, 179, 182, 222, 227–228, 259n40
Just war theory, 184

Kagan, Frederick, 195, 200–201, 204
Kaiser, David, 127, 139, 158–159, 161, 164, 168
Kashmir, 32, 191
Kattenburg, Paul, 168
Keegan, John, 206–207
Keeley, Lawrence, 10–11
Keitel, Wilhelm, 103, 106
Kennedy, Edward, 210, 214
Kennedy, John F., 25–26, 51, 108–113, 115–124, 126–127, 129–130, 134–141, 154, 158–159, 161–162, 166, 168–169, 177, 179, 182, 190
Kennedy, Paul, 68, 71
Kennedy, Robert, 110, 120–121, 138
Keynes, John Maynard, 85, 91, 97
Khrushchev, Nikita, 108–113, 115, 118–119, 121–124, 129, 173, 175, 177, 186, 190, 255n5
Kirshner, Jonathan, 246n70
Kissinger, Henry, 156, 227
Kitchener, Horatio Herbert, 78
Klar, Yechiel, 83–84
Korean War, 32–33, 127, 130, 132, 156, 164
Kowert, Paul, 49, 182
Kubrick, Stanley, 162–163
Kuwait, 195, 202

Lansdowne, Marquis of (Henry Petty-Fitzmaurice), 69
Laos, 135, 139, 142, 148, 159, 182
Law, Andrew Bonar, 98
Leadership, 23–26
Learning, 221
Lebow, Richard Ned, 3, 31, 108, 112, 119, 139, 173–174, 190
Leclerc, General, 151–152
LeMay, Curtis, 116–117, 148
Lerchenfeld, Count, 73
LeShan, Lawrence, 2, 23, 47

Levin, Carl, 208
Lincoln, Abraham, 24
Lindsay, Lawrence, 207
Lloyd George, David, 62, 98
Logevall, Fredrik, 127, 141, 158–160, 171

MacArthur, Douglas, 32–33
MacDougall, Alice Foote, 173
Malaya, 23, 156
Mann, Thomas, 75
Mansfield, Mike, 132, 135, 138
Manstein, Fritz von, 105
Mao Zedong, 32
Marshall, Joshua, 193
Martel, Gordon, 31, 62, 68–69, 79–80
May, Ernest, 49, 81–82, 129, 136, 141, 165, 169
McCain, John, 208
McCarthy, Joseph, 159
McCone, John, 117
McConnell, John P., 148
McDermott, Rose, 230
McNamara, Robert, 51, 115, 125, 135, 139, 143, 145, 150–151, 157, 161, 163–164, 167–168, 182
McNoughton, John, 129–130
Mearsheimer, John, 93, 247n74, 253n14
Meier, Norman, 22
Mercer, Jonathan, 188
Merriman, John, 65, 67, 74, 84, 98
Mikoyan, Anastas, 255n8
Mikoyan, Sergo, 255n8
Military Assistance Advisory Group, 132, 135
Military Assistance Command, Vietnam, 140, 143, 145, 166–167, 259n40
Milosevic, Slobodan, 14
Misperceptions/miscalculations, 13, 29–30, 92, 100, 113, 157, 165, 186–187, 234, 241n21
Moltke, Helmuth von, 73
Mombauer, Annika, 62, 76–77, 251n39
Morgenthau, Hans, 187
Moyers, Bill, 149, 151–152
Munich crisis, 50, 55, 85–107, 129, 173–175, 177–178, 180–181, 249n31;

background, 86–87; Britain, 87–94; Germany, 94–97; positive illusions in, 97–100; and World War II, 100–107
Mussolini, Benito, 12, 89–90, 96, 253n18

Napoleon Bonaparte, 14, 26, 39, 70, 221
Nasser, Gamal Abdel, 18
Nathan, James, 182
National Institute of Mental Health, 10
Nationalism, 22, 62, 64, 75, 163, 177
Nazis, 21, 86, 102
Nazi-Soviet pact, 90
Negotiations, 4, 144, 156, 160, 245n59, 260n64. See also Diplomacy
Neorealism, 28–31, 187–188
Nettle, David, 13, 188, 222, 224–226, 228
Niebuhr, Reinhold, 187
Nitze, Paul, 117
Nixon, Richard M., 126, 130, 153–156, 158, 160, 179, 227–228
North Atlantic Treaty Organization, 111, 114
North Korea, 15, 32–33
North Vietnam, 14, 125–172, 174–177, 261n78
Nuclear war, 109–110, 118, 122–124, 186, 190

Occupation, 193, 199, 201–210, 215–216
Open debate, 48–49, 174–179, 181–183
Operation Iraqi Freedom, 266n32
Operation Rolling Thunder, 148–149
Opponent deception, 6, 9, 11–13. See also Bluffing
Optimism, 2–7, 170; valid vs. false, 4, 29–30, 64; vs. pessimism, 11; and morale, 14
Ottoman Empire. See Turkey
Out-group positive illusions, 22–23
Overconfidence, 2–5; adaptive, 5–18; and conscious/subconscious strategies, 28; and relative power, 29–30; antecedent conditions for, 47–49; types of,

Overconfidence *(continued)*
53–54; in World War I, 77–78, 80–82;
in World War II, 102–107; during
Cuban missile crisis, 112, 117–119; in
Vietnam war, 145–146, 152–154, 162,
165–166; during invasion of Iraq,
194–200, 216–217; alternative origins,
221–222, 249n23; versus accuracy,
222–226

Pakistan, 3, 32, 181, 186, 265n22
Palestine/Palestinians, 33, 221
Pape, Robert, 163–164
Pentagon Papers, 126–128, 148, 157,
169, 176
Performance enhancement, 11–13
Perkins, David, 216
Pessimism, 11, 152, 170
Peterson, Christopher, 7, 37
Pizarro, Francisco, 1–2, 239n1
Poland, 98, 103–104, 107, 253n14
Policy Planning Council, 148
Pollack, Kenneth, 196, 200, 210, 214–215
Positive illusions, 7–9, 173–175, 188–
190; advantages, 9–15; in today's
world, 15–18; empirical evidence, 18–
23; of individuals, 18–20; group, 20–
23; of leaders, 23–26; theoretical basis,
26–31; historical basis, 31–34; antecedent conditions for, 39–47; and regime type, 48, 180–181; and openness
of debate, 48–49, 174–179, 181–183;
evidence for, 52–55; in World War I,
58, 64–84; and Munich crisis, 85–86,
97–107; and Cuban missile crisis, 108,
112–113, 116–124; in Vietnam war,
133–134, 138–141, 147–153, 156–172;
and gamble of war, 184–186; and deterrence, 186–187; and realism, 187–
188; and invasion of Iraq, 192, 203,
209–213, 216, 218; extremes of, 226–
233; individually adaptive/globally
maladaptive, 233–235
Positive illusions theory of war, 35–36,
242n28, 249n28; sources of variation,
37; individual variation, 38–39; and
antecedent conditions for positive

illusions, 39–47; and antecedent conditions for overconfidence, 47–49;
case studies, 50–51; eliminating alternative proximate factors, 51–52; evidence for positive illusions, 52–55;
tests, 55–57; results of case studies,
175–179; importance of context, 179–
183; implications for theory, 184–188;
summary of hypotheses/predictions,
236–238
Prisoner's dilemma, game of, 122
Prospect theory, 184–186
Provocation, 247n75
Proximate factors, 29–31; alternative,
elimination of, 51–52
Psychological basis to overconfidence,
5–7, 10, 15, 17
Pyrrhic victories, 4

Qaeda, al, 199, 265n22

Race, Jeffrey, 161
Rankin, Jeannette, 229
Rational choice theory, 8, 27–28
Realism, 28–31, 187–188
Rearmament, 88–89, 91, 99, 102
Reconstruction, 202, 205, 207–210,
215–216, 266n32
Regime type, 48, 180–181
Religion, 22–23, 221–222
Reproductive success, 10–11, 15
Resolve, 6, 12–14, 17, 28, 104, 185
Richardson, James, 89, 93, 99–100
Ricks, Thomas, 195, 199
Ridgway, Matthew B., 132
Ridley, Matt, 221
Rilke, Rainer Maria, 75
Risk: perceived invulnerability to, 45;
willingness to engage in, 79–80; gam-
ble of war, 184–186
Robins, Richard, 16
Rommel, Erwin, 105
Rostow, Walt, 135–136, 146, 148–149,
182, 259n40
Rumsfeld, Donald, 193, 199, 201–203,
207, 212, 214, 216

Rusk, Dean, 123, 129, 136–137, 149, 154, 161, 168
Russia, 31, 100; in World War I, 58–84. *See also* Soviet Union
Russo-Japanese War, 31, 68, 83, 100

Saddam Hussein, 13, 39, 124, 187, 189, 192–197, 199, 204, 206–207, 209–213
Sanger, David, 198, 208
Saracens, 2, 221
Saris, Willem, 116
Saving face, 129–130, 136
Schelling strategy, 164, 261n77
Schlesinger, James, 227
Schlieffen plan, 60–61, 67, 81
Schmidt, Christian, 122
Schoenbrun, David, 137
Sedgwick, John, 2
Self-deception, 8–9, 11–12, 97, 147, 212
Self-fulfilling prophecies, 9–10, 16
Self-perceptions, 9–10
Seligman, Martin, 7
September 11, 2001, terrorist attacks, 192–193
Serbia, 3, 14, 60, 73, 216
Seven Years' War, 185
Shalikashvili, John, 209
Sharon, Ariel, 183
Shattered illusions, 82–84, 101, 150–152
Shenkman, Richard, 24–25
Shinseki, Eric K., 201
Simon, John, 85
Smith, Margaret Chase, 229
Snyder, Glenn, 85
Snyder, Jack, 78–79
Social dilemma games, 122–123, 234
Social identity theory, 20–21, 188
Sorensen, Ted, 120
Soukhomlinov, General, 68
Southeast Asia Treaty Organization, 137
South Korea, 32–33, 145
South Vietnam, 125–172, 182, 261n78
Soviet Union, 3, 8, 14, 127, 129, 186, 232; during Munich crisis, 87, 89–90, 94; in World War II, 101, 103–107;

during Cuban missile crisis, 108–124, 173–175, 177, 186, 190, 245n59, 256n20. *See also* Russia
Stalemate, 4, 83, 128
Stalin, Joseph, 8, 89, 222, 232
Stevens, Ted, 229
Stoessinger, John, 3, 29, 84, 141, 172
Strategy: offensive, 62–63, 91; defensive, 63
Subconscious strategies, 12, 28
Sudetenland, 87, 90, 93, 96
Suez crisis, 3, 232
Suppression of information, 167–169, 182, 199–200
Switzerland, 74
Sylvan, Donald, 118

Tajfel, Henri, 20
Taliban, 15, 189, 264n7, 265n22
Taylor, A. J. P., 96–97, 106
Taylor, Maxwell D., 108, 117, 121, 135–136, 139–140, 144–145, 163, 168, 259n40
Taylor, Shelley, 7, 9, 11, 35, 39, 41, 44, 188–189, 231
Terrorism, 192–193, 199
Testosterone, 7
Tet offensive, 151–152, 155, 174, 177
t'Hart, Paul, 245n59
Thatcher, Margaret, 228, 230
Thayer, Bradley, 187
Thielmann, Greg, 215
Tho, Le Duc, 156
Thomas, Baylis, 33
Thorson, Stuart, 118
Threat level, danger vs. no danger, 46–47
Tiger, Lionel, 6, 38
Tinbergen, Niko, 18
Tirpitz, Alfred von, 81
Tonkin Gulf Resolution, 144, 215
Tra, Tran Van, 155
Traits, behavioral, 37–38
Treaty of Versailles, 89, 93
Triggering responses, 17–18, 46–47
Triple Entente, 58–84, 173–175
Trivers, Robert, 8–9, 188

Truman, Harry, 126, 131, 134, 169, 179
Tuchman, Barbara, 5, 25, 119, 125, 127,
    130, 134–136, 139, 142, 150, 152,
    154–155, 157–162, 167–169, 171, 180,
    263n11
Turkey, 60, 77–78, 110, 112, 114, 119,
    122, 198, 255n5
Turner, John, 20
Tyranny, 48, 192, 204

U Thant, 144
U-2 flights, 109, 113, 115, 124, 256n20
Uncertainty, 27, 29
United Nations, 32, 124, 192, 196–197,
    201, 204, 213–214
United States, 24–25, 38, 48, 50, 64,
    186, 232; during invasion of Iraq, 3,
    12–13, 21–22, 124, 189–190, 191–218,
    266n32; in Vietnam War, 14, 46, 55,
    125–172, 173–183, 185, 189, 195, 208,
    215, 222, 227, 259n40, 261n78; dur-
    ing Cuban missile crisis, 26, 108–124,
    173–175, 177, 181–182, 186, 190,
    255n5, 256n20; in Korean War, 32–
    33; in World War II, 94, 101, 104,
    113

Vagts, Alfred, 3, 65
Van Evera, Stephen, 3, 22, 29–30, 58,
    64–65, 68, 72, 75–77, 113, 189
Vann, John, 168
Verifiability, high vs. low, 40–41
Viet Cong, 135, 139, 145–147, 154–156,
    164, 168, 259n33
Viet Minh, 132
Vietnam Task Force, 139–140
Vietnam war, 3, 14, 46, 50, 55, 111, 125–
    172, 173–183, 185, 189, 195, 208, 215,
    222, 227, 249n31, 259n40, 261n78;
    background, 126–131; Eisenhower ad-
    ministration, 131–134; Kennedy ad-
    ministration, 134–141; Johnson ad-
    ministration, 141–153; Nixon
    administration, 153–154; North Viet-

nam in, 154–156; positive illusions in,
    156–172
Volkan, Vladimir, 22

Walker, Stephen, 94
War: as puzzle, 4, 27, 34, 173, 189; as
    positive activity, 64, 75–76; momen-
    tum of, 170; gamble of, 184–186;
    short war expectation, 252n46
Weapons of mass destruction, 13, 192–
    194, 196–197, 199–200, 202, 209,
    211–212, 214
Welch, David, 37
Wellington, Duke of (Arthur Wellesley),
    2
Westmoreland, William, 145–147, 152,
    167, 259n40
Wheeler, General, 143, 147
White, Thomas, 203
Wilhelm II, 61, 70–71, 81–82
Wilson, Henry, 69
Wohlforth, William, 232
Wolfowitz, Paul, 191, 201, 203, 205, 208
Woodward, Bob, 216
Working Group on Vietnam, 142, 168
World War I, 3, 6, 50, 58–84, 90–91,
    119, 173–175, 189, 229, 249n31,
    251n39, 252n46; background, 59–66;
    Triple Entente, 66–71; Central
    Powers, 71–76; positive illusions in,
    76–84
World War II, 3, 6, 22–23, 42, 92, 113,
    138, 150, 164, 178, 185, 205, 229,
    253n14; and Munich crisis, 100–107
Wrangham, Richard, 10–11, 13, 46, 188,
    228, 233, 235

Yom Kippur War, 2, 33
Yugoslavia, 3, 14, 216

Zinni, Anthony, 203
Zizek, Slavoj, 198, 212